Bibliography
of the
Little Golden Books

RECENT TITLES IN
BIBLIOGRAPHIES AND INDEXES IN AMERICAN LITERATURE

The Native American in American Literature:
A Selectively Annotated Bibliography
Roger O. Rock

Science Fiction in America, 1870s-1930s:
An Annotated Bibliography of Primary Sources
Thomas D. Clareson

Joseph Conrad and American Writers:
A Bibliographical Study of Affinities, Influences,and Relations
Robert Secor and Debra Moddelmog

Melville's Classical Allusions:
A Comprehensive Index and Glossary
Gail H. Coffler

An "Oliver Optic" Checklist:
An Annotated Catalog-Index to the Series, Nonseries Stories,
and Magazine Publications of William Taylor Adams
Dolores B. Jones

Women in Southern Literature:
An Index
Patricia Sweeney

Bibliography
of the
Little Golden Books

Compiled by
Dolores B. Jones

Bibliographies and Indexes in American Literature, Number 7

GREENWOOD PRESS
New York • Westport, Connecticut • London

LIBRARY OF CONGRESS CATALOGING-IN-PUBLICATION DATA

Jones, Dolores Blythe.
  Bibliography of the little golden books.

  (Bibliographies and indexes in American literature,
ISSN 0742-6860 ; no. 7)
    Includes indexes.
    1. Little golden books—Bibliography.
2. Children's literature in series—Bibliography.
3. Children's literature, American—Bibliography.
I. Title. II. Series.
Z473.L765J66 1987   011'.62   86-27090
ISBN 0-313-25025-1 (lib. bdg. : alk. paper)

Library of Congress Catalog Card Number: 86-27090
ISBN: 0-313-25025-1
ISSN: 0742-6860

First published in 1987

Greenwood Press, Inc.
88 Post Road West, Westport, Connecticut 06881

Printed in the United States of America

The paper used in this book complies with the
Permanent Paper Standard issued by the National
Information Standards Organization (Z39.48-1984).

10 9 8 7 6 5 4 3 2 1

To my "other" parents
The Joneses

Contents

Preface	ix
Acknowledgments	xi
Introduction	xiii
Abbreviations	xxi
Title List	3
Series List	97
Name Index	127
Format Index	170

Preface

Bibliography of the Little Golden Books provides a comprehensive listing of all Little Golden Book titles issued by Simon & Schuster (later Golden Press and Western) from the series inception in 1942 through 1985. Included are all titles issued in the familiar Little Golden Book format, 8" x 6 3/4," gold foil spine and 44 pages (reduced to 24 in later years). Various subseries (e.g., Ding Dong School Books, Giant Little Golden Books, Little Golden Activity Books, Walt Disney Books) will later be discussed in detail.

The main section of the book, TITLE LIST, arranges the Little Golden Books alphabetically by title. Each distinct title has an entry number ranging from 001 - 815. The basic title entry is signified by the three digit number without qualifiers. (e.g., 588). This base entry is used for the publisher's initial issuance of the title.

Depending upon the particular title, the base entry includes: complete title, author(s), illustrator(s), place of publication, publisher, and date. Additional information may include the Library of Congress card number (LC#), copyright registration number and date, copyright renewal registration number and date, and a series statement. The series name appears in upper case letters within parenthesis. In some cases, the same Little Golden Book series number was used for more than one title. To distinguish between the two titles, an X has been added to the Little Golden Book series number of the second title to be assigned the number (e.g., LITTLE GOLDEN BOOK 108X).

Subsequent printings in book form with a new copyright date, new Little Golden Book series number, or a new subseries are signified with the same three digit number as the base entry with the addition of a qualifier (e.g., 588a, 588b, 588c).

Over the years, Little Golden Book stories have been issued in a variety of formats. Each different format has a qualifier added to the base number. For example, a filmstrip version of The poky little puppy (base number 588) is designated as 588FS, a motion picture is 588MP and a sound recording of the same title is 588SR. Twenty of the Little Golden Book titles were made accessible to blind children

through the efforts of the American Brotherhood for the
Blind. These braille books are distinguished by the addition
of "B" to the base number (ØØ3B).

The next section, SERIES LIST, enumerates all series
and subseries issued in the Little Golden Book format.
Information regarding each series and a description of the
arrangement is detailed in that section. In general, all
titles within a given series are listed, with a cross-
reference back to the main TITLE LIST. This reference is
provided by means of the entry number in parenthesis
following each title.

For additional information, there are two indexes, NAME
INDEX and FORMAT INDEX. The first index is arranged by name
of the author, illustrator, narrator, songwriter, producer,
etc. A person's real name is considered as the main entry,
with cross-references to pseudonyms, maiden names, and
variant forms. Therefore, all titles in which the person had
creative input are gathered together under one listing.
Reference to all pertinent entries in the main TITLE LIST is
provided by means of the entry number in parenthesis
following the title.

The FORMAT INDEX lists the various formats in which the
Little Golden Book stories have appeared. Under each format
(e.g., Braille, cassette, filmstrip, recording) appear all
titles so issued. Cross-reference is made to the main TITLE
LIST by means of the entry number in parenthesis following
the title.

The task of compiling information on all Little Golden
Book titles is a difficult one due to several factors. The
first limiting factor is the unavailability of complete and
accurate bibliographic control for literature considered to
be ephemeral, even by the publishers. Information in basic
reference sources such as the National Union Catalog...,
Publisher's Trade List Annual..., Cumulative Book Index...,
and Publishers' Weekly from 1942-196Ø is relatively complete
and accurate. But in the early 196Øs, for unknown reasons,
the publisher of Little Golden Books began to see them as
merely a continuation of an existing series. Each title was
not important in itself, but was merely one of eight or ten
new titles being added to the series. At that point,
bibliographic information became nonexistent; even publisher
catalogs did not list the titles separately. Publisher files
and records are inaccessible to researchers, totally closing
an important avenue of investigation.

Despite the limitations created by the aforementioned
problems, every attempt has been made to secure as much
accurate information as possible from available sources.
This bibliography provides substantial information pertinent
to the study of the publishing history of twentieth-century
children's books and mass-market publishing techniques,
series books, and children's books' illustrators. Students
and specialists of children's literature, as well as
librarians, teachers, book collectors, and booksellers, will
find this book to be helpful in their various pursuits.

Acknowledgments

Because of their ephemeral nature, Little Golden Books are very difficult to locate. To help in my search for elusive titles, I enlisted the aid of many librarians, booksellers, private collectors and friends.

I am indebted to the following people who made their library collections available to me: Margaret Coughlan, Reference Specialist, Children's Literature Center, Library of Congress; Janet M. Hamilton, Head, Technical Services, Alabama Public Library Service; John Kelly, Curator, de Grummond Collection, University of Southern Mississippi; Alfred H. Lane, Director, Crouse Library for Publishing Arts; Nancy Lee, Librarian, Popular Culture Collection, Bowling Green State University; DianeJude L. McDowell, Assistant Head, Central Children's Dept., Free Library of Philadelphia; and David R. Smith, Archivist, Walt Disney Archives.

Private collectors Billie M. Levy of West Hartford, Connecticut and Dorothy Tharpe of Hattiesburg, Mississippi provided much needed information on titles, series, authors, and illustrators.

Special thanks go to Steve Santi who unselfishly allowed me to use information provided in A guide to little golden books. His wealth of experience derived from years of collecting Little Golden Books provided me with information on many hard-to-find titles.

Booksellers Carol Docheff of Berkeley, California and Helen Younger of Aleph-Bet Books, Valley Cottage, New York provided additional bibliographic information, as well as the discovery that Little Golden Books were issued with dust jackets.

Others who shared their children's collections of Little Golden Books with me are Doris Blythe, Patricia Blythe, Cathy Gaskin and Joyce Sanders.

Once again, my task was made easier because of the thoughtful, insightful suggestions of my editor, Marilyn Brownstein.

I would also like to thank my husband and son for their tolerance and support, without which I could never have completed this work.

Introduction

The story of Little Golden Books began in the early 1940s
with the foresight of Georges Duplaix, Lucille Ogle, Albert
Leventhal and Leon Shimkin.

Georges Duplaix, head of Artists and Writers Guild,
together with his assistant, Lucille Ogle, had contemplated
the possibility of creating a line of modestly priced
full-color children's books. Their idea began to take shape
when Duplaix discussed the possibilities with Leon Shimkin,
an executive with Simon & Schuster. With Shimkin's positive
reception of their idea, Duplaix and Ogle set to work,
preparing twelve prospective books.

Albert Leventhal, vice-president of Simon & Schuster,
worked with Duplaix and Ogle in developing their concept.
They knew that the only possible way to produce a quality,
full-color book selling for only 25 cents was to sell
hundreds of thousands of copies of each title. With this in
mind, they set about the task of creating a market for their
new product. Their advertising campaign began with a
four-page insert in the September 19, 1942 issue of
Publishers' Weekly.

The advertisement contained a full-page color
illustration by Miss Elliott from Mother Goose. Publisher
statements "about the how's, why's and wherefores of Little
Golden Books" include the following information: "On October
1st, 1942 Essandess [S&S] will publish the first twelve
titles in a new series of books for children. The purpose
. . . is to create a new type of low-priced juvenile books
that are outstanding from the standpoints of quality and
taste, books that are durable . . . produced in a uniform
and easily identifiable format."[1]

To assure buyers that the books were educationally sound,
the advertisement continues, "The editor supervising the
entire series is Dr. Mary Reed of Teachers College, Columbia
University."[2]

Manufacturing details stated that "each book has 44
pages, a four color jacket, 8 1/4" x 6 3/4", 14 pages in
full color, 30 pages illustrated in black and white, each
book has stained edges in blue, yellow or green."[3] There is
not much information on the dust jacket, but some have

survived the ravages of time and children. The jacket is a
duplication of the front cover of the book. It is not known
for how long the books were issued with jackets, but it
seems to have been only briefly. The books were initially
issued with a dark blue paper spine, later changed to a
marbled gold paper spine. The distinctive gold foil spine
that has become a hallmark of the series was not used until
later in their production.

Simon & Schuster executives boasted about their impending
success based on advance sales figures. "The first printing
of Little Golden Books is 600,000 copies -- 50,000 [of] each
of the 12 titles. It now looks as though this entire
quantity may be sold out by publication."[4]   Prepublication
orders included 50 gross to Marshall Field, 18 gross to
F.A.O. Schwarz, 50 gross to Womrath in New York and 20 gross
to Stix, Baer & Fuller in St. Louis.

"The first twelve Little Golden Books, a name proposed by
Tom Bevans, rolled off Western Printing's presses in the
fall of 1942, for the project had been set up with S&S
carrying out the creative editorial, art, and sales part of
it, and Western the production and manufacturing end, with
the two firms partners in the enterprise."[5]

Simon & Schuster's prediction of rapid sales was
fulfilled as three editions of each of the twelve titles
were printed and sold during the first five months. That
amounted to 1,500,000 books, or 125,000 of each title. Sales
of that magnitude far exceeded expectations in a statement
made by the publishers in a letter to the trade, "It is our
belief that as many as 1,000,000 copies of these little
books can be sold each year."[6]

Paper shortages caused by World War II, coupled with
tremendous demand for the Little Golden Books, led the
publishers to create an elaborate rationing scheme which
controlled their distribution. Simon & Schuster shipped
600,000 books from January to June 1943. There were,
however, an additional 2,000,000 copies back ordered, most
of which were never filled.

Little Golden Books were initially marketed in 800 book
and department stores. Their popularity spread distribution
to syndicated variety stores like Woolworth, Kress, and
Grant. In addition, the little books were sold in toy
stores, drug stores, newsstands, stationery stores and
finally entered the biggest of all outlets -- the
supermarkets. By 1957, Little Golden Books were sold in
120,000 outlets throughout the United States.

Simon & Schuster soon became well established in their
role of providing reading material for young children. Their
phenomenal success in the creation of the Little Golden Book
series was followed by others, including the Giant Golden
Books, Tiny Golden Books and Big Golden Books. These
promotional wizards were quick to realize that children
enjoyed hearing a record just as much as they enjoyed
reading a book, perhaps even more. Thus, Little Golden
Records were introduced to the trade at the American
Booksellers' Association Convention in 1948. Twelve
different records, priced at 20 cents each, were offered for

sale in the summer of 1948. The unbreakable yellow plastic
records came in a heavy paper folder, the same size as the
Little Golden Books. A brief story and color illustrations
were printed on the folder.[7]   True to form, the 10,000-
record stock of one Los Angeles store was sold out within
three days.

Another Little Golden Book spin-off was My Little Golden
Writing Paper, introduced in the fall of 1951. Each box
contained twelve single sheets, six double sheets, twelve
post cards, and twelve envelopes, all decorated in color
with Golden Book characters.

The overwhelming success of Little Golden Books was not
limited to the United States. Translations appeared in
France, Germany, Norway, Sweden, Mexico, Saudi Arabia,
Portugal, and Japan. English versions were also marketed in
England and Canada. By 1958, Little Golden Books appeared
regularly in translation in 13 languages.

Little Golden Books were the first of the 25-cent
children's books, but they were not without imitators for
long. Wonder Books, Jolly Books, Treasure Books, Bonnie
Books, Elf Books, and Cozy Corner Books soon provided
competition with similarly designed series.

Although the future of the 25-cent mass market book
seemed quite bright, it could not remain equally bright for
all competing publishers. By 1953, most publishers and
distributors agreed that "the immediate future will see a
period of overproduction and overexpansion, followed by an
inevitable shake-out. There will then remain four or five or
six publishers to supply . . . well-printed, well-edited,
colorful pre-school books at the lowest possible price."[8]
Obviously, Simon & Schuster weathered the shake-out and
survived. But, despite their survival in the 25-cent book
market, they were receptive to an offer from Western to buy
out their half interest. On November 12, 1958, an
announcement was made of the formation of Golden Press, Inc.
jointly owned by Western Printing & Lithographing Co. and
Affiliated Publishers, Inc., later Pocket Books. Albert R.
Leventhal was named president, but also continued in his
position as president of the Artists and Writers Guild, the
creative book division of Western Printing. Golden Press
prospered throughout the years, and in 1964, Western bought
out Pocket Books' interest, becoming sole owner of the many
Golden Book lines.

The subject content of Little Golden Books covered the
normal fare of nursery rhymes, fairy tales, poetry, songs,
ABC books, and animal stories. In addition to their frequent
use of time-honored classics, the editors of Little Golden
Books looked to contemporary writers for original stories.

One of the most famous was Margaret Wise Brown, who
created eighteen lively stories for the series, including
works such as The two little gardeners, Five little firemen,
The sleepy book, Seven little postmen, and The wonderful
house. Edith Thacher Hurd collaborated with Brown on many of
these titles.

Several stories were contributed by Helen Palmer, better
known as the first wife of Dr. Seuss. Scuffy the tugboat

and <u>Tootle</u> were two of the memorable characters created by
Gertrude Crampton. The team of Kathryn and Byron Jackson was
responsible for bringing us <u>The saggy baggy elephant</u> and <u>The
tawny scrawny lion,</u> while founder, Georges Duplaix created
<u>The lively little rabbit,</u> <u>The topsy turvy circus,</u> and <u>The
big brown bear.</u>

Kathleen Daly and Jane Werner Watson were both members of
the editorial staff of Western and were involved in the
writing of numerous stories and adaptations.

More recent authors include Joan Chase Bowden, David Lee
Harrison, Barbara Shook Hazen, Charlotte Zolotow, Charles
Spain Verral, and Adelaide Holl. Patricia Scarry, wife of
Richard Scarry, has authored twenty titles for the Little
Golden Book series.

The advertisement for Little Golden Books that appeared
in the September 19, 1942 <u>Publishers' Weekly</u> stated that
"each book is illustrated by one of the country's top
juvenile artists."[9] The first list included Gustav
Tenggren, Rudolf Freund, Corinne Malvern and Masha. Another
early illustrator was Feodor Rojankovsky, brought to America
in 1941 by Georges Duplaix.

Eloise Wilkin, Tibor Gergely, Garth Williams, and Lilian
Obligado were prolific Little Golden Book illustrators, each
bringing his or her own distinctive style to the series.
Richard Scarry was a Simon & Schuster discovery. The first
book he ever illustrated was <u>Duck and his friends,</u> a Little
Golden Book published in 1949.

The Walt Disney Book subseries was begun with the
publication of <u>Through the picture frame</u> in 1944. This
collaboration with the Disney Studio brought more
illustrators into the Little Golden Book family. Alice and
Martin Provensen (awarded the Caldecott Medal in 1984), J.P.
Miller, and Mel Crawford were all staff artists for Disney
before they began illustrating Little Golden Books. Another
Caldecott award winner who illustrated Little Golden Books
early in her career was Trina Schart Hyman.

Several of the most successful Little Golden Book titles
were tied to promotional endorsements of commercial
products. The first was <u>Dr. Dan, the bandage man,</u> written by
Helen Gaspard with illustrations by Corinne Malvern. Simon &
Schuster had reached an agreement with Johnson & Johnson,
makers of Band-Aids, in which a predicted eighteen million
Band-Aids would be supplied to be given away with books
sold. The first printing of 1,600,000 was the largest first
edition of a Little Golden Book ever produced at the time.
"The book is intended to explain the rudiments of first aid
for pre-school children, and each copy will have in it six
real Band-Aids."[10] Johnson & Johnson advertised Dr. Dan on
their television programs and purchased 400,000 copies to be
sold in drugstores. The book was issued in January 1951 with
"what the publishers believe to be 'unquestionably the most
extensive advertising and promotional campaign ever staged
for a low-priced book.'"[11]

Simon & Schuster was soon to outdo even themselves with
the largest promotional campaign ever mounted, this for

Little Lulu and her magic tricks. Released on May 1, 1954 with a first printing of 2,250,000 copies, "probably the largest initial run of any book ever published in this country."[12]   Little Lulu contained a packet of Kleenex tissues with instructions for making a doll, a carnation, and a bunny. Full-page ads in Life, Look, Woman's Day, and Family Circle constituted part of the immense advertising campaign. A demonstration of the tricks from the book was presented on the "Arthur Godfrey Show," reaching an estimated 7,500,000 families. Direction sheets were included in 100 million boxes of Kleenex distributed during May, June, and July. An animated battery-run figure of Little Lulu holding a Little Golden Book was available for high-traffic outlets. A first pressing of 400,000 copies of a new Little Golden Record was also promoted along with the book.

Regardless of which imprint graced the title page of a Little Golden Book, the sales figures were astounding. By their tenth anniversary in 1952, Little Golden Books had sold 182,615,000 copies. Of the 161 titles, 86 had sold more than one million copies each; 13 titles had sold in excess of two million; 4 others sold three million copies and The night before Christmas had sold more than four million copies.[13] By 1954, the total number sold had jumped to 300 million. The 400 million mark was reached in 1957.[14] By 1958, 150 of the titles had sold more than one million copies each, with several reaching the five million mark. At the time of the twentieth anniversary in 1962, 452 Little Golden Book titles had been issued. In celebration of the fortieth anniversary in 1982, sales figures had reached 800 million, with the perennial favorite, The poky little puppy accounting for more than six million copies.[15]

In spite of the marketing success of the Little Golden Book series, the titles are ignored by reviewers, are absent from library shelves, and are denounced as the junk food of children's literature. They have been passed over by award programs, with the notable exception of I can fly, which was named an Honor Book in the New York Herald Tribune Spring Book Festival proceedings in 1951.

Despite their poor image with literary critics, librarians, and teachers, Little Golden Books do have a place in the history of children's literature. In his masterful work on the history of book publishing in the United States, John Tebbel offers the following comment concerning the impact of the Little Golden Book series on children's literature : "certainly one of the most significant, far-reaching and successful of the developments during that period [1940-1960] was the creation and marketing of the various Golden Book lines. . . ."[16]

Down the Rabbit Hole by Selma Lanes devotes an entire chapter to the impact of mass-market books on children's literature in general. The chapter concludes with the following, "While the thread binding them to children's literature may often be tenuous, merchandise books serve a number of positive ends. . . . Merchandise publishing brings an awareness of books to countless children who never set foot in a library. Whatever one may think of many of

the texts, the books' design is often excellent and the
illustrations are engaging, tasteful and, on occasion,
first-rate. For a child whose only extended exposure to
books is through school texts or the comics, these
merchandise products provide portals to the possibility
of reading pleasure. One safe generalization about
merchandise books is that they stick close to the
common experiences and interests of childhood. No child
is ever likely to be intimidated by the subject matter
of a merchandise book, and few parents will be stopped
by their prices. They are not investments to be
protected and handled only with clean hands in the
presence of a responsible adult. From a child's point
of view, they probably help to give reading a good
name."17

Little Golden Books are now into their fourth decade of
publishing. New series are created each year, utilizing
characters and situations from the past, present, and
future. The newest Little Golden Book spin-off is the First
Little Golden Book series. These books are identical in
format to the familiar Little Golden Books, but with smaller
dimensions.

Familiar characters live on in new adventures. The poky
little puppy goes to the fair, pulls wash from the line,
loses his bone, and even learns how to count. The saggy
baggy elephant meets new friends, dances a new dance, and
counts just as well as the poky little puppy in his own
counting book.

Although the controversy regarding the relative value of
children's merchandise books and "quality" children's books
continues, we may find that there is a need, as well as a
plentiful market, for both types of books.

Notes

1.   "Announcing little golden books," Publishers' Weekly,
September 19, 1942, unpaged advertising supplement.
2.   Ibid.
3.   Ibid.
4.   Ibid.
5.   Peter Schwed, Turning the pages : an insider's story
of Simon & Schuster 1924-1984 (New York: Macmillan, 1984),
p. 167.
6.   Albert R. Leventhal, "The children's book in the mass
market," Publishers' Weekly, November 21, 1953, p. 2106.
7.   "Little golden records to be introduced at
convention," Publishers' Weekly, May 15, 1948, p. 2095.
8.   Ibid. , pp. 2107-08.
9.   "Announcing little golden books," Publishers' Weekly,
September 19, 1942, unpaged advertising supplement.
10.   "Tips for the booksellers," Publishers' Weekly,
December 23, 1950, p. 2568.
11.   Ibid.
12.   "Spring promotions for 25-cent children's book
lines," Publishers' Weekly, March 20, 1954, p. 1448.

13. "Golden numbers," Publishers' Weekly, July 26, 1952, p. 354.

14. Schwed, Turning the pages, p. 168.

15. "A birthday celebration for golden books," Publishers' Weekly, April 9, 1982, p. 24.

16. John Tebbel, A history of book publishing in the United States. Vol. IV The great change, 1940-1980. (New York: R. R. Bowker, 1981), p. 468.

17. Selma G. Lanes, Down the rabbit hole: adventures & misadventures in the realm of children's literature. (New York: Atheneum, 1972), pp. 126-27.

Abbreviations

A	Little Golden Activity Book
B	Braille book
c	copyright date
ca.	circa
col.	color
D	Walt Disney Book
Din	Ding Dong School Book
fr.	frames
FS	filmstrip
GB	Golden Book
GP	Golden Press
GR	Golden Record
ill.	illustrated
illus	illustrator
in.	inch
ips	inch per second
LC#	Library of Congress card number
mm	millimeter
min.	minute
mono.	monaural
MP	motion picture
pseud	pseudonym
rpm	revolutions per minute
S&S	Simon & Schuster
sec.	second
SR	sound recording
V	variant
VC	videocassette

Title List

001. <u>ABC around the house</u> by Sharon Holaves, ill. by Fred Irvin; NY: GP, c1978. (LITTLE GOLDEN BOOK 176X).

001a. ---- NY: S&S, c1957. (LITTLE GOLDEN ACTIVITY BOOK A18).

001b. ---- NY: GP, c1962. (LITTLE GOLDEN ACTIVITY BOOK A44).

001c. ---- reissued (LITTLE GOLDEN BOOK 200-25).

002. <u>ABC is for Christmas</u> by Jane Werner Watson, ill. by Sally Augustiny; NY: GP, c1974. (LITTLE GOLDEN BOOK 108X).

002a. ---- reissued (LITTLE GOLDEN BOOK 454-1).

003. <u>ABC rhymes</u> by Carl Memling, ill. by Roland Rodegast and Grace Clarke; NY: GP, c1964. Copyright A690710 dated 26 Mar 64. (LITTLE GOLDEN BOOK 543).

003B. ---- [braille] Tarzana, CA: American Brotherhood for the Blind, Twin Vision Publication Division; reprint of the c1964 ed. Opposite pages in braille. (TWIN VISION BOOK).

003SR. ---- [sound recording] NY: Golden Record, [197-]. 1 disc (45 rpm, mono.; 7 in.) + book, c1964. Narrated by Doris Baran. (READ AND HEAR GR 00233).

003a. ---- reissued (LITTLE GOLDEN BOOK 200-3).

004. <u>Adventures of goat, The</u> by Lucille Hammond, ill. by Eugenie; NY: GP, c1984. LC# 83-80022. (LITTLE GOLDEN BOOK 201-10).

005. <u>Adventures of Lassie, The</u> NY: S&S, c1957. Authorized ed. Contents: <u>Lassie and her day in the sun</u> / Charles Spain Verral, ill. by Mel Crawford (381) -- <u>Lassie and the daring rescue</u> / Charles Spain Verral, ill. by E. Joseph Dreany (383) -- <u>Lassie shows the way</u> / Monica Hill, ill. by Lee Ames (385). (GIANT LITTLE GOLDEN BOOK 5012).

006. Airplanes by Ruth Mabee Lachman, ill. by Lenora and Herbert Combes; NY: S&S, c1953. LC# 53-4502. Copyright A114601 dated 22 Oct 53; renewal RE-109-124 dated 29 Oct 81. (LITTLE GOLDEN BOOK 180).

006a. ---- ill. by Steele Savage; NY: GP, c1959. Copyright A415430 dated 21 Sept 59. (LITTLE GOLDEN BOOK 373).

007. Aladdin and his magic lamp. A story from A thousand and one Arabian nights by Kathleen N. Daly, ill. by Lowell Hess; NY: GP, c1959. Copyright A430194 dated 29 Oct 59. (LITTLE GOLDEN BOOK 371).

008. Albert's zoo : a stencil book by Jane Werner, ill. by Richard Scarry; NY: S&S, c1951. LC# 51-39072rev. Copyright A60626 dated 6 Mar 51; renewal RE-42-803 dated 7 Nov 79. Contains 7 pages of stencils. (LITTLE GOLDEN BOOK 112).

009. Ali Baba and the forty thieves. A story from A thousand and one Arabian nights ill. by Lowell Hess; NY: GP, c1958. Copyright AA357017 dated 21 May 58. (LITTLE GOLDEN BOOK 323).

009SR. ---- [sound recording] NY: Golden Record. 1 disc (45 rpm, mono.; 7 in.) + book. (READ AND HEAR).

010. Alice in Wonderland finds the garden of live flowers, Walt Disney's told by Jane Werner, pictures by the Walt Disney Studio, adapted by Campbell Grant from the motion picture "Alice in Wonderland" based on the story by Lewis Carroll; NY: S&S, c1951. LC# 51-40026. (WALT DISNEY BOOK D20).

011. Alice in Wonderland meets the White Rabbit, Walt Disney's retold by Jane Werner, pictures by the Walt Disney Studio adapted by Al Dempster from the motion picture "Alice in Wonderland" based on the story by Lewis Carroll; NY: S&S, c1951. LC# 51-13084. (WALT DISNEY BOOK D19).

011a. ---- reissued (LITTLE GOLDEN BOOK 103-41).

012. All aboard! by Marion Conger, ill. by Corinne Malvern; NY: S&S, c1952. LC# 52-11750. Copyright A68949 dated 18 Jun 52; renewal RE-68-197 dated 20 Oct 80. (LITTLE GOLDEN BOOK 152).

013. Alphabet from A to Z, The by Leah Gale, ill. by Vivienne Blake; NY: S&S, c1942. LC# 42-24232. Copyright A168877 dated 13 Nov 42. First printing Sept 42. (LITTLE GOLDEN BOOK 3).

014. Amanda's first day of school story and pictures by Joan Elizabeth Goodman; NY: GB, c1985. LC# 84-72864. (LITTLE GOLDEN BOOK 204-56).

015. Amazing Mumford forgets the magic words!, The by
Patricia Thackray, ill. by Normand Chartier, featuring Jim
Henson's Muppets; Racine: Western, in conjunction with
Children's Television Workshop, c1979. (LITTLE GOLDEN BOOK
108-45); (SESAME STREET BOOK).

016. Animal alphabet from A to Z by Barbara Shook Hazen,
ill. by Adele Werber; NY: GP, c1959. Copyright AA380261
dated 29 Dec 58. (LITTLE GOLDEN BOOK 349).

017. Animal babies by Kathryn and Byron Jackson, ill. by
Adele Werber; NY: S&S, c1947. LC# 47-11889. Copyright A19678
dated 27 Oct 47; renewal R589656 dated 4 Nov 74. (LITTLE
GOLDEN BOOK 39).

Animal book. See My little golden animal book (515).

018. Animal counting book adapted from "Over in the meadow"
an old nursery poem, ill. by Moritz Kennel; NY: GP, c1969.
(LITTLE GOLDEN BOOK 584).

019. Animal daddies and my daddy by Barbara Shook Hazen,
ill. by Ilse-Margret Vogel, NY: GP, c1968. (LITTLE GOLDEN
BOOK 576).

019a. ---- reissued (LITTLE GOLDEN BOOK 208-3).

020. Animal dictionary by Jane Werner Watson, ill. by Feodor
Rojankovsky; NY: GP, c1960. Copyright A458299 dated 25 May
60. (LITTLE GOLDEN BOOK 379).

020a. ---- reissued (LITTLE GOLDEN BOOK 533X).

020b. ---- reissued (LITTLE GOLDEN BOOK 205-1).

021. Animal friends by Jane Werner, ill. by Garth Williams;
NY: S&S, c1953. LC# 52-12327rev. Copyright A99467 dated 27
May 53; renewal RE-109-103 dated 29 Oct 81. (LITTLE GOLDEN
BOOK 167).
    Later issued with title The very best home for me
(774).

021a. ---- reissued in 1959 (LITTLE GOLDEN BOOK 365).

021b. ---- reissued (LITTLE GOLDEN BOOK 560).

021c. ---- reissued (LITTLE GOLDEN BOOK 304-25).

022. Animal gym by Beth Greiner Hoffman, ill. by Tibor
Gergely; NY: S&S, c1956. LC# 56-1861. Copyright A237063
dated 24 Feb 56; renewal RE 223-016 dated 21 Nov 84.
(LITTLE GOLDEN BOOK 249).

023. Animal orchestra by Ilo Orleans, ill. by Tibor Gergely;
NY: GP, c1958. Copyright AA380257 dated 19 Nov 58. (LITTLE
GOLDEN BOOK 334).

024. Animal quiz by Nancy Fielding Hulick, ill. by Mel Crawford; NY: GP, c1960. Copyright A477192 dated 17 Nov 60. (LITTLE GOLDEN BOOK 396).

024a. ---- reissued (LITTLE GOLDEN BOOK 201-10).

025. Animal quiz book by Edith T. Kunhardt, ill. by Kelly Oechsli; NY: GP, c1983. LC# 82-83066/AC. (LITTLE GOLDEN BOOK 308-44; 308-54).

026. Animal stamps by Kathleen N. Daly and James Gordon Irving, drawings by William J. Dugan; NY: S&S, c1955. LC# 56-13514. (LITTLE GOLDEN ACTIVITY BOOK A7).

Animal stories. See Giant little golden book of animal stories (270).

027. Animals and their babies by Barbara Shook Hazen, ill. by Lilian Obligado; NY: GP, c1959. (LITTLE GOLDEN ACTIVITY BOOK A29).

028. Animals' Christmas eve, The by Gale Wiersum, ill. by Jim Robison; NY: GP, c1977. (LITTLE GOLDEN BOOK 154X).

028a. ---- reissued (LITTLE GOLDEN BOOK 456-1).

029. Animals' Merry Christmas, The by Kathryn Jackson, ill. by Richard Scarry; NY: S&S, c1950. Copyright A47924 dated 13 Sept 50; renewal R672902 dated 28 Sept 77. (LITTLE GOLDEN BOOK 329).

029a. ---- reissued in 1958; copyright AA358151 dated 18 June 58.

030. Animals of Farmer Jones, The by Leah Gale, ill. by Rudolf Freund; NY: S&S, c1942. LC# 42-24235rev. Copyright A168879 dated 13 Nov 42. First printing Sept 42. (LITTLE GOLDEN BOOK 11).

030SR. ---- [sound recording] Copyright KK46591 dated 1 Mar 49 (LITTLE GOLDEN RECORD 13).

030a. ---- ill. by Richard Scarry; NY: S&S, c1953. LC# 53-4414. Copyright A114600 dated 1 Oct 53; renewal RE-109-123 dated 29 Oct 81. (LITTLE GOLDEN BOOK 211).

030aSR. ---- [sound recording] NY: Golden Record, [197-]. 1 disc (45 rpm, mono.; 7 in.) + book, c1953. Narrated by Miss Laine; music director, Ralph Stein. (READ AND HEAR GR 00218).

030b. ---- ill. by Richard Scarry; NY: S&S, c1956. (LITTLE GOLDEN BOOK 282).

030c. ---- reissued (LITTLE GOLDEN BOOK 303-23).

031. Animals on the farm written and ill. by Jan Pfloog; NY:
GP, c1963. (LITTLE GOLDEN BOOK 573).

031a. ---- reissued (LITTLE GOLDEN BOOK 200-41; 203-3).

032. Annie Oakley and the rustlers by Ann McGovern, ill. by
Mel Crawford; NY: S&S, c1955. LC# 55-1613. (LITTLE GOLDEN
BOOK 221).

033. Annie Oakley, sharpshooter by Charles Spain Verral,
ill. by E. Joseph Dreany; NY: S&S, c1956. LC# 57-1087.
(LITTLE GOLDEN BOOK 275).

034. Aren't you glad? by Charlotte Zolotow, ill. by Elaine
Kurtz; NY: GP, c1962. Copyright A609558 dated 22 Nov 62.
(LITTLE GOLDEN BOOK 489X).

035. Aristocats, Walt Disney Productions presents the
Authorized edition based on the popular motion picture. NY:
GP, c1970. (WALT DISNEY BOOK D122).

036. Babes in toyland, Walt Disney's based on the Walt
Disney motion picture "Babes in toyland" told by Barbara
Shook Hazen, pictures by the Walt Disney Studio, adapted by
Earl and Carol Marshall; NY: GP, c1961. (WALT DISNEY BOOK
D97).

037. Baby animals written and ill. by Garth Williams; NY:
S&S, c1956. LC# 57-1089. Copyright A273106 dated 12 Dec 56;
renewal RE-223-055 dated 11 Nov 84. (LITTLE GOLDEN BOOK
274).

037a. ---- reissued in 1963 (LITTLE GOLDEN BOOK 517).

037b. ---- reissued (LITTLE GOLDEN BOOK 204-22).

038. Baby Dear by Esther Wilkin, ill. by Eloise Wilkin; NY:
GP, c1962. Copyright A569104 dated 11 Apr 62. (LITTLE GOLDEN
BOOK 466).
    "Baby Dear" is a registered trademark of a doll designed
by Eloise Wilkin and manufactured exclusively by Vogue
Dolls.

038a. ---- reissued (LITTLE GOLDEN BOOK 209-4).

039. Baby farm animals [written and ill.] by Garth Williams;
NY: S&S, c1958. Copyright AA358150 dated 25 Jun 58; renewal
RE-109-109 dated 29 Oct 81. (LITTLE GOLDEN BOOK 333).

039a. ---- reissued in 1961 (LITTLE GOLDEN BOOK 464).

039b. ---- reissued (LITTLE GOLDEN BOOK 203-22).

040. Baby Jesus stamps by Jane Werner Watson, ill. by Eloise
Wilkin; NY: S&S, c1957. (LITTLE GOLDEN ACTIVITY BOOK A12).

041. <u>Baby listens</u> by Esther Wilkin, ill. by Eloise Wilkin;
NY: GP, c1960. Copyright A458642 dated 25 May 60. (LITTLE
GOLDEN BOOK 383.)

042. <u>Baby looks</u> by Esther Wilkin, ill. by Eloise Wilkin; NY:
GP, c1960. Copyright A498319 dated 14 Dec 60. (LITTLE GOLDEN
BOOK 404).

043. <u>Baby's birthday</u> [by Patricia Mowers], ill. by Eloise
Wilkin; NY: GP, c1972. Copyright A377979 dated 28 Sept 72.
(LITTLE GOLDEN BOOK 365X).

043a. ---- reissued (LITTLE GOLDEN BOOK 209-5).

044. <u>Baby's book</u> [by Janette Lowrey], ill. by Bob Smith; NY:
S&S, c1942. LC# 42-25479. Copyright A168874 dated 13 Nov 42.
First printing 1 Oct 42. (LITTLE GOLDEN BOOK 10).
    Later issued with title <u>My first book</u> (507).

045. <u>Baby's first book</u> [written and ill.] by Garth Williams;
NY: S&S, c1955. LC# 55-1685. Copyright A180485 dated 16 Feb
55; renewal RE-185-986 dated 5 Dec 83. (LITTLE GOLDEN BOOK
358).

045a. ---- reissued in 1959 (LITTLE GOLDEN BOOK 489).

046. <u>Baby's first Christmas</u> by Esther Wilkin, ill. by Eloise
Wilkin; NY: GP, c1959. Copyright A404077 dated 17 Jun 59.
(LITTLE GOLDEN BOOK 368).

047. <u>Baby's house</u> by Gelolo McHugh, ill. by Mary Blair; NY:
S&S, c1950. LC# 50-6275. Copyright A41544 dated 18 Jan 50;
renewal R658086 dated 4 Feb 77. With jigsaw puzzle in back
cover. (LITTLE GOLDEN BOOK 80).

047a. ---- reissued in 1963 (LITTLE GOLDEN BOOK 524).

048. <u>Baby's Mother Goose</u> ill. by Aurelius Battaglia; NY:
S&S, c1957. (LITTLE GOLDEN BOOK 303).
    Originally issued with title <u>Pat-a-cake: A baby's
Mother Goose</u> (574).

048a. ---- reissued (LITTLE GOLDEN BOOK 422).

049. <u>Bambi, Walt Disney's</u> based on the original story by
Felix Salten, ill. by the Walt Disney Studio, adapted by Bob
Grant from the Walt Disney motion picture "Bambi;" NY: S&S,
c1948. LC# 48-6666. (WALT DISNEY BOOK D7); (MICKEY MOUSE
CLUB BOOK D7).

049B. ---- [braille] Tarzana, CA: American Brotherhood for
the Blind, Twin Vision Publication Division; reprint of the
c1948 ed. Opposite pages in braille. (TWIN VISION BOOK).

049a. ---- reissued in 1960 (WALT DISNEY BOOK D90).

049b. ---- reissued (LITTLE GOLDEN BOOK 106-9; 106-41).

050. Bambi, friends of the forest, Walt Disney's by Felix Salten, ill. by the Walt Disney Studios; NY: GP, c1975. (WALT DISNEY BOOK D132).

050a. ---- reissued (LITTLE GOLDEN BOOK 106-42).

051. Bamm-Bamm, with Pebbles Flintstone by Jean Lewis, ill. by Hawley Pratt and Norm McGary; NY: GP, c1963. (LITTLE GOLDEN BOOK 540).

052. Barbie by Betty Biesterveld, ill. by Fred Irvin; NY: GP, c1974. Features Barbie and Ken. (LITTLE GOLDEN BOOK 125X).

Barbie. See also Superstar Barbie (700).

053. Beaney goes to sea, Bob Clampett's by Monica Hill, ill. by Hawley Pratt and Bill Lorencz; NY: GP, c1963. (LITTLE GOLDEN BOOK 537).

054. Bear in the boat, The written and ill. by Ilse-Margret Vogel; NY: GP, c1972. Copyright A409624 dated 29 Jan 73 (1972 notice). (LITTLE GOLDEN BOOK 397).

055. Bear's surprise party by Joan Bowden, ill. by Jerry Scott; NY: GP, c1975. (LITTLE GOLDEN BOOK 809); (EAGER READER).

056. Bedknobs and broomsticks, Walt Disney Productions presents, based on the popular motion picture; NY: GP, c1971. Authorized ed. (WALT DISNEY BOOK D93).

057. Bedtime stories. NY: GP, c1969. Contents: The golden sleepy book / Margaret Wise Brown (286) -- The new baby / Ruth and Harold Shane (534) -- The sailor dog / Margaret Wise Brown (663) -- The kitten who thought he was a mouse / Miriam Norton (374) -- Daddies / Janet Frank (173) -- The wonderful house / Margaret Wise Brown (816) -- Indian, Indian / Charlotte Zolotow (350) -- Baby animals / Garth Williams (037) -- What if? / Helen and Henry Tanous (788) -- Daniel Boone / Irwin Shapiro (177) -- The merry shipwreck / Georges Duplaix (467) -- Busy Timmy / Kathryn and Byron Jackson (118) -- Hush, hush, it's sleepytime / Peggy Parish (342). LC# 72-89089. (LITTLE GOLDEN BOOK LIBRARY).

058. Bedtime stories [revisions by Leah Gale], ill. by Gustaf Tenggren. NY: Artists & Writers Guild, dist. by S&S, c1942. Contents: Chicken Little -- The three bears -- The three little pigs -- Little Red Riding Hood -- The gingerbread man. LC# 42-24230. Copyright A168875 dated 13 Nov 42. First printing Sept 42. (LITTLE GOLDEN BOOK 2).

058a. ---- reissued in 1955 (LITTLE GOLDEN BOOK 239).

Ø58b. ---- reissued in 1959 (LITTLE GOLDEN BOOK 364).

Ø58c. ---- reissued (LITTLE GOLDEN BOOK 538).

Ø58d. ---- reissued (LITTLE GOLDEN BOOK 311-22).

Ø59. Ben and me, Walt Disney's based on the book by Robert
Lawson, pictures by the Walt Disney Studio, adapted by
Campbell Grant from the motion picture "Ben and Me;" NY:
S&S, c1954. LC# 54-14961. (WALT DISNEY BOOK D37).

Ø6Ø. Benji, fastest dog in the West, Joe Camp's by Gina
Ingoglia, ill. by Werner Willis; NY: GP, c1978. (LITTLE
GOLDEN BOOK 165X).

Ø6Øa. ---- reissued (LITTLE GOLDEN BOOK 111-6).

Ø61. Bert's hall of great inventions by Ravena Dwight, ill.
by Roger Bradfield, featuring Bert and Ernie and other Jim
Henson Muppets; Racine: Western, in conjunction with
Children's Television Workshop, c1972. (LITTLE GOLDEN BOOK
321); (SESAME STREET BOOK).

Ø61a. ---- reissued (LITTLE GOLDEN BOOK 1Ø9-23).

Ø62. Best friends by Catherine Kenworthy, ill. by DyAnne
DiSalvo-RyAn; NY: GP, c1983. LC# 82-82285/AC. (LITTLE GOLDEN
BOOK 2Ø9-56).

Ø63. Best of all! A story about the farm, The by Cecily Ruth
Hogan, ill. by Lorinda Bryan Cauley; NY: GP, c1978.
Copyright TX-33-675 dated 9 Aug 79. (LITTLE GOLDEN BOOK
17ØX).

Ø63a. ---- reissued (LITTLE GOLDEN BOOK 2Ø3-4).

Ø64. Betsy McCall, paper doll story book by Selma Robinson,
ill. by Ginnie Hofmann; NY: GP, c1965. (LITTLE GOLDEN BOOK
559).

Ø65. Bialosky's Christmas by Leslie McGuire, ill. by Jerry
Joyner, [created by Peggy and Alan Bialosky]; NY: GB, c1984.
LC# 84-80551. (LITTLE GOLDEN BOOK ---).

Ø66. Bialosky's special picnic by Leslie McGuire, ill. by
Jerry Joyner; created by Peggy and Alan Bialosky; NY: GB,
c1985. (LITTLE GOLDEN BOOK 2Ø4-55).

Bible stories. See My first book of Bible stories (5Ø8).

Ø67. Bible stories from the Old Testament by Sing Lee, ill.
by Jim Robison; NY: GP, c1977. (LITTLE GOLDEN BOOK 153X).

Ø67a. ---- reissued (LITTLE GOLDEN BOOK 4Ø9-1).

068. <u>Bible stories of boys and girls</u> retold by Jane Werner,
ill. by Rachel Taft Dixon and Marjorie Hartwell; NY: S&S,
c1953. LC# 53-3747rev. Copyright A105646 dated 22 Jul 53;
renewal RE-109-107 dated 29 Oct 81. (LITTLE GOLDEN BOOK
174).

068a. ---- reissued (LITTLE GOLDEN BOOK 404-1).

069. <u>Big Bird brings Spring to Sesame Street</u> by Lauren
Collier Swindler, ill. by Marsha Winborn; featuring Jim
Henson's Sesame Street Muppets; NY: Sesame Street/Golden
Press Book, c1985. LC# 83-82194. (LITTLE GOLDEN BOOK
108-57); (SESAME STREET BOOK).

069VC. ---- [videocassette] Racine: Western, c1985. <u>5
Sesame Street stories</u> [including <u>Big Bird brings Spring to
Sesame Street</u>]. 1 videocassette (30 min., sd., col., 1/2
in.) VHS (GOLDEN BOOK VIDEO) #13863.

070. <u>Big Bird's day on the farm</u> by Cathi Rosenberg-Turow,
ill. by Maggie Swanson, inspired by "Sesame Street presents:
Follow that bird;" screenplay by Tony Geiss and Judy
Freudberg; featuring Jim Henson's Sesame Street Muppets; NY:
Sesame Street/Golden Press Book, c1985. LC# 84-72876.
(LITTLE GOLDEN BOOK 107-61); (SESAME STREET BOOK).

071. <u>Big Bird's red book</u> by Rosanne and Jonathan Cerf, ill.
by Michael J. Smollin; featuring Jim Henson's Muppets;
Racine: Western, in conjunction with Children's Televison
Workshop, c1977. (LITTLE GOLDEN BOOK 157X); (SESAME STREET
BOOK).

071a. ---- reissued (LITTLE GOLDEN BOOK 108-22).

Big blue marble. See <u>The runaway squash</u> (659).

072. <u>Big brown bear, The</u> by Georges Duplaix, ill. by Gustaf
Tenggren; NY: S&S, c1947. Copyright A20051 dated 1 Dec 47.
(LITTLE GOLDEN BOOK 89).

072SR. ---- [sound recording] Copyright KK38751 dated 1 Sep
48 (LITTLE GOLDEN RECORD 11).

072SR. ---- [sound recording] NY: Golden Record, [197-]. 1
disc (45 rpm, mono.; 7 in.) + book, c1947. Narrated by Jerry
Roberts; music director, Ralph Stein. (READ AND HEAR
GR 00220).

072a. ---- reissued in 1959 (LITTLE GOLDEN BOOK 335).

072b. ---- reissued in 1975; LC# 82-83097. Copyright renewal
R595810 dated 6 Jan 75. (LITTLE GOLDEN BOOK 304-41).

073. <u>Big enough helper, The</u> by Nancy Hall, ill. by Tom
O'Sullivan; NY: GP, c1978. (LITTLE GOLDEN BOOK 152X).

073a. ---- reissued (LITTLE GOLDEN BOOK 208-5; 208-41).

074. Big little book, The by Dorothy Hall Smith, ill. by
Moritz Kennel; NY: GP, c1962. Copyright A591060 dated 28
Sept 62. (LITTLE GOLDEN BOOK 482).

075. Big Red, Walt Disney's based on the Walt Disney motion
picture "Big Red," story adapted by Kathleen N. Daly, ill.
by Mel Crawford; NY: GP, c1962. (WALT DISNEY BOOK D102).

076. Biggest most beautiful Christmas tree, The story and
pictures by Amye Rosenberg; NY: GB, c1985. LC# 84-72867.
(LITTLE GOLDEN BOOK 459-8).

077. Bird stamps by Kathleen N. Daly and James Gordon
Irving; NY: S&S, c1955. LC# 56-13516. (LITTLE GOLDEN
ACTIVITY BOOK A8).

078. Birds by Jane Werner Watson, ill. by Eloise Wilkin; NY:
GP, c1958. (LITTLE GOLDEN BOOK 184X).

078a. ---- reissued (LITTLE GOLDEN BOOK 202-1).

Birds. See also Giant little golden book of birds (271);
Golden book of birds (279).

079. Birds of all kinds written and ill. by Walter Ferguson;
NY: GP, c1959. Copyright A430097 dated 24 Nov 59. (LITTLE
GOLDEN BOOK 380).

080. Biskitts in double trouble, The by Gina Ingoglia, ill.
by John Costanza; NY: GB, c1984. (LITTLE GOLDEN BOOK
107-47).

081. Black cauldron - Taran finds a friend, Walt Disney
Pictures The NY: GB, c1985. LC# 84-72874. (LITTLE GOLDEN
BOOK 105-54).

082. Black hole, The by Walt Disney Productions; NY:
Western, c1979. (LITTLE GOLDEN BOOK 501X).

083. Blue book of fairy tales: three stories with pictures,
The by Barbara Shook Hazen, ill. by Gordon Laite; NY: GP,
c1959. Copyright A430096 dated 24 Nov 59. (LITTLE GOLDEN
BOOK 374).

084. Boats by Ruth Mabee Lachman, ill. by Lenora and Herbert
Combes; NY: S&S, c1951. LC# 51-13831. Copyright A62296 dated
9 Oct 51; renewal RE-46-391 dated 7 Nov 79. (LITTLE GOLDEN
BOOK 125).

084a. ---- reissued in 1959 (LITTLE GOLDEN BOOK 339).

084b. ---- reissued in 1962 (LITTLE GOLDEN BOOK 501).

085. Bobby and his airplanes by Helen Palmer, ill. by Tibor
Gergely; NY: S&S, c1949. LC# 49-48154. Copyright A37023
dated 1 Aug 49; renewal R641073 dated 10 Sept 76. (LITTLE
GOLDEN BOOK 69).

086. Bobby the dog written and ill. by Pierre Probst; NY:
GP, c1961. Copyright A513331 dated 16 May 61. (LITTLE GOLDEN
BOOK 440).

087. Bongo, Walt Disney's illustrated by the Walt Disney
Studio, adapted by Campbell Grant, based on the Walt Disney
motion picture adaptation of the original story Bongo by
Sinclair Lewis; NY: S&S, c1948. LC# 49-131. (WALT DISNEY
BOOK D9); (MICKEY MOUSE CLUB BOOK D9).

087a. ---- reissued in 1957; LC# 57-1221 (WALT DISNEY BOOK
D62).

088. Boo and the flying Flews by Joan Chase Bacon, ill. by
Donald Leake; NY: GP, c1974. (LITTLE GOLDEN BOOK 803);
(EAGER READER).

089. Book of God's gifts, A by Ruth Hannon, ill. by Rick
Schreter; NY: GP, c1972. Bound with: I sing a song of
praise. Adapted from Psalm 103 by Mary Michaels White, ill.
by Idellette Bordigoni. (LITTLE GOLDEN BOOK 112X).

089a. ---- reissued (LITTLE GOLDEN BOOK 411-1).

090. Bouncy baby bunny finds his bed, The by Joan Bowden,
ill. by Christine Westerberg; NY: GP, c1974. Copyright
A596535 dated 19 Nov 74. (LITTLE GOLDEN BOOK 129X).

090SR. ---- [sound recording] Racine: Western, [1977]. 1
cassette (2 track, mono.) + text and teacher's guide by
Joanne Wylie. Copyright N45526 dated 25 Jun 77. (LITTLE
GOLDEN READ ALONG 3500).

091. Bow wow! Meow! A first book of sounds by Melanie
Bellah, ill. by Trina Schart; NY: GP, c1963. Copyright
A647678 dated 31 Jul 63. (LITTLE GOLDEN BOOK 523).

091a. ---- reissued (LITTLE GOLDEN BOOK 207-3).

092. Boy with a drum, The by David L. Harrison, ill. by
Eloise Wilkin; NY: GP, c1969. (LITTLE GOLDEN BOOK 588).

092SR. ---- [sound recording] NY: Golden Record, [197-]. 1
disc (45 rpm, mono.; 7 in.) + book, c1969. Narrated by David
Teig. (READ AND HEAR GR 00254).

092a. ---- reissued (LITTLE GOLDEN BOOK 311-5).

093. Bozo and the hide 'n' seek elephant by William
Johnston, ill. by Allan Hubbard and Milli Jancar; NY: GP,
[ca. 1971]. (LITTLE GOLDEN BOOK 598).

094. Bozo finds a friend, Larry Harmon's TV by Tom Golberg,
ill. by Hawley Pratt and Al White; NY: GP, c1962. (LITTLE
GOLDEN BOOK 485).

094SR. ---- [sound recording] NY: Golden Record, [197-]. 1
disc (45 rpm, mono., 7 in.) + book, c1962. Narrated by Larry
Harmon. (READ AND HEAR GR 00169).

095. Bozo the clown by Carl Buettner, ill. by Charles
Satterfield and Al White; NY: GP, c1961. (LITTLE GOLDEN BOOK
446).

095SR. ---- [sound recording] NY: Golden Record. 1 disc (45
rpm, mono., 7 in.) + book, c1961. Narrated by Larry Harmon.
(READ AND HEAR GR 00212).

096. Brave cowboy Bill by Kathryn and Byron Jackson, ill. by
Richard Scarry; NY: S&S, c1950. LC# 50-10027. Copyright
A47920 dated 31 Aug 50; renewal R670840 dated 6 Sept 77.
With jigsaw puzzle in back cover. (LITTLE GOLDEN BOOK 93).

097. Brave Eagle by Charles Spain Verral, ill. by Si
Vanderlaan; NY: S&S, c1957. Authorized edition based on the
"Brave Eagle" television program. (LITTLE GOLDEN BOOK 294).

098. Brave little tailor, The [a new version of the old folk
tale from Grimm], ill. by J. P. Miller; NY: S&S, c1953. LC#
53-4534. Copyright A114599 dated 22 Sept 53; renewal RE-
109-122 dated 29 Oct 81. (LITTLE GOLDEN BOOK 178).

099. Bravest of all by Kate Emery Pogue, ill. by Al
Andersen; NY: GP, c1973. LGB 402. Copyright A422416 dated 9
Feb 73. (LITTLE GOLDEN BOOK 402).

099SR. ---- [sound recording] NY: Golden Record, [197-]. 1
disc (45 rpm, mono., 7 in.) + book, c1973. Narrated by Jim
Dukas. (READ AND HEAR GR 00260).

099a. ---- reissued (LITTLE GOLDEN BOOK 208-4).

100. Broken arrow by Charles Spain Verral, ill. by Mel
Crawford; NY: S&S, c1957. (LITTLE GOLDEN BOOK 299).

101. Brownie scouts by Lillian Gardner Soskin, ill. by
Louise Rumely; NY: GP, c1961. Copyright A508379 dated 18 Apr
61. (LITTLE GOLDEN BOOK 409).

102. Buck Rogers and the children of Hopetown by Ravena
Dwight, ill. by Kurt Schaffenberger; NY: GP, c1979. (LITTLE
GOLDEN BOOK 500X).

103. Buffalo Bill, Jr. and the Indian chief by Gladys Wyatt,
ill. by Hamilton Greene; NY: S&S, c1956. LC# 56-3059.
(LITTLE GOLDEN BOOK 254).

104. Bugs Bunny by Warner Bros. Cartoons, ill. by Warner
Bros. Cartoons, ill. adapted by Tom McKimson and Al
Dempster; NY: S&S, c1949. LC# 49-5071. (LITTLE GOLDEN BOOK
72).

104B. ---- [braille] Tarzana, CA: American Brotherhood for
the Blind, Twin Vision Publication Division; reprint of the
c1949 ed. Opposite pages in braille. (TWIN VISION BOOK).

104a. ---- reissued in 1958 (LITTLE GOLDEN BOOK 312).

104b. ---- reissued in 1962 (LITTLE GOLDEN BOOK 475).

105. Bugs Bunny and the Indians told by Annie North Bedford,
pictures by Warner Bros. Cartoons, adapted by Richmond I.
Kelsey and Tom McKimson; NY: S&S, c1951. LC# 51-40438.
Copyright A60928 dated 20 Sept 51. (LITTLE GOLDEN BOOK 120).

105a. ---- reissued in 1961 (LITTLE GOLDEN BOOK 430).

106. Bugs Bunny at the county fair told by Elizabeth
Beecher, pictures by Warner Bros. Cartoons, adapted by Fred
Abranz and Don MacLaughlin; NY: S&S, c1953. LC# 53-2869.
(LITTLE GOLDEN BOOK 164).

107. Bugs Bunny at the Easter party told by Kathryn Hitte,
pictures by Warner Bros. Cartoons, adapted by Tony Strobl
and Ben Kudo; NY: S&S, c1953. LC# 54-1134. (LITTLE GOLDEN
BOOK 183).

108. Bugs Bunny gets a job told by Annie North Bedford,
pictures by Warner Bros. Cartoons, adapted by Tony Strobl
and Don MacLaughlin; NY: S&S, c1952. LC# 52-11749. Copyright
A70782 dated 23 Sept 52. (LITTLE GOLDEN BOOK 136).

109. Bugs Bunny marooned! by Justine Korman, ill. by Joe
Messerli; NY: GB, c1985. LC# 84-72875. (LITTLE GOLDEN BOOK
110-55).

110. Bugs Bunny, pioneer by Fern G. Brown, ill. by Darrell
Baker, NY: GP, c1977. (LITTLE GOLDEN BOOK 161X).

110a. ---- reissued (LITTLE GOLDEN BOOK 110-44).

111. Bugs Bunny - too many carrots by Jean Lewis, ill. by
Peter Alvarado and Bob Totten; NY: GP, c1976. (LITTLE GOLDEN
BOOK 145X).

111a. ---- reissued (LITTLE GOLDEN BOOK 110-21; 110-41).

112. Bugs Bunny's birthday by Warner Bros. Cartoons, adapted
by Elizabeth Beecher, pictures by Warner Bros. Cartoons,
ill. adapted by Ralph Heimdahl and Al Dempster; NY: S&S,
c1950. LC# 50-11850. (LITTLE GOLDEN BOOK 98).

113. Bugs Bunny's carrot machine by Clark Carlisle, ill. by
Anthony Strobl and Bob Totten; NY: GP, c1971. (LITTLE GOLDEN
BOOK 127).

113a. ---- reissued (LITTLE GOLDEN BOOK 110-23).

114. <u>Bullwinkle</u> by David Corwyn, ill. by Hawley Pratt and Harry Garo; NY: GP, c1962. (LITTLE GOLDEN BOOK 462).

115. <u>Bunny book, The</u> by Patsy Scarry, ill. by Richard Scarry; NY: S&S, c1955. LC# 55-1632. Copyright A179209 dated 26 Jan 55; renewal RE-187-856 dated 22 Dec 83. (LITTLE GOLDEN BOOK 215).

115a. ---- reissued (LITTLE GOLDEN BOOK 311-43; 473-21).

116. <u>Bunny book, Walt Disney's</u> told by Jane Werner, ill. by the Walt Disney Studio, adapted by Dick Kelsey and Bill Justice; NY: S&S, c1951. (WALT DISNEY BOOK D111).

117. <u>Bunny's magic tricks</u> by Janet and Alex D'Amato, ill. by Judy and Barry Martin; NY: GP, c1962. Copyright A552540 dated 25 Jan 62. (LITTLE GOLDEN BOOK 441).

118. <u>Busy Timmy</u> by Kathryn and Byron Jackson, ill. by Eloise Wilkin; NY: S&S, c1948. LC# 48-7820. Copyright A24381 dated 30 Jun 48; renewal R609180 dated 7 Jul 75. (LITTLE GOLDEN BOOK 50).

118a. ---- reissued in 1961 (LITTLE GOLDEN BOOK 452).

119. <u>Captain Kangaroo: Three stories</u>, CBS Television's NY: GP, c1959. Contents: <u>Captain Kangaroo</u> / Kathleen Daly, ill. by Art Seiden (120) -- <u>Captain Kangaroo and the panda</u> / Kathleen Daly, ill. by Edwin Schmidt (122) -- <u>Captain Kangaroo's surprise party</u> / Barbara Lindsay, ill. by Edwin Schmidt (123). (GIANT LITTLE GOLDEN BOOK 5021).

120. <u>Captain Kangaroo, CBS Television's</u> by Kathleen N. Daly, ill. by Art Seiden; NY: S&S, c1956. LC# 56-4761. (LITTLE GOLDEN BOOK 261).
    See also <u>Captain Kangaroo: Three stories</u> (119).

121. <u>Captain Kangaroo and the beaver, CBS Television's</u> by Carl Memling, ill. by Marie Nonnast; NY: GP, c1961. (LITTLE GOLDEN BOOK 427).

122. <u>Captain Kangaroo and the panda, CBS Television's</u> by Kathleen N. Daly, ill. by Edwin Schmidt; NY: S&S, c1957. LC# 57-13726. (LITTLE GOLDEN BOOK 278).
    See also <u>Captain Kangaroo: Three stories</u> (119).

122a. ---- reissued in 1960 (LITTLE GOLDEN BOOK 421).

123. <u>Captain Kangaroo's surprise party</u> by Barbara Lindsay, ill. by Edwin Schmidt; NY: GP, c1958. (LITTLE GOLDEN BOOK 341).
    See also <u>Captain Kangaroo: Three stories</u> (119).

124. <u>Car and truck stamps</u> by Kathleen Daly, ill. by E. Joseph Dreany; NY: S&S, c1957. (LITTLE GOLDEN ACTIVITY BOOK A20).

125. <u>Cars</u> by Kathryn Jackson, ill. by William J. Dugan; NY: S&S, c1956. LC# 56-2047. Copyright AA237065 dated 24 Feb 56; renewal RE-223-018 dated 21 Nov 84. (LITTLE GOLDEN BOOK 251).

125a. ---- by Bob Ottum, ill. by William Dugan; NY: GP, c1973. (LITTLE GOLDEN BOOK 566).

125b. ---- reissued (LITTLE GOLDEN BOOK 211-3).

126. <u>Cars and trucks</u> ill. by Richard Scarry; NY: GP, c1959. Copyright A404079 dated 29 May 59. (LITTLE GOLDEN BOOK 366).

126a. ---- reissued (LITTLE GOLDEN BOOK 211-22).

127. <u>Cat who stamped his feet, The</u> by Betty Ren Wright, ill. by Tom O'Sullivan; NY: GP, c1974. (LITTLE GOLDEN BOOK 806); (EAGER READER).

128. <u>Cats</u> by Laura French, ill. by Mel Crawford; NY: GP, c1976. Copyright A781045 dated 12 Aug 76. (LITTLE GOLDEN BOOK 150X).

128a. ---- reissued (LITTLE GOLDEN BOOK 202-7; 309-44).

129. <u>Cave kids</u> by Bruce Carrick, ill. by Mel Crawford; NY: GP, c1964. (LITTLE GOLDEN BOOK 539).

130. <u>Charlie</u> by Diane Fox Downs, ill. by Lilian Obligado; NY: GP, c1970. LC# 82-83098. (LITTLE GOLDEN BOOK 587).

130a. ---- reissued (LITTLE GOLDEN BOOK 302-44).

131. <u>Charmin' Chatty</u> by Barbara Shook Hazen, ill. by Dagmar Wilson; NY: GP, c1964. (LITTLE GOLDEN BOOK 554).

132. <u>Cheyenne, the famous scout, Warner Bros.'</u> told by Charles Spain Verral, ill. by Al Schmidt; NY: S&S, c1958. Authorized ed. (LITTLE GOLDEN BOOK 318).

133. <u>Chicken Little</u> adapted by Vivienne Benstead, ill. by Richard Scarry; NY: GP, c1960. Copyright A481098 dated 23 Sept 60. (LITTLE GOLDEN BOOK 413).

133SR. ---- [sound recording] NY: Golden Record. 1 disc (45 rpm, mono., 7 in.) + book, c1960. Narrated by Kari. (READ AND HEAR GR 00162).

133a. ---- retold by Stella Williams Nathan, ill. by June Goldsborough. (LITTLE GOLDEN BOOK 524).

134. <u>Child's garden of verses, A</u> by Robert Louis Stevenson, selected and ill. by Eloise Wilkin; NY: S&S, c1957. LC# 57-1222. Copyright AA283236 dated 22 Feb 57. (LITTLE GOLDEN BOOK 289).

134a. ---- reissued in 1962 (LITTLE GOLDEN BOOK 493).

134aSR. ---- [sound recording] NY: Golden Record. 1 disc (45 rpm, mono., 7 in.) + book, c1962. (READ AND HEAR GR 00236).

135. Chip 'n' Dale at the zoo, Walt Disney's told by Annie North Bedford, ill. by the Walt Disney Studio, adapted by Bill Bosche from the motion picture "Working for peanuts;" NY: S&S, c1954. LC# 54-3718. (WALT DISNEY BOOK D38).

136. Chip Chip by Norman Wright, ill. by Nino Carbe; NY: S&S, c1947. LC# 47-20095. Copyright A12600 dated 20 Mar 47; renewal R573521 dated 25 Mar 74. (LITTLE GOLDEN BOOK 28).

137. Chipmunk's ABC by Roberta Miller, ill. by Richard Scarry; NY: GP, c1963. LC# 82-82619. Copyright A634179 dated 25 Apr 63. (LITTLE GOLDEN BOOK 512).

138. Chipmunks' merry Christmas, The by David Corwin, ill. by Richard Scarry; NY: GP, c1959. Authorized ed. (LITTLE GOLDEN BOOK 375).

139. Chitty Chitty Bang Bang adapted by Jean Lewis, ill. by Gordon Laite; NY: GP, c1968. (LITTLE GOLDEN BOOK 581).

139B. ---- [braille] Tarzana, CA: American Brotherhood for the Blind, Twin Vision Publication Division; reprint of the c1968 ed. Opposite pages in braille. (TWIN VISION BOOK).

139SR. ---- [sound recording] NY: Golden Record, [197-]. 1 disc (45 rpm, mono., 7 in.) + book, c1968. Narrated by Joel Crager. (READ AND HEAR GR 00238).

140. Christmas ABC, The by Florence Johnson, ill. by Eloise Wilkin; NY: GP, c1962. Copyright A591061 dated 28 Sept 62. (LITTLE GOLDEN BOOK 478).

Christmas book. See My little golden Christmas book (521).

141. Christmas carols arranged by Marjorie Wyckoff, ill. by Corinne Malvern; NY: S&S, c1946. LC# 47-346. Copyright A9014 dated 29 Nov 46; renewal R565049 dated 5 Dec 73. With piano accompaniment. (LITTLE GOLDEN BOOK 26).

141a. ---- reissued in 1972; copyright A355885 dated 23 Jun 72. (LITTLE GOLDEN BOOK 595).

142. Christmas donkey, The by T. William Taylor, ill. by Andrea Brooks; NY: GB, c1984. LC# 83-82200. (LITTLE GOLDEN BOOK 460-41).

143. Christmas in the country by Barbara Collyer and John R. Foley, ill. by Retta Worcester; NY: S&S, c1950. LC# 50-10018. Copyright A58340 dated 10 Aug 50; renewal R670846 dated 6 Sept 77. (LITTLE GOLDEN BOOK 95).

Christmas manger. See <u>Little golden Christmas manger</u> (420).

144. <u>Christmas story, The</u> adapted from the Bible by Jane
Werner, ill. by Eloise Wilkin; NY: S&S, c1952. LC# 52-12287.
Copyright A70783 dated 23 Jul 52; renewal RE 68-202 dated 20
Oct 80. LC# 82-80763. (LITTLE GOLDEN BOOK 158).

145. <u>Christopher and the Columbus</u> by Kathryn and Byron
Jackson, ill. by Tibor Gergely; NY: S&S, c1951. LC#
51-13056. Copyright A60572 dated 30 Jul 51; renewal RE
46-373 dated 7 Nov 79. (LITTLE GOLDEN BOOK 103).

146. <u>Cinderella, Walt Disney's</u> ill. by the Walt Disney
Studio, adapted by Campbell Grant from the Walt Disney
motion picture "Cinderella;" NY: S&S, c1950. LC# 50-8298.
(WALT DISNEY BOOK D13); (MICKEY MOUSE CLUB BOOK D13).

146a. ---- reissued in 1957 (WALT DISNEY BOOK D59).

146b. ---- reissued in 1965 (WALT DISNEY BOOK D114).

146c. ---- reissued (LITTLE GOLDEN BOOK 103-43).

147. <u>Cinderella paper dolls to cut out and dress</u> by Kathleen
N. Daly, ill. by Gordon Laite; NY: GP, c1960. (LITTLE GOLDEN
ACTIVITY BOOK A36).

148. <u>Cinderella's friends, Walt Disney's</u> told by Jane
Werner, ill. by the Walt Disney Studio, adapted by Al
Dempster from the motion picture "Cinderella;" NY: S&S,
c1950. LC# 50-11854. (WALT DISNEY BOOK D17).

148B. ---- [braille] Tarzana, CA: American Brotherhood for
the Blind, Twin Vision Publication Division; reprint of the
c1950 ed. Opposite pages in braille. (TWIN VISION BOOK).

148a. ---- reissued in 1957 (WALT DISNEY BOOK D58); (MICKEY
MOUSE CLUB BOOK D58).

148b. ---- reissued in 1965 (WALT DISNEY BOOK D115).

149. <u>Cindy bear, Hanna-Barbera's</u> by Jean Klinordlinger, ill.
by Harvey Eisenberg and Milli Jancar; NY: GP, c1961. (LITTLE
GOLDEN BOOK 442).

149B. ---- [braille] Tarzana, CA: American Brotherhood for
the Blind, Twin Vision Publication Division; reprint of the
c1961 ed. Opposite pages in braille. (TWIN VISION BOOK).

150. <u>Circus ABC, The</u> by Kathryn Jackson, ill. by J. P.
Miller; NY: S&S, c1955. LC# 55-14341. Copyright A180486
dated 18 Feb 55; renewal RE-185-987 dated 5 Dec 83. (LITTLE
GOLDEN BOOK 222).

151. <u>Circus boy</u> told by Irwin Shapiro, ill. by Joan Walsh
Anglund; NY: S&S, c1957. Authorized ed. Based on the "Circus
Boy" television program. LC# 60-29903. (LITTLE GOLDEN BOOK
290).

152. Circus is in town: a counting book,The by David L. Harrison, ill. by Larry Ross; NY: GP, c1978. (LITTLE GOLDEN BOOK 168X).

152a. ---- reissued (LITTLE GOLDEN BOOK 201-4).

153. Circus time by Marion Conger, ill. by Tibor Gergely; NY: S&S, c1948. LC# 48-6668. Copyright A23291 dated 5 Apr 48. (LITTLE GOLDEN BOOK 31).

153FS. ---- [filmstrip] NY: S&S, released by Young America Films, 1951. 1 filmstrip (34 fr., col., 35 mm) + teacher's guide. LC# fia52-1743. (GOLDEN BOOK SERIES. SET NO. 3).

153SR. ---- [sound recording] NY: Golden Record, [197-]. 1 disc (45 rpm, mono., 7 in.) + book, c1948. Narrated by Cecelia Scott. (READ AND HEAR GR 00239).

153SR. ---- [sound recording] Burbank, CA: Disneyland Records, c1976. 1 disc (33 1/3 rpm, 7 in.) + book. Songs: "Circus time " and "What a pretty parade" by Jeff Stern. (LITTLE GOLDEN BOOK AND RECORD).

153SR. ---- [sound recording] Copyright KK38746 dated 1 Sep 48 (LITTLE GOLDEN RECORD 6).

153a. ---- NY: S&S, c1955. LC# 55-4901. (LITTLE GOLDEN ACTIVITY BOOK A2).

154. Cleo by Irwin Shapiro, photographs by Durward B. Graybill; NY: S&S, c1957. LC# 57-13729. (LITTLE GOLDEN BOOK 287).

155. Cold-blooded penguin, The from the Walt Disney picture, "The Three Caballeros," adapted from the screen version by Robert Edmunds, ill. by the Walt Disney Studio; NY: S&S, c1944. LC# 44-51040. First printing Sept 44. (WALT DISNEY BOOK D2).

156. Color kittens, The by Margaret Wise Brown, ill. by Alice and Martin Provensen; NY: S&S, c1949. LC# 50-5777. Copyright A40465 dated 11 Jan 50; renewal R658082 dated 4 Feb 77. (LITTLE GOLDEN BOOK 86).

156FS. ---- [filmstrip] NY: S&S, released by Young America Films, 1951. 1 filmstrip (33 fr., col., 35 mm) + teacher's guide. LC# fia52-1744. (GOLDEN BOOK SERIES. SET NO. 3).

156SR. ---- [sound recording] Burbank, CA: Disneyland, 1976. 1 disc (33 1/3 rpm, 7 in.) + book. Song by Larry Groce. (LITTLE GOLDEN BOOK AND RECORD).

156a. ---- reissued in 1958; LC# 65-19376.

156b. ---- reissued in 1961 (LITTLE GOLDEN BOOK 436).

156c. ---- reissued (LITTLE GOLDEN BOOK 202-28; 205-41).

157. Colors are nice by Adelaide Holl, ill. by Leonard
Shortall; NY: GP, c1962. LC# 66-9447. Copyright A609563
dated 20 Dec 62. (LITTLE GOLDEN BOOK 496).

157a. ---- reissued (LITTLE GOLDEN BOOK 207-21).

158. Come play house by Edith Osswald, ill. by Eloise
Wilkin; NY: S&S, c1948. LC# 48-6211. Copyright A16757 dated
8 Mar 48; renewal R601948 dated 28 Mar 75. (LITTLE GOLDEN
BOOK 44).
    Also issued with title Come play with me (159).

159. Come play with me by Edith Osswald, ill. by Eloise
Wilkin; NY: S&S, c1948. LC# 48-6211/L. (LITTLE GOLDEN BOOK
44V).
    Also issued with title Come play house (158).

160. Cookie Monster and the cookie tree by David Korr, ill.
by Joe Mathieu, featuring Jim Henson's Muppets; Racine:
Western, in conjunction with Children's Television Workshop,
c1977. (LITTLE GOLDEN BOOK 159X); (SESAME STREET BOOK).

160SR. ---- [sound recording] NY: Children's Television
Workshop. 1 cassette (1 7/8 ips) + book.

160SR. ---- [sound recording] NY: Children's Television
Workshop, 1981. 1 disc (5 min., 33 1/3 rpm, 7 in.).

160a. ---- reissued (LITTLE GOLDEN BOOK 109-22).

161. Corky by Patricia Scarry, ill. by Irma Wilde; NY: GP,
c1962. Copyright A595324 dated 12 Oct 62. (LITTLE GOLDEN
BOOK 486).

162. Corky's hiccups by Nicolete Meredith Stack, ill. by Tom
O'Sullivan; NY: GP, c1968. (LITTLE GOLDEN BOOK 503).

162SR. ---- [sound recording] NY: Golden Record, [197-]. 1
disc (45 rpm, mono., 7 in.) + book, c1968. Narrated by Jim
Dukas. (READ AND HEAR GR 00262).

162SR. ---- [sound recording] Racine: Western, 1977. 1
cassette (8 min. 30 sec., 2 track, mono.) + text and
teacher's guide by Joanne Wylie. (LITTLE GOLDEN READ ALONG
3501).

163. Count all the way to Sesame Street by Dina Anastasio,
ill. by Richard Brown; inspired by "Sesame Street presents:
Follow the bird" screenplay by Tony Geiss and Judy
Freudberg, featuring Jim Henson's Sesame Street Muppets; NY:
Sesame Street/Golden Press Book, c1985. LC# 84-72877.
(LITTLE GOLDEN BOOK 203-56); (SESAME STREET BOOK).

Counting book. See My first counting book (510).

164. Count to ten by Lilian Moore, ill. by Beth Krush; NY:
S&S, c1957. (LITTLE GOLDEN ACTIVITY BOOK A16).

164a. ---- reissued (LITTLE GOLDEN ACTIVITY BOOK A43).

165. Counting rhymes ill. by Corinne Malvern; NY: S&S, c1946. LC# 47-1531. Copyright A10191 dated 15 Jan 47; renewal R569102 dated 28 Jan 74. (LITTLE GOLDEN BOOK 12).
     Originally issued with title This little piggy and other counting rhymes (720).

165a. ---- reissued in 1956 (LITTLE GOLDEN BOOK 257).

165b. ---- ill. by Sharon Kane; NY: GP, c1960. Copyright A477194 dated 2 Aug 60. (LITTLE GOLDEN BOOK 361).

165c. ---- reissued (LITTLE GOLDEN BOOK 311-1).

166. Country mouse and the city mouse, The. Three Aesop fables told by Patricia Scarry, ill. by Richard Scarry; NY: GP, c1961. Other contents: The dog and his bone and The fox and the crow. LC# 82-83092. Copyright A526566 dated 18 Jul 61. (LITTLE GOLDEN BOOK 426).

167. Cow and the elephant, The by Claude Clayton Smith, ill. by R.Z. Whitlock; NY: GP, c1983. LC# 82-84023. (LITTLE GOLDEN BOOK 304-58).

168. Cow went over the mountain, The by Jeanette Krinsley, ill. by Feodor Rojankovsky; NY: GP, c1963. LC# 82-83090. Copyright A634183 dated 22 May 63. (LITTLE GOLDEN BOOK 516).

169. Cowboy ABC by Gladys R. Saxon, ill. by Jerry Smath; NY: GP, c1960. Copyright A444241 dated 11 Mar 60. (LITTLE GOLDEN BOOK 389).

170. Cowboy stamps by John Lyle Shimek, ill. by Richard Scarry; NY: S&S, c1957. (LITTLE GOLDEN ACTIVITY BOOK A11).

171. Cowboys and Indians by Willis Lindquist, ill. by Richard Scarry; NY: S&S, c1958. Copyright AA380259 dated 6 Nov 58. (GIANT LITTLE GOLDEN BOOK 5019).

172. Cub Scouts by Bruce Brian, with foreward by Ben Satzman, ill. by Mel Crawford; NY: GP, c1959. LC# 59-1565. Copyright A382019 dated 16 Feb 59. (GIANT LITTLE GOLDEN BOOK 5022).

173. Daddies by Janet Frank, ill. by Tibor Gergely; NY: S&S, c1953. LC# 54-1147. Copyright A127267 dated 28 Jan 54. (LITTLE GOLDEN BOOK 187).

174. Daisy Dog's wake-up book written and ill. by Ilse-Margret Vogel; NY: GP, c1974. Copyright A506805 dated 11 Jan 74. (LITTLE GOLDEN BOOK 102X).

175. Dale Evans and the coyote by Gladys Wyatt, ill. by E. Joseph Dreany; NY: S&S, c1956. LC# 56-3058. (LITTLE GOLDEN BOOK 253).

176. Dale Evans and the lost gold mine by Monica Hill, ill. by Mel Crawford; NY: S&S, c1954. LC# 55-1596rev. (LITTLE GOLDEN BOOK 213).

177. Daniel Boone by Irwin Shapiro, ill. by Miriam Story Hurford and Arch Hurford; NY: S&S, c1956. LC# 56-3079. Copyright AA245588 dated 10 May 56. (LITTLE GOLDEN BOOK 256).

178. Danny Beaver's secret by Patsy Scarry, ill. by Richard Scarry; NY: S&S, c1953. LC# 53-3029. Copyright A92983 dated 18 Mar 53; renewal RE-109-093 dated 29 Oct 81. (LITTLE GOLDEN BOOK 160).

179. Darby O'Gill, Walt Disney's told by Annie Bedford, ill. by the Walt Disney Studio, ill. adapted by David Gantz; NY: GP, c1959. (WALT DISNEY BOOK D81).

180. David and Goliath by Barbara Shook Hazen, ill. by Robert J. Lee; NY: GP, c1968. (LITTLE GOLDEN BOOK 110X).

180SR. ---- [sound recording] Burbank, CA: Disneyland Vista Records, c1976. 1 disc (33 1/3 rpm, 7 in.) + book. Songs: "The shepherd song" and "God will protect me" by Larry Groce.

180a. ---- reissued in 1974; copyright A548774 dated 14 May 74.

180b. ---- reissued (LITTLE GOLDEN BOOK 401-1).

181. Davy Crockett, king of the wild frontier, Walt Disney's told by Irwin Shapiro, ill. by the Walt Disney Studio, adapted by Mel Crawford; NY: S&S, c1955. LC# 55-14724. (WALT DISNEY BOOK D45); (MICKEY MOUSE CLUB BOOK D45).

182. Davy Crockett's keelboat race, Walt Disney's told by Irwin Shapiro, pictures by the Walt Disney Studio, adapted by Mel Crawford; NY: S&S, c1955. Copyright A210808 dated 15 Nov 55. (WALT DISNEY BOOK D47); (MICKEY MOUSE CLUB BOOK D47).

183. Day at the beach, A by Kathryn and Byron Jackson, ill. by Corinne Malvern; NY: S&S, c1951. LC# 51-11262. Copyright A60566 dated 13 Jun 51; renewal RE-46-367 dated 7 Nov 79. (LITTLE GOLDEN BOOK 110).

184. Day at the playground, A by Miriam Schlein, ill. by Eloise Wilkin; NY: S&S, c1951. LC# 51-11223. Copyright A60568 dated 13 Jun 51; renewal RE-46-369 dated 7 Nov 79. (LITTLE GOLDEN BOOK 119).

185. Day at the zoo, A by Marion Conger, ill. by Tibor Gergely; NY: S&S, c1950. LC# 50-11855. Copyright A49619 dated 26 Oct 50. "A day at the zoo" words & music by Ethel Crowninshield on p [42]. (LITTLE GOLDEN BOOK 88).

185a. ---- reissued in 1958 (LITTLE GOLDEN BOOK 324).

186. Day in the jungle, A by Janette Sebring Lowrey, ill. by
Tibor Gergely; NY: Artists & Writers Guild, dist. by S&S,
c1943. LC# 44-4502. Copyright A179736 dated 31 Mar 44;
renewal R497039 dated 15 Dec 70. (LITTLE GOLDEN BOOK 18).

187. Day on the farm, A by Nancy Fielding Hulick, ill. by
John P. Miller; NY: GP, c1960. Copyright A477191 dated 20
Oct 60. (LITTLE GOLDEN BOOK 407).

187SR. ---- [sound recording] NY: Golden Record, [197-]. 1
disc (45 rpm, mono., 7 in.) + book, c1960. Narrated by Anne
Costello. (READ AND HEAR GR 00235).

187a. ---- reissued (LITTLE GOLDEN BOOK 203-21).

188. Day with Donald Duck, Walt Disney's A by Annie North
Bedford, ill. by the Walt Disney Studio, adapted by Samuel
Armstrong; NY: S&S, c1956. (LITTLE GOLDEN BOOK D55X);
(MICKEY MOUSE CLUB BOOK D55X).

189. Deep blue sea, The by Bertha Morris Parker and Kathleen
N. Daly, ill. by Tibor Gergely; NY: S&S, c1958. Copyright
AA358152 dated 6 Jun 58. (LITTLE GOLDEN BOOK 338).

190. Dennis the Menace. A quiet afternoon by Carl Memling
based on the character created by Hank Ketcham, ill. by Lee
Holley; NY: GP, c1960. (LITTLE GOLDEN BOOK 412).

191. Dennis the Menace and Ruff by Carl Memling, [based on
the character created by Hank Ketcham], ill. by Hawley Pratt
and Lee Holley; NY: GP, c1959. (LITTLE GOLDEN BOOK 386).

191a. ---- ill. by Gene Fawcett; NY: GP, c1964. (LITTLE
GOLDEN BOOK 535).

192. Dennis the Menace waits for Santa by Carl Memling,
[based on the character created by Hank Ketcham]; ill. by Al
Weisman; NY: GP, c1961. (LITTLE GOLDEN BOOK 432).

193. Dick Tracy by Carl Memling, ill. by Hawley Pratt and Al
White; NY: GP, c1962. (LITTLE GOLDEN BOOK 497).

Dictionary. See My little golden dictionary (522).

Dinosaur. See My little dinosaur (514).

194. Dinosaurs by Jane Werner Watson, ill. by William de J.
Rutherfoord, NY: GP, c1959. Copyright A381765 dated 12 Jan
59. (LITTLE GOLDEN BOOK 355).

194a. ---- reissued (LITTLE GOLDEN BOOK 202-26).

195. Disneyland on the air, Walt Disney's told by Annie
North Bedford, ill. by the Walt Disney Studio, adapted by
Samuel Armstrong; NY: S&S, c1955. LC# 55-41?0. (WALT DISNEY
BOOK D43); (MICKEY MOUSE CLUB BOOK D43).

196. Disneyland parade with Donald Duck, Walt Disney's NY:
GP, c1971. Authorized ed. (WALT DISNEY BOOK D123).

197. Doctor Dan at the circus by Pauline Wilkins, ill. by
Katherine Sampson; NY: GP, c1960. Copyright A458443 dated 16
Jun 60. (LITTLE GOLDEN BOOK 399).

198. Doctor Dan the bandage man by Helen Gaspard, ill. by
Corinne Malvern; NY: S&S, c1950. LC# 51-9472. Copyright
A52309 dated 13 Dec 50; renewal R681826 dated 19 Dec 77.
With six real Band-aids. (LITTLE GOLDEN BOOK 111).

198a. ---- reissued; Copyright AA295631 dated 1 May 57.
(LITTLE GOLDEN BOOK 295).

199. Doctor Squash, the doll doctor by Margaret Wise Brown,
ill. by J.P. Miller; NY: S&S, c1952. LC# 52- 10797.
Copyright A68607 dated 8 May 52; renewal RE-68-194 dated 20
Oct 80. (LITTLE GOLDEN BOOK 157).

Dog and his bone. See Country mouse and the city mouse
(166).

200. Dog stamps by Ann McGovern, ill. by Edwin Megargee; NY:
S&S, c1955. LC# 56-13519. (LITTLE GOLDEN ACTIVITY BOOK A9).

201. Dogs by Jean Lewis, ill. by Turi MacCombie; NY: GP,
c1983. LC# 82-60202, 82-83379/AC. (LITTLE GOLDEN BOOK 532X).

Dogs. See also Giant little golden book of dogs (272);
Little golden book of dogs (411).

Donald Duck. See Day with Donald Duck (188).

202. Donald Duck and Santa Claus, Walt Disney's told by
Annie North Bedford, ill. by the Walt Disney Studio, adapted
by Al Dempster; NY: S&S, c1952. (WALT DISNEY BOOK D27).

203. Donald Duck and the Mousketeers, Walt Disney's told by
Annie North Bedford, pictures by the Walt Disney Studio,
adapted by Samuel Armstrong; NY: S&S, c1956. LC# 56-59041.
(WALT DISNEY BOOK D55); (MICKEY MOUSE CLUB BOOK D55).

204. Donald Duck and the one bear: a turn-about tale, Walt
Disney's NY: GP, c1978. (WALT DISNEY BOOK D139).

205. Donald Duck and the witch told by Annie North Bedford,
ill. by the Walt Disney Studio, adapted by Dick Kelsey;
based on the motion picture "Tricks or treats;" NY: S&S,
c1953. LC# 53-3497. Copyright A105653 dated 13 Jul 53. (WALT
DISNEY BOOK D34).
    See also Donald Duck treasury (213).

206. Donald Duck and the witch next door, Walt Disney's NY: GP, c1974. (WALT DISNEY BOOK D127).

207. Donald Duck in America on parade, Walt Disney's NY: GP, c1975. (WALT DISNEY BOOK D131).

208. Donald Duck in Disneyland, Walt Disney's told by Annie North Bedford, ill. by the Walt Disney Studio, adapted by Campbell Grant; NY: S&S, c1955. LC# 55-2057. (WALT DISNEY BOOK D44); (MICKEY MOUSE CLUB BOOK D44).

208a. ---- reissued (WALT DISNEY BOOK D92).

208b. ---- reissued (WALT DISNEY BOOK D109).

209. Donald Duck, instant millionaire, Walt Disney's NY: GP, c1978. (WALT DISNEY BOOK D140).

209a. ---- reissued (LITTLE GOLDEN BOOK 102-44).

210. Donald Duck, lost and found, Walt Disney's by Carl Buettner, ill. by Bob Grant and Bob Totten; NY: GP, c1960. (WALT DISNEY BOOK D86).

211. Donald Duck, private eye, Walt Disney's by Carl Buettner, ill. by the Walt Disney Studio, adapted by Al White and Homer Jonas; NY: GP, c1961. (WALT DISNEY BOOK D94).

212. Donald Duck, prize driver, Walt Disney's told by Annie North Bedford, pictures from the Walt Disney Studio, adapted by Neil Boyle; NY: S&S, c1956. LC# 56-1965. (WALT DISNEY BOOK D49); (MICKEY MOUSE CLUB BOOK D49).

213. Donald Duck treasury, Walt Disney's NY: S&S, c1957. Contents: Donald Duck's toy train (219) -- Donald Duck's adventure (214) -- Donald Duck and the witch (205). (GIANT LITTLE GOLDEN BOOK 5005).

214. Donald Duck's adventure, Walt Disney's told by Annie North Bedford, ill. by the Walt Disney Studio, adapted by Campbell Grant; NY; S&S, c1950. LC# 50-12176. (WALT DISNEY BOOK D14); (MICKEY MOUSE CLUB BOOK D14).
      See also Donald Duck treasury (213).

215. Donald Duck's Christmas carol, Walt Disney's told by Annie North Bedford, ill. by the Walt Disney Studio, adapted by Norm McGary; NY: GP, c1960. (WALT DISNEY BOOK D84).

216. Donald Duck's Christmas tree, Walt Disney's told by Annie North Bedford, ill. by the Walt Disney Studio, adapted by Bob Moore; NY: S&S, c1954. LC# 55-411. (WALT DISNEY BOOK D39).

217. Donald Duck's safety book, Walt Disney's told by Annie
North Bedford, ill. by the Walt Disney Studio, adapted by
Manuel Gonzales and George Wheeler; NY: S&S, c1954. LC#
55-1000. (WALT DISNEY BOOK D41); (MICKEY MOUSE CLUB BOOK
D41).

218. Donald Duck's toy sailboat, Walt Disney's told by Annie
North Bedford, pictures by Walt Disney Studio, ill. adapted
by Samuel Armstrong from the motion picture "Chips Ahoy;"
NY: S&S, c1954. LC# 54-14963. (WALT DISNEY BOOK D40).

219. Donald Duck's toy train, Walt Disney's told by Jane
Werner, pictures by the Walt Disney Studio, ill. adapted by
Dick Kelsey and Bill Justice from the motion picture "Out of
scale;" NY: S&S, c1950. LC# 51-1837. (WALT DISNEY BOOK D18);
(MICKEY MOUSE CLUB BOOK D18).
    See also Donald Duck treasury (213).

220. Donny and Marie - The top secret project by Laura
French, ill. by Jan Neely; NY: GP, c1977. (LITTLE GOLDEN
BOOK 160X).

220a. ---- reissued (LITTLE GOLDEN BOOK 111-7).

Dorothy saves the Emerald City. See Return to Oz (632).

221. Dragon in a wagon, A by Janette Rainwater, ill. by John
Martin Gilbert; NY: GP, c1966. (LITTLE GOLDEN BOOK 565).

221FS. ---- [filmstrip] Racine: Western Publishing Co.,
Education Division, 1972. 1 filmstrip (48 fr., col., 35 mm)
+ disc (6 min., 33 1/3 rpm, 7 in.) + teacher's guide by
Adelaide Holl. (EDUCATIONAL EXPERIENCES SOUND FILMSTRIPS:
IMAGINATIVE PLAY).

222. Duck and his friends by K[athryn] and B[yron] Jackson,
ill. by Richard Scarry; NY: S&S, c1949. LC# 50-5794.
Copyright A40464 dated 11 Jan 50; renewal R658081 dated 4
Feb 77. (LITTLE GOLDEN BOOK 81).

222a. ---- reissued (LITTLE GOLDEN BOOK 475-21).

223. Dumbo, Walt Disney's ill. by the Walt Disney Studio
adapted by Bob Moore; NY: S&S, c1947. LC# 47-1968. (WALT
DISNEY BOOK D3); (MICKEY MOUSE CLUB BOOK D3).
    See also Favorite stories, Walt Disney's (234).

223B. ---- [braille] Tarzana, CA: American Brotherhood for
the Blind, Twin Vision Publication Division; reprint of the
c1947 ed. Opposite pages in braille. (TWIN VISION BOOK).

223a. ---- reissued (LITTLE GOLDEN BOOK 104-34).

224. Elephant on wheels by Alida McKay Thacher, ill. by
Jerry Scott based on sketches by Ted Schroeder; NY: GP,
c1974. (LITTLE GOLDEN BOOK 807); (EAGER READER).

225. Elves and the shoemaker, The retold by Eric Suben, ill. by Lloyd Bloom; NY: GP, c1983. LC# 82-82287. (LITTLE GOLDEN BOOK 307-56).

226. Emerald City of Oz, The by Lyman Frank Baum, adapted by Peter Archer, ill. by Harry McNaught; NY: S&S, c1952. LC# 52-2380. (LITTLE GOLDEN BOOK 151).

227. Ernie's work of art by Valjean McLenighan, ill. by Joe Mathieu, featuring the Jim Henson Muppets; Racine: Western, in conjunction with Children's Television Workshop, c1979. (LITTLE GOLDEN BOOK 109-5; 109-25); (SESAME STREET BOOK).

Escape from the witch's castle. See Return to Oz (631).

228. Exploring space: a true story about the rockets of today and a glimpse of the rockets that are to come by Rose Wyler, ill. by Tibor Gergely, cover by George Solonewitsch; NY: S&S, c1958. Copyright AA369642 dated 23 Oct 58. (LITTLE GOLDEN BOOK 342).

229. Fairy tales by Hans Christian Andersen, adapted by Anne Terry White, ill. by Lowell Hess; NY: S&S, c1958. LC# 59-1338. Copyright AA380260 dated 6 Nov 58. (GIANT LITTLE GOLDEN BOOK 5020).

Fairy tales. See also Blue book of fairy tales (083); Golden book of fairy tales (280,281).

230. Fairy tales and rhymes NY: GP, c1969. Contents: A little golden Mother Goose (423) -- Little Red Riding Hood / Elizabeth Orton Jones (437) -- Thumbelina / Hans Christian Andersen (729) -- The three bears (722) -- Hansel and Gretel / Brothers Grimm (302) -- The twelve dancing princesses / retold by Jane Werner (762) -- The brave little tailor (098) -- More Mother Goose rhymes (486) -- Snow White and Rose Red (688) -- The little red hen (436) -- A child's garden of verses / Robert Louis Stevenson (134) -- Three little kittens (725) -- Jack and the beanstalk (357) -- Puss in boots / retold by Kathryn Jackson (610) -- The night before Christmas / Clement C. Moore (542). LC# 79-89088. (LITTLE GOLDEN BOOK LIBRARY).

231. Farm stamps by Kathryn Jackson, ill. by Adriana Mazza Saviozzi; NY: S&S, c1957. (LITTLE GOLDEN ACTIVITY BOOK A19).

232. Farmyard friends story and kodachromes by William P. Gottlieb; NY: S&S, c1956. LC# 56-59040. Copyright A269066 dated 21 Sept 56; renewal RE-223-003 dated 21 Nov 84. (LITTLE GOLDEN BOOK 272).

232a. ---- reissued in 1960 (LITTLE GOLDEN BOOK 429).

233. Favorite nursery tales, Walt Disney's. The Gingerbread man and The golden goose ill. by the Walt Disney Studio; NY: GP, c1965. (WALT DISNEY BOOK D125).

233a. ---- reissued (LITTLE GOLDEN BOOK 106-4).

234. Favorite stories, Walt Disney's ill. by the Walt Disney
Studio, adapted by Bob Moore, Milt Banta, Al Dempster, and
Bob Grant; NY: S&S, c1957. Contents: Dumbo (223) -- The
three little pigs (727) -- Uncle Remus stories (771). (GIANT
LITTLE GOLDEN BOOK 5004).

235. Feelings from A to Z by Pat Visser, ill. by Rod Ruth;
NY: GP, c1979. (LITTLE GOLDEN BOOK 200-6).

236. Fire engines ill. by Tibor Gergely; NY: GP, c1959.
(LITTLE GOLDEN BOOK 382).

236a. ---- reissued (LITTLE GOLDEN BOOK 210-2).

237. Fire fighters' counting book, The by Polly Curren, ill.
by Pat Stewart; NY: GP, c1983. LC# 82-83071. (LITTLE GOLDEN
BOOK 203-55).

238. Fireball XL5 by Barbara Shook Hazen, ill. by Hawley
Pratt and Al White; NY: GP, c1964. (LITTLE GOLDEN BOOK 546).

239. Fireman and fire engine stamps by Jane Goldsmith, ill.
by Richard Scarry and Rick Estrada; NY: GP, c1959. (LITTLE
GOLDEN ACTIVITY BOOK A27).

240. First Bible stories retold by Jane Werner, ill. by
Eloise Wilkin; NY: S&S, c1954. LC# 54-14540rev. Copyright
A159056 dated 24 Jun 54; renewal RE-143-629 dated 15 Nov 82.
(LITTLE GOLDEN BOOK 198).

241. First golden geography: a beginner's introduction to
our world, The by Jane Werner Watson, ill. by William
Sayles; NY: S&S, c1955. (LITTLE GOLDEN BOOK 534).
    Originally issued with title Our world (565).

First little golden book of fairy tales. See Golden book of
fairy tales (281).

242. Fish by Herbert S. Zim, ill. by Jean Zallinger; NY: GP,
c1959. LC# AC68-1784. Copyright A395441 dated 30 Mar 59.
(GIANT LITTLE GOLDEN BOOK 5023).

243. Five bedtime stories ill. by Gustaf Tenggren; NY: S&S,
c1957. Contents: Little Red Riding Hood -- Gingerbread man
-- The golden Goose -- Chicken Little -- Jack and the
beanstalk. Copyright AA313054 dated 9 Sept 57. (GIANT LITTLE
GOLDEN BOOK 5002).

244. Five little firemen by Margaret Wise Brown and Edith
Thacher Hurd, ill. by Tibor Gergely; NY: S&S, c1949. LC#
49-7117. Copyright A28614 dated 13 Dec 48; renewal R623880
dated 8 Jan 76. (LITTLE GOLDEN BOOK 64).

244SR. ---- [sound recording] NY: Golden Record, [197-]. 1
disc (45 rpm, mono., 7 in.) + book, c1949. Narrated by Jim
Ryerson. (READ AND HEAR GR 00241).

244a. ---- reissued in 1957 (LITTLE GOLDEN BOOK 301).

245. 5 pennies to spend by Miriam Young, ill. by Corinne
Malvern; NY: S&S, c1955. LC# 55-14371. Copyright A186512
dated 30 Mar 55; renewal RE-185-995 dated 5 Dec 83. (LITTLE
GOLDEN BOOK 238).

5 Sesame Street stories [videocassette]. See Big Bird brings
Spring to Sesame Street (069VC).

246. Fix it, please! by Lucy Sprague Mitchell, ill. by
Eloise Wilkin; NY: S&S, c1947. LC# 48-1846. Copyright
AA73623 dated 26 Dec 47; renewal R595812 dated 6 Jan 75.
(LITTLE GOLDEN BOOK 32); (BANK STREET BOOK).

246FS. ---- [filmstrip] NY: S&S, released by Young America
Films, 1951. 1 filmstrip (33 fr., col., 35 mm) + teacher's
guide. LC# fia52-1745. (GOLDEN BOOK SERIES. SET NO. 3).

247. Flintstones, The written and ill. by Mel Crawford; NY:
GP, c1961. (LITTLE GOLDEN BOOK 450).

Flowers. See Golden book of flowers (282).

248. Fly high written and ill. by Virginia Parsons; NY: GP,
c1971. Copyright A291860 dated 1 Nov 71. (LITTLE GOLDEN BOOK
597).

249. Flying car, Walt Disney's The adapted by Charles Spain
Verral from the Walt Disney motion picture "The absent-
minded professor," ill. by Fred Irvin; NY: GP, c1961. (WALT
DISNEY BOOK D96).

250. Forest hotel: a counting story by Barbara Steincrohn
Davis, ill. by Benvenuti; NY: GP, c1972. Copyright A378008
dated 30 Aug 72. (LITTLE GOLDEN BOOK 350).

250SR. ---- [sound recording] Racine: Western, [1977]. 1
cassette (2 track, mono.) + text and teacher's guide by
Joanne Wylie. (LITTLE GOLDEN READ ALONG 3502).

250a. ---- reissued (LITTLE GOLDEN BOOK 201-25).

251. Four little kittens by Kathleen N. Daly, ill. by
Adriana Mazza Saviozzi; NY: S&S, c1957. Copyright AA324813
dated 20 Dec 57. (LITTLE GOLDEN BOOK 322).

251a. ---- reissued in 1963 (LITTLE GOLDEN BOOK 530).

251b. ---- reissued (LITTLE GOLDEN BOOK 302-21).

252. Four puppies by Anne Heathers, ill. by Lilian Obligado;
NY: GP, c1960. Copyright A477189 dated 19 Aug 60. (LITTLE
GOLDEN BOOK 405).

252a. ---- reissued (LITTLE GOLDEN BOOK 202-4).

253. Four seasons, The by Tony Geiss, ill. by Tom Cooke,
featuring Jim Henson's Muppets; Racine: Western, in
conjunction with Children's Television Workshop, c1979.
(LITTLE GOLDEN BOOK 108-24; 108-44); (SESAME STREET BOOK).

Fox and the crow. See Country mouse and the city mouse
(166).

254. Fox and the hound: Hide and seek, Walt Disney
Productions The NY: GP, c1981. LC# 80-85425. (LITTLE GOLDEN
BOOK 104-44).

255. Friendly book, The by Margaret Wise Brown, ill. by
Garth Williams; NY: S&S, c1954. LC# 54-9024. Copyright
A135846 dated 23 Feb 54; renewal RE-143-921 dated 15 Nov 82.
(LITTLE GOLDEN BOOK 199).

255a. ---- reissued (LITTLE GOLDEN BOOK 592).

255b. ---- reissued (LITTLE GOLDEN BOOK 206-24; 209-41).

256. Fritzie goes home by Kate Emery Pogue, ill. by Sally
Augustiny; NY: GP, c1974. Copyright A528528 dated 4 Mar 74.
(LITTLE GOLDEN BOOK 103X).

257. From then to now by John Philip Leventhal, ill. by
Tibor Gergely; NY: S&S, c1954. LC# 55-842. Copyright A172866
dated 9 Sept 54; renewal RE-143-611 dated 15 Nov 82. (LITTLE
GOLDEN BOOK 201).

258. Frosty the snowman adapted from the song of the same
name; retold by Annie North Bedford, ill. by Corinne
Malvern; NY: S&S, c1950. LC# 51-13064. Copyright A58967
dated 13 Aug 51. (LITTLE GOLDEN BOOK 142).

258SR. ---- [sound recording] NY: Golden Record. 1 disc (45
rpm, mono., 7 in.) + book, c1951. (READ AND HEAR GR 00179).

258a. ---- reissued (LITTLE GOLDEN BOOK 451-1).

259. Fun for Hunky Dory by May Justus, ill. by Sue
d'Avignon; NY: GP, c1963. Copyright A625539 dated 28 Mar 63.
(LITTLE GOLDEN BOOK 521).

260. Fun with decals by Elsa Ruth Nast, ill. by Corinne
Malvern; NY: S&S, c1952. LC# 53-2460rev. Copyright A94968
dated 2 Feb 53. With a page of real decals. (LITTLE GOLDEN
BOOK 139).

Funny book. See Little golden funny book (421).

261. Fury by Kathleen Irwin, ill. by Mel Crawford; NY: S&S, c1957. Authorized edition based on the "Fury" television program. LC# 57-13728. (LITTLE GOLDEN BOOK 286).

262. Fury takes the jump by Seymour Reit, ill. by Mel Crawford; NY: GP, c1958. Authorized edition based on the "Fury" Television program. (LITTLE GOLDEN BOOK 336X).

263. Fuzzy duckling, The by Jane Werner Watson, ill. by Alice and Martin Provensen; NY: S&S, c1949. LC# 49-8904. Copyright A33515 dated 1 May 49; renewal R634086 dated 28 May 76. (LITTLE GOLDEN BOOK 78).

263FS. ---- [filmstrip] NY: S&S, released by Young America Films, 1951. 1 filmstrip (25 fr., col., 35 mm). LC# fia52-1746. (GOLDEN BOOK SERIES. SET 3).

263SR. ---- [sound recording] NY: Golden Record, [197-]. 1 disc (45 rpm, mono., 7 in.) + book, c1949. Narrated by Cecelia Scott. (READ AND HEAR GR 00256).

263a. ---- reissued in 1963 (LITTLE GOLDEN BOOK 533).

263b. ---- reissued in 1965 (LITTLE GOLDEN BOOK 557).

263c. ---- reissued (LITTLE GOLDEN BOOK 482-21).

264. Gaston and Josephine by Georges Duplaix, ill. by Feodor Rojankovsky; NY: S&S, c1948. LC# 49-3882. Copyright A32501 dated 18 Apr 49. (LITTLE GOLDEN BOOK 65).

265. Gay purr-ee, UPA Pictures' based on the U.P.A. motion picture "Gay purr-ee" adapted by Carl Memling, ill. by Hawley Pratt, Harland Young, and Herb Fillmore; NY: GP, c1962. (LITTLE GOLDEN BOOK 488).

266. Gene Autry by Steffi Fletcher, ill. by Mel Crawford; NY: S&S, c1955. LC# 55-3222. (LITTLE GOLDEN BOOK 230).

267. Gene Autry and Champion by Monica Hill, ill. by Frank Bolle; NY: S&S, c1956. LC# 57-13505. (LITTLE GOLDEN BOOK 267).

268. Georgie finds a Grandpa by Miriam Young, ill. by Eloise Wilkin; NY: S&S, c1954. LC# 55-1067. Copyright A172868 dated 9 Sept 54; renewal RE-148-059 dated 13 Dec 82. (LITTLE GOLDEN BOOK 196).

269. Giant little golden book about plants and animals, A by Jane Werner Watson, ill. by Ted Chaiko; NY: S&S, c1958. LC# 60-131. Copyright A369637 dated 6 Oct 58. (GIANT LITTLE GOLDEN BOOK 5017).

270. Giant little golden book of animal stories, A NY: S&S, c1957. Stories by Miryam, Georges Duplaix, and Beth Greiner Hoffman, all ill. by Tibor Gergely. Copyright AA324811 dated 17 Oct 57. (GIANT LITTLE GOLDEN BOOK 5006).

271. Giant little golden book of birds, A by Jane Werner
Watson, ill. by Eloise Wilkin; NY: S&S, c1958. LC# 58-3952.
Copyright AA345955 dated 17 Mar 58. (GIANT LITTLE GOLDEN
BOOK 5011).

272. Giant little golden book of dogs, The by Kathleen N.
Daly, ill. by Tibor Gergely; NY: S&S, c1957. LC# A59-1522.
Copyright AA324814 dated 18 Nov 57. (GIANT LITTLE GOLDEN
BOOK 5008).

273. Giant little golden book of kittens, The NY: S&S,
c1958. Contents: The three little kittens / ill. by Masha
(725) -- The shy little kitten / Cathleen Schurr, ill. by
Gustaf Tenggren (678) -- My kitten / Patricia Scarry; ill.
by Eloise Wilkin (513). Copyright AA345957 dated 9 Apr 58.
(GIANT LITTLE GOLDEN BOOK 5013).

274. Giant who wanted company, The by Lee Priestly, ill. by
Dennis Hockerman; NY: GP, c1979. (LITTLE GOLDEN BOOK 207-4).

275. Giant with the three golden hairs, Tenggren's The
adapted from the Brothers Grimm, ill. by Gustaf Tenggren;
NY: S&S, c1955. LC# 55-1633. Copyright A179208 dated 26 Jan
55; renewal RE-187-855 dated 22 Dec 83. (LITTLE GOLDEN BOOK
219).

276. Gingerbread man, The told by Nancy Nolte, ill. by
Richard Scarry; NY: S&S, c1953. LC# 53-2893. Copyright
A99469 dated 11 May 53; renewal RE-109-104 dated 29 Oct 81.
(LITTLE GOLDEN BOOK 165).
    See also Favorite nursery tales (233).

276a. ---- reissued; copyright A513335 dated 16 May 61
(LITTLE GOLDEN BOOK 437).

276aSR. ---- [sound recording] NY: Golden Record, [197-]. 1
disc (45 rpm, mono., 7 in.) + book, c1961. Narrated by Rita
and Ed. (READ AND HEAR GR 00164).

276aVC. ---- [videocassette] Racine: Western, c1985. 3
Richard Scarry animal nursery tales [including The
gingerbread man]. 1 videocassette (30 min., sd., col., 1/2
in.) VHS (GOLDEN BOOK VIDEO) #13871.

276b. ---- ill. by Elfrieda; NY: GP, c1972. Copyright
A340567 dated 8 May 72. (LITTLE GOLDEN BOOK 182).

276c. ---- reissued (LITTLE GOLDEN BOOK 310-21).

277. Gingerbread shop: a story from Mary Poppins, The by
Pamela L. Travers, ill. by Gertrude Elliott; NY: S&S, c1952.
LC# 52-9933. Copyright A66990 dated 18 Mar 52. (LITTLE
GOLDEN BOOK 126).

278. <u>Ginghams: The backward picnic, The</u> by Joan Chase Bowden, ill. by JoAnne E. Koenig / Creative Studios I, Inc.; NY: GP, c1976. Copyright A787172 dated 23 Sept 76. (LITTLE GOLDEN BOOK 148X).

278a. ---- reissued (LITTLE GOLDEN BOOK 311-7).

279. <u>Golden book of birds, The</u> by Hazel Lockwood, ill. by Feodor Rojankovsky; NY: S&S, c1943. LC# 43-13706. Copyright A175688 dated 27 Aug 43. First printing Apr 43. (LITTLE GOLDEN BOOK 13).

280. <u>Golden book of fairy tales, The</u> [revisions by Leah Gale], ill. by Winfield Hoskins; NY: S&S, c1942. Copyright A168878 dated 13 Nov 42. First printing Sept 42. (LITTLE GOLDEN BOOK 9).

281. <u>Golden book of fairy tales, The</u> ill. by Gertrude Elliott; NY: S&S, c1946. LC# 47-1301. Copyright A10193 dated 15 Jan 47. Cover title: The first little golden book of fairy tales. (LITTLE GOLDEN BOOK 9).

282. <u>Golden book of flowers</u> by Mabel Foote Witman, ill. by m.[ac] h.[arshberger]; NY: Artists & Writers Guild, dist. by S&S, c1943. LC# 43-16554. Copyright A175685 dated 27 Aug 43. First printing Sept 43. Issued with dust jacket. (LITTLE GOLDEN BOOK 16).

283. <u>Golden egg book, The</u> by Margaret Wise Brown, ill. by Lilian Obligado; NY: GP, c1962. Copyright A560062 dated 15 Mar 62. (LITTLE GOLDEN BOOK 456).

283FS. ---- [filmstrip] Racine: Western Publishing Co., Education Division, 1972. 1 filmstrip (45 fr., col., 35 mm) + disc (6 min., 33 1/3 rpm, 7 in.) + teacher's guide by Adelaide Holl. (EDUCATIONAL EXPERIENCES SOUND FILMSTRIPS: ABOUT MAKE-BELIEVE ANIMALS).

283SR. ---- [sound recording] Copyright KK38750 dated 1 Sep 48. (LITTLE GOLDEN RECORD 10).

283a. ---- reissued 478-21.

284. <u>Golden favorites</u> NY: GP, c1969. Contents: <u>The poky little puppy</u> / Janette S. Lowrey (600) -- <u>Tootle</u> / Gertrude Crampton (747) -- <u>Little boy with a big horn</u> / Jack Bechdolt (401) -- <u>Ukelele and her new doll</u> / Clara L. Grant (769) -- <u>Five little firemen</u> / Margaret Wise Brown and Edith Thacher Hurd (244) -- <u>Tawny scrawny lion</u> / Kathryn Jackson (711) -- The taxi that hurried / Lucy Sprague Mitchell (713) -- <u>Pets for Peter</u> / Jane Werner (587) -- The train to Timbuctoo / Margaret Wise Brown (754) -- <u>I can fly</u> / Ruth Krauss (343) -- <u>The little fat policeman</u> / Margaret Wise Brown and Edith Thacher Hurd (406) -- <u>The saggy baggy elephant</u> / Kathryn and Byron Jackson (662) -- <u>Scuffy the tugboat and his adventures down the river</u> / Gertrude Crampton (671) -- <u>Seven little postmen</u> / Margaret Wise Brown and Edith Thacher Hurd (673). LC# 77-89090. (LITTLE GOLDEN BOOK LIBRARY).

285. Golden goose, The by the Brothers Grimm, ill. by Gustaf
Tenggren; NY: S&S, c1954. LC# 54-14444. Copyright A159054
dated 3 Aug 54; renewal RE-143-630 dated 15 Nov 82. (LITTLE
GOLDEN BOOK 200).
    See also Favorite nursery tales (223).

285a. ---- reissued in 1962 (LITTLE GOLDEN BOOK 487).

286. Golden sleepy book, The by Margaret Wise Brown, ill. by
Garth Williams; NY: S&S, c1948. LC# 48-8169. Copyright
A29589 dated 10 Aug 48. (LITTLE GOLDEN BOOK 46).

286a. ---- reissued (LITTLE GOLDEN BOOK 209-27).

287. Goliath II, Walt Disney's written and ill. by Bill
Peet; NY: GP, c1959. (WALT DISNEY BOOK D83).

287SR. ---- [sound recording] Burbank, CA: Disneyland, 1978.
1 disc (33 1/3 rpm, mono., 12 in.). Narrated by Sterling
Holloway.

288. Good-by day, The by Leone Castell Anderson, ill. by
Eugenie [Fernandes]; NY: GB, c1984. LC# 83-80025. (LITTLE
GOLDEN BOOK 209-57).

289. Good-bye tonsils by Anne Welsh Guy, ill. by Frank
Vaughn; NY: GP, c1966. (LITTLE GOLDEN BOOK 327).

290. Good Humor man, The by Kathleen N. Daly, ill. by Tibor
Gergely; NY: GP, c1964. Copyright A703863 dated 5 May 64.
(LITTLE GOLDEN BOOK 550).

291. Good little, bad little girl by Esther Wilkin, ill. by
Eloise Wilkin; NY: GP, c1965. (LITTLE GOLDEN BOOK 562).

292. Good morning and good night by Jane Werner, ill. by
Eloise Wilkin; NY: S&S, c1948. LC# 49-8905rev. Copyright
A32500 dated 18 Apr 49. (LITTLE GOLDEN BOOK 61).

293. Good night, Aunt Lilly by Margaret Madigan, ill. by
Diane Dawson; NY: GP, c1983. LC# 82-84022/AC. (LITTLE GOLDEN
BOOK 208-54).

294. Good night, Little Bear by Patsy Scarry, ill. by
Richard Scarry; NY: GP, c1961. LC# 82-83095. Copyright
A543595 dated 12 Dec 61. (LITTLE GOLDEN BOOK 447).

295. Goofy, movie star, Walt Disney's by Annie North
Bedford, based on the Disneyland television show. Pictures
by the Walt Disney Studio, adapted by Samuel Armstrong; NY:
S&S, c1956. LC# 56-3060. (WALT DISNEY BOOK D52); (MICKEY
MOUSE CLUB BOOK D52).

296. Grandma and Grandpa Smith by Edith Kunhardt, ill. by
Terri Super; NY: GB, c1985. LC# 85-70338. (LITTLE GOLDEN
BOOK 305-55).

297. Grandpa Bunny, Walt Disney's told by Jane Werner, ill.
by the Walt Disney Studio, adapted by Dick Kelsey and Bill
Justice from the motion picture "Funny little bunnies;" NY:
S&S, c1951. LC# 51-39070. (WALT DISNEY BOOK D21).

298. Grover's own alphabet letters by Sal Murdocca featuring
Grover, a Jim Henson Sesame Street Muppet; Racine: Western,
in conjunction with Children's Television Workshop, c1978.
LC# 81-84276. (LITTLE GOLDEN BOOK 108-46; 108-56); (SESAME
STREET BOOK).

299. Guess who lives here? by Louise Woodcock, ill. by
Eloise Wilkin; NY: S&S, c1949. LC# 49-9976. Copyright A37027
dated 7 Jun 49. (LITTLE GOLDEN BOOK 60); (BANK STREET BOOK).

300. Gull that lost the sea, The by Claude Clayton Smith,
ill. by Lucinda McQueen; NY: GB, c1984. LC# 83-80023.
(LITTLE GOLDEN BOOK 206-55).

301. Gunsmoke by Seymour Reit, ill. by E. Joseph Dreany; NY:
GP, c1958. (LITTLE GOLDEN BOOK 320).

302. Hansel and Gretel by Jacob and William [sic] Grimm,
ill. by Erika Weihs; NY: S&S, c1945.LC# 48-3503. Copyright
A1198 dated 26 Sept 45; renewal R538989 dated 26 Oct 72.
First printing Jun 45. (LITTLE GOLDEN BOOK 17).

302a. ---- by the Brothers Grimm, ill. by Eloise Wilkin; NY:
S&S, c1954. LC# 54-1135. Copyright A127269 dated 22 Jan 54;
renewal RE-143-918 dated 15 Nov 82. (LITTLE GOLDEN BOOK
217).

302aSR. ---- [sound recording] NY: Golden Record. 1 disc (45
rpm, mono., 7 in.) + book, c1954. (READ AND HEAR GR 00151).

302b. ---- reissued (LITTLE GOLDEN BOOK 491).

302c. ---- reissued (LITTLE GOLDEN BOOK 207-41; 308-22).

303. Hansel and Gretel: a paper doll story book by Judy and
Barry Martin; NY: GP, c1961. (LITTLE GOLDEN ACTIVITY BOOK
A41).

Happy birthday. See How to have a happy birthday (327).

304. Happy days: what children do the whole day through by
Janet Frank, ill. by Eleanor Dart; NY: S&S, c1955. LC#
55-12633. Copyright A224342 dated 12 Dec 55; renewal
RE-187-875 dated 5 Dec 83. (LITTLE GOLDEN BOOK 247).

304SR. ---- [sound recording] NY: Golden Record, [197-]. 1
disc (45 rpm, mono., 7 in.) + book, c1955. Narrated by
Cecelia Scott. (READ AND HEAR GR 00252).

305. Happy family, The story by Nicole, ill. by Gertrude
Elliott; NY: S&S, c1947. LC# 47-3634. Copyright A12601 dated
20 Mar 47. (LITTLE GOLDEN BOOK 35).

305a. ---- ill. by Corinne Malvern; NY: S&S, c1955. LC#
55-1614. Copyright A179207 dated 26 Jan 55; renewal
RE-187-854 dated 22 Dec 83. (LITTLE GOLDEN BOOK 216).

306. Happy golden ABC, The ill. by Joan Allen; NY: GP,
c1972. Copyright A377976 dated 30 Aug 72. (LITTLE GOLDEN
BOOK 344).

306a. ---- reissued (LITTLE GOLDEN BOOK 200-2).

307. Happy little whale, The told to Jane Werner Watson by
Kenneth Norris, ill. by Tibor Gergely; NY: GP, c1960. LC#
79-4897. Copyright A444861 dated 11 Mar 60. (LITTLE GOLDEN
BOOK 393).

308. Happy man and his dump truck, The by Miryam
[Yardumian], ill. by Tibor Gergely; NY: S&S, c1950. LC#
50-6280. Copyright A41542 dated 18 Jan 50; renewal R658084
dated 4 Feb 77. (LITTLE GOLDEN BOOK 77).

308SR. ---- [sound recording] NY: Golden Record, [197-]. 1
disc (45 rpm, mono., 7 in.) + book, c1950. Narrated by Jerry
Roberts; Music director, Ralph Stein. (READ AND HEAR GR
00219).

308a. ---- reissued in 1963 (LITTLE GOLDEN BOOK 520).

308aSR. ---- [sound recording] Burbank, CA: Disneyland Vista
Records, 1976. 1 cassette (1 7/8 ips, mono., 3 7/8 x 2 1/2
in.; 1/8 in. tape) + book. "Dump truck song" by Larry Groce.
(DISNEYLAND STORYTELLER CASSETTE 213B).

308aSR. ---- [sound recording] Burbank, CA: Disneyland
Records, c1976. 1 disc (33 1/3 rpm, 7 in.) + book. "Dump
truck song" by Larry Groce. (LITTLE GOLDEN BOOK AND RECORD).

309. Hat for the queen, A story by Joan Chase Bacon, ill. by
Olindo Giacomini; NY: GP, c1974. (LITTLE GOLDEN BOOK 802);
(EAGER READER).

310. Heidi adapted from the original story by Johanna Spyri,
ill. by Corinne Malvern; NY: S&S, c1954. LC# 54-2639.
Copyright A138908 dated 23 Apr 54; renewal RE-143-926 dated
15 Nov 82. (LITTLE GOLDEN BOOK 192).

310SR. ---- [sound recording] NY: Golden Record. 1 disc (45
rpm, mono., 7 in.) + book, c1954. Narrated by Susan Douglas.
(READ AND HEAR GR 00152).

310a. ---- reissued in 1956 (LITTLE GOLDEN BOOK 258).

310b. ---- reissued in 1962 (LITTLE GOLDEN BOOK 470).

310c. ---- reissued (LITTLE GOLDEN BOOK 308-1; 308-21).

Helicopters. See Little golden book of helicopters (412).

311. Here comes the band by Dr. Frances R. Horwich, ill. by
William Timmins; NY: GP, c1960. (DING DONG SCHOOL BOOK
Din5).

312. Here comes the parade by Kathryn Jackson, ill. by
Richard Scarry; NY: S&S, c1951. LC# 51-13055. Copyright
A60567 dated 16 Aug 51; renewal RE-46-368 dated 7 Nov 79.
(LITTLE GOLDEN BOOK 143).

313. Heroes of the Bible by Jane Werner Watson, ill. by
Rachel Taft Dixon and Marjorie Hartwell; NY: S&S, c1955. LC#
55-3229. Copyright A201878 dated 24 Jun 55; renewal RE
186-013 dated 5 Dec 83. (LITTLE GOLDEN BOOK 236).

313a. ---- reissued (LITTLE GOLDEN BOOK 406-1).

314. Hey there - It's Yogi Bear!, Hanna-Barbera by Carl
Memling, ill. by Hawley Pratt and Al White; NY: GP, c1964.
(LITTLE GOLDEN BOOK 542).

315. Hi ho! Three in a row by Louise Woodcock, ill. by
Eloise Wilkin; NY: S&S, c1954. LC# 54-1145. Copyright
A127270 dated 22 Jan 54; renewal RE-143-919 dated 15 Nov 82.
(LITTLE GOLDEN BOOK 188).

316. Hiawatha, Walt Disney's based on the Walt Disney motion
picture "Hiawatha"; NY: S&S, c1953. LC# 53-8195. (WALT
DISNEY BOOK D31).

317. Hiram's red shirt by Mabel Watts, ill. by Aurelius
Battaglia; NY: GP, c1981. LC# 80-85027/AC. (LITTLE GOLDEN
BOOK 204-43).

318. Hokey Wolf and Ding-a-Ling featuring Huckleberry Hound,
Hanna-Barbera's by S. Quentin Hyatt, ill. by Frans van
Lamsweerde; NY: GP, c1961. (LITTLE GOLDEN BOOK 444).

Holiday book. See Little golden holiday book (422).

319. Home for a bunny by Margaret Wise Brown, ill. by Garth
Williams; NY: GP, c1961. Copyright A498390 dated 10 Feb 61;
renewal RE-223-020 dated 21 Nov 84. (LITTLE GOLDEN BOOK
428).

319a. ---- reissued (LITTLE GOLDEN BOOK 477-21).

320. Hop, little kangaroo by Patricia Scarry, ill. by Feodor
Rojankovsky; NY: GP, c1965. (LITTLE GOLDEN BOOK 558).

321. Hopalong Cassidy and the Bar 20 cowboy: starring
William Boyd based on characters created by Clarence E.
Mulford, adapted by Elizabeth Beecher, ill. by Sahula-Dycke;
NY: S&S, c1952. LC# 52-9881. (LITTLE GOLDEN BOOK 147).

322. Horses by Blanche Chenery Perrin, ill. by Hamilton
Greene; NY: GP, c1962. Copyright A552594 dated 25 Jan 62.
(LITTLE GOLDEN BOOK 459).

322a. ---- reissued (LITTLE GOLDEN BOOK 202-2).

323. House that Jack built: a Mother Goose rhyme, The ill.
by J.P. Miller; NY: S&S, c1954. LC# 55-1066. Copyright
A179203 dated 3 Jan 55 (notice 1954). (LITTLE GOLDEN BOOK
218).

324. Houses by Elsa Jane Werner, ill. by Tibor Gergely; NY:
S&S, c1955. LC# 55-2056rev. Copyright A193401 dated 28 Apr
55; renewal RE-185-999 dated 5 Dec 83. (LITTLE GOLDEN BOOK
229).

325. How big? written and ill. by Corinne Malvern; NY: S&S,
c1949. LC# 49-48152. Copyright A37024 dated 1 Aug 49;
renewal R641074 dated 10 Sept 76. (LITTLE GOLDEN BOOK 83).

326. How does your garden grow? by Pat Patterson, ill. by
Brenda Clark and Debi Perna; Racine: An Owl Magazine/Golden
Press Book, c1985. LC# 85-70828. (LITTLE GOLDEN BOOK
308-55).

327. How to have a happy birthday: a party cut-out book by
Elsa Ruth Nast, ill. by Retta Worcester; NY: S&S, c1952.
LC# 53-236. Copyright A73718 dated 17 Nov 52. "A very
special little golden book with party cut-outs, favors,
games, invitations, place cards, candy cups." Cover title:
Happy birthday. (LITTLE GOLDEN BOOK 123).

327a. ---- reissued; copyright A458442 dated 22 Jun 60.
(LITTLE GOLDEN BOOK 384).

328. How to tell time by Jane Werner Watson, ill. by Eleanor
Dart; NY: S&S, c1957. LC# 57-13730. Copyright AA290943 dated
8 Mar 57. (LITTLE GOLDEN BOOK 285).

328B. ---- [braille] Tarzana, CA: American Brotherhood for
the Blind, Twin Vision Publication Division; reprint of the
c1957 ed. Opposite pages in braille. (TWIN VISION BOOK).

328a. ---- (LITTLE GOLDEN ACTIVITY BOOK).

Howdy Doody time. See It's Howdy Doody time (354).

329. Howdy Doody and Clarabell by Edward Kean, ill. by Art
Seiden; NY: S&S, c1951. LC# 52-6594. (LITTLE GOLDEN BOOK
121).

330. Howdy Doody and his magic hat based on the UPA cartoon
by Edward Kean, ill. by Art Seiden; NY: S&S, c1954. LC#
54-2153rev. (LITTLE GOLDEN BOOK 184).

331. Howdy Doody and Mr. Bluster by Edward Kean, ill. by
Elias Marge; NY: S&S, c1954. LC# 54-14962. (LITTLE GOLDEN
BOOK 204).

332. Howdy Doody and Santa Claus by Edward Kean, ill. by Art Seiden; NY: S&S, c1955. LC# 55-4120. (LITTLE GOLDEN BOOK 237).

333. Howdy Doody and the Princess by Edward Kean, ill. by Art Seiden; NY: S&S, c1952. LC# 52-4278. (LITTLE GOLDEN BOOK 135).

334. Howdy Doody in funland by Edward Kean, ill. by Art Seiden; NY: S&S, c1953. LC# 53-4350. (LITTLE GOLDEN BOOK 172).

335. Howdy Doody's animal friends by Kathleen N. Daly, ill. by Art Seiden; NY: S&S, c1956. LC# 56-1899. (LITTLE GOLDEN BOOK 252).

336. Howdy Doody's circus by Edward Kean, ill. by Liz Dauber and Dan Gormley; NY: S&S, c1950. LC# 50-11852rev. Song: "It's Howdy Doody time" on last page. (LITTLE GOLDEN BOOK 99).

337. Howdy Doody's lucky trip by Edward Kean, ill. by Harry McNaught; NY: S&S, c1953. LC# 53-3481. (LITTLE GOLDEN BOOK 171).

338. Huckleberry Hound and his friends by Pat Cherr, ill. by Ben De Nunez and Bob Totten; NY: GP, c1960. (LITTLE GOLDEN BOOK 406).

339. Huckleberry Hound and the Christmas sleigh by Pat Cherr, ill. by Ben De Nunez and Chuck Satterfield; NY: GP, c1960. (LITTLE GOLDEN BOOK 403).

340. Huckleberry Hound builds a house by Ann McGovern, ill. by Harvey Eisenberg and Al White; NY: GP, c1959. (LITTLE GOLDEN BOOK 376).

341. Huckleberry Hound safety signs, Hanna-Barbera's by Ann McGovern, ill. by Al White; NY: GP, c1961. (LITTLE GOLDEN BOOK 458).

342. Hush, hush, it's sleepytime by Peggy Parish, ill. by Leonid Pinchevsky; NY: GP, c1968. Copyright A2823 dated 1968. (LITTLE GOLDEN BOOK 577).

342a. ---- reissued (LITTLE GOLDEN BOOK 301-53).

Hymns. See Little golden book of hymns (414).

343. I can fly by Ruth Krauss, ill. by Mary Blair; NY: S&S, c1950. LC# 51-9477. Copyright A52311 dated 22 Jan 51; renewal RE-21-290 dated 14 Feb 79. Song: "I can fly" words by Hilda Marx, music by Alec Wilder. (LITTLE GOLDEN BOOK 92); (BANK STREET BOOK).

I do my best. See I think about God (346).

344. <u>I have a secret: a first counting book</u> by Carl Memling,
ill. by Joseph Giordano; NY: GP, c1962. Copyright A609562
dated 15 Nov 62. (LITTLE GOLDEN BOOK 495).

345. <u>I like to live in the city</u> by Margaret Hillert, ill. by
Lilian Obligado; NY: GP, c1970. (LITTLE GOLDEN BOOK 593).

<u>I sing a song of praise.</u> See <u>Book of God's gifts</u> (089).

346. <u>I think about God: two stories about my day</u> by Sue Val,
ill. by Christiane Cassan; NY: GP, 1974, c1965. Bound with <u>I
do my best</u> by Norah Smaridge, ill. by Trina Hyman. (LITTLE
GOLDEN BOOK 111X).

346a. ---- reissued (LITTLE GOLDEN BOOK 410-1).

347. <u>I think that it is wonderful</u> by David Korr, ill. by A.
Delaney; featuring Jim Henson's Sesame Street Muppets. A
Sesame Street/Golden Press Book, c1984. LC# 82-82288.
(LITTLE GOLDEN BOOK 109-9); (SESAME STREET BOOK).

348. <u>I'm an Indian today</u> by Kathryn Hitte, ill. by William
Dugan; NY: GP, c1961. Copyright A498322 dated 6 Apr 61.
(LITTLE GOLDEN BOOK 425).

349. <u>If I had a dog</u> written and ill. by Lilian Obligado; NY:
GB, c1984. LC# 83-80024. (LITTLE GOLDEN BOOK 205-51).

350. <u>Indian, Indian</u> by Charlotte Zolotow, ill. by Leonard
Weisgard; NY: S&S, c1952. LC# 52-8717. Copyright A65901
dated 6 Mar 52; renewal RE-68-190 dated 20 Oct 80. (LITTLE
GOLDEN BOOK 149).

351. <u>Indian stamps</u> by Ed Huberman, ill. by Edwin Schmidt;
NY: S&S, c1957. (LITTLE GOLDEN ACTIVITY BOOK A13).

352. <u>Insect stamps</u> by Richard A. Martin, ill. by Jean
Zallinger; NY: S&S, c1958. (LITTLE GOLDEN ACTIVITY BOOK
A25).

353. <u>Inspector Gadget in Africa</u> by Sandra Beris, ill. by
David Gantz; NY: GB, c1984. LC# 83-83290. (LITTLE GOLDEN
BOOK 107-59).

354. <u>It's Howdy Doody time</u> by Edward Kean, ill. by Art
Seiden; NY: S&S, c1955. LC# 55-1612. (LITTLE GOLDEN BOOK
223).

355. <u>J. Fred Muggs</u> by Irwin Shapiro, ill. by Edwin Schmidt;
NY: S&S, c1955. Authorized ed. LC# 55-3178. (LITTLE GOLDEN
BOOK 234).

356. <u>Jack and the beanstalk</u> retold by Stella Williams
Nathan, ill. by Dora Leder; NY: GP, c1973. Copyright A453487
dated 25 Jun 73. (LITTLE GOLDEN BOOK 545).

356a. ---- reissued (LITTLE GOLDEN BOOK 307-23).

357. Jack and the beanstalk: an English folk tale,
Tenggren's ill. by Gustaf Tenggren; NY: S&S, c1953. LC#
54-1082. Copyright A126757 dated 31 Dec 53. (LITTLE GOLDEN
BOOK 179).

357a. ---- reissued; LC# 56-12982. Copyright A269064 dated 5
Sept 56; renewal RE-223-002 dated 21 Nov 84. (LITTLE GOLDEN
BOOK 181X).

357aSR. ---- [sound recording] NY: Golden Record. 1 disc (45
rpm, mono., 7 in.) + book, c1956.(READ AND HEAR GR 00163).

357b. ---- reissued in 1956 (LITTLE GOLDEN BOOK 281).

357c. ---- reissued in 1960 (LITTLE GOLDEN BOOK 420).

358. Jack's adventure by Edith Thacher Hurd, ill. by John P.
Miller; NY: S&S, c1958. Copyright AA345953 dated 21 Apr 58.
(LITTLE GOLDEN BOOK 308).

359. Jamie looks by Adelaide Holl, ill. by Eloise Wilkin;
NY: GP, c1963. Copyright A647679 dated 3 Jul 63. (LITTLE
GOLDEN BOOK 522).

360. Jenny's new brother by Elaine Evans, ill. by Joan
Esley; NY: GP, c1970. (LITTLE GOLDEN BOOK 596).

360B. ---- [braille] Tarzana, CA: American Brotherhood for
the Blind, Twin Vision Publication Division; reprint of the
c1970 ed. Opposite pages in braille. (TWIN VISION BOOK).

361. Jenny's surprise summer written and ill. by Eugenie;
NY: GP, c1981. LC# 80-85033/AC. (LITTLE GOLDEN BOOK ---).

362. Jerry at school by Kathryn and Byron Jackson, ill. by
Corinne Malvern; NY: S&S, c1950. LC# 50-10645. Copyright
A49617 dated 6 Oct 50. With jig-saw puzzle in back cover.
(LITTLE GOLDEN BOOK 94).

363. Jetsons, Hanna-Barbera The by Carl Memling, ill. by Al
White and Hawley Pratt; NY: GP, c1962. (LITTLE GOLDEN BOOK
500).

364. Jiminy Cricket, fire fighter, Walt Disney's told by
Annie North Bedford, ill. by the Walt Disney Studio, adapted
by Samuel Armstrong; NY: S&S, c1956. LC# 56-1898. (WALT
DISNEY BOOK D50); (MICKEY MOUSE CLUB BOOK D50).

365. Jingle bell Jack by Dr. Frances R. Horwich, ill. by
Katherine Evans; NY: GP, c1959. (DING DONG SCHOOL BOOK
Din1).

366. <u>Jingle bells: a new story based on the traditional Christmas carol</u> by Kathleen N. Daly, ill. by J. P. Miller; NY: GP, c1964. Copyright A724538 dated 21 Sept 64. (LITTLE GOLDEN BOOK 553).

367. <u>Johnny Appleseed, Walt Disney's</u> ill. by the Walt Disney Studio, adapted by Ted Parmalee from the Walt Disney movie, "Melody time;" NY: S&S, c1949. LC# 49-9960. (WALT DISNEY BOOK D11).

368. <u>Johnny's machines</u> by Helen Palmer, ill. by Cornelius DeWitt; NY: S&S, c1949. Copyright A40467 dated 9 Nov 49. LC# 50-5804. (LITTLE GOLDEN BOOK 71).

Jokes. See <u>My little golden book of jokes</u> (519).

Jokes and riddles. See <u>Little golden book of jokes & riddles</u> (415).

369. <u>Jolly barnyard, The</u> by Annie North Bedford, ill. by Tibor Gergely; NY: S&S, c1950. LC# 50-4093. Copyright A44291 dated 16 Mar 50. With jigsaw puzzle in back cover. (LITTLE GOLDEN BOOK 67).

369a. ---- reissued (LITTLE GOLDEN BOOK 200-44; 303-22).

370. <u>Jungle book, The</u> told by Annie North Bedford, ill. adapted by Mel Crawford; NY: GP, c1967. (WALT DISNEY BOOK D120).

371. <u>Just for fun</u> by Patricia Scarry, ill. by Richard Scarry; NY: GP, c1960. (LITTLE GOLDEN BOOK 264).

371a. ---- reissued (LITTLE GOLDEN BOOK 311-26).

372. <u>Just watch me! Funny things to be and see</u> by Eileen Daly, ill. by Frank Aloise; NY: GP, c1975. (LITTLE GOLDEN BOOK 104).

373. <u>Katie the kitten</u> by Kathryn and Byron Jackson, ill. by Alice and Martin Provensen; NY: S&S, c1949. LC# 49-8895. Copyright A33516 dated 1 May 49. (LITTLE GOLDEN BOOK 75).

373FS. ---- [filmstrip] NY: S&S, released by Young America Films, 1951. 1 filmstrip (28 fr., col., 35 mm) + teacher's guide. LC# fia52-1741. (GOLDEN BOOK SERIES. SET NO. 3).

374. <u>Kitten who thought he was a mouse, The</u> by Miriam Norton, ill. by Garth Williams; NY: S&S, c1954. LC# 55-1001. Copyright A180484 dated 6 Dec 54; renewal RE-149-965 dated 30 Dec 82. (LITTLE GOLDEN BOOK 210).

375. <u>Kitten's surprise, The</u> by Nina, ill. by Feodor Rojankovsky; NY: S&S, c1951. LC# 51-40028. Copyright A60571 dated 4 Jul 51; renewal RE-46-372 dated 7 Nov 79. (LITTLE GOLDEN BOOK 107).

Kittens. See Giant little golden book of kittens (273).

376. Laddie and the little rabbit story and pictures by Bill
Gottlieb; NY: S&S, c1952 [photos c1950]. LC# 52-4204.
Copyright A70779 dated 28 Jul 52. (LITTLE GOLDEN BOOK 116).

377. Laddie the superdog story and pictures by William P.
Gottlieb; adapted from a filmstrip produced by Curriculum
Films, Inc; NY: S&S, c1954. LC# 54-9026. Copyright A135847
dated 23 Feb 54; renewal RE-143-922 dated 15 Nov 82. (LITTLE
GOLDEN BOOK 185).

378. Lady, Walt Disney's from the motion picture "Lady and
the Tramp" based on the story by Ward Greene; illustrations
by the Walt Disney Studio, adapted by Samuel Armstrong; NY:
S&S, c1954. LC# 55-1615. (WALT DISNEY BOOK D42); (MICKEY
MOUSE CLUB BOOK D42).

378a. ---- reissued in 1962 (WALT DISNEY BOOK D-103).

378b. ---- reissued (LITTLE GOLDEN BOOK 105-45).

379. Land of the lost: the surprise guests by Kennon Graham,
ill. by Fred Irvin; NY: GP, c1975. (LITTLE GOLDEN BOOK
136X).

380. Large and growly bear, The by Gertrude Crampton, ill.
by John Miller; NY: GP, c1961. (LITTLE GOLDEN BOOK 510).

380FS. ---- [filmstrip] Racine: Western Publishing Co.,
Education Division, 1972. 1 filmstrip (46 fr., col., 35 mm)
+ disc (6 min., 33 1/3 rpm, 7 in.) + teacher's guide by
Adelaide Holl. LC# 72-777479/F. (EDUCATIONAL EXPERIENCES
FILMSTRIPS: ABOUT MAKE-BELIEVE ANIMALS).

380SR. ---- [sound recording] Racine: Western, 1977. 1
cassette (9 min. 30 sec., 2 track, mono.) + text and
teacher's guide by Joanne Wylie. (LITTLE GOLDEN READ ALONG
3503).

380SR. ---- [sound recording] Burbank, CA: Buena Vista,
c1976. 1 disc (33 1/3 rpm, 7 in.) + book. (LITTLE GOLDEN
BOOK AND RECORD).

380a. ---- reissued (LITTLE GOLDEN BOOK 304-21; 304-42).

Lassie, Adventures of. See Adventures of Lassie (005).

381. Lassie and her day in the sun by Charles Spain Verral,
ill. by Mel Crawford; NY: GP, c1958. (LITTLE GOLDEN BOOK
307).
    See also Adventures of Lassie (005).

381a. ---- reissued in 1963 (LITTLE GOLDEN BOOK 518).

381b. ---- reissued (LITTLE GOLDEN BOOK 301-23).

382. <u>Lassie and the big clean-up day</u> by Kennon Graham, ill. by Bob Schaar; NY: GP, c1971. (LITTLE GOLDEN BOOK 572).

382a. ---- reissued (LITTLE GOLDEN BOOK 301-4).

383. <u>Lassie and the daring rescue</u> by Charles Spain Verral, ill. by E. Joseph Dreany; NY: S&S, c1956. Authorized ed. LC# 57-1088. (LITTLE GOLDEN BOOK 277).
    See also <u>Adventures of Lassie</u> (005).

384. <u>Lassie and the lost explorer</u> by Leon Lazarus, ill. by Frank Bolle; NY: GP, c1958. (LITTLE GOLDEN BOOK 343).

385. <u>Lassie shows the way</u> by Monica Hill, ill. by Lee Ames; NY: S&S, c1956. Authorized ed. LC# 56-30161. Copyright A245590 dated 10 May 56. (LITTLE GOLDEN BOOK 255).
    See also <u>Adventures of Lassie</u> (005).

385a. ---- reissued in 1960 (LITTLE GOLDEN BOOK 415).

386. <u>Leave it to Beaver</u> by Lawrence Alson, ill. by Mel Crawford; NY: GP, c1959. (LITTLE GOLDEN BOOK 347).

387. <u>Let's go shopping with Peter and Penny</u> written and ill. by Lenora Combes; NY: S&S, c1948. LC# 48-7812. Copyright A24382 dated 30 Jun 48. (LITTLE GOLDEN BOOK 33).

388. <u>Let's go, trucks!</u> by David L. Harrison, ill. by Bill Dugan; NY: GP, c1973. Copyright A493289 dated 29 Nov 73. (LITTLE GOLDEN BOOK 185X).

388a. ---- reissued (LITTLE GOLDEN BOOK 211-1).

389. <u>Let's save money</u> by Loyta Higgins, ill. by Violet LaMont; NY: S&S, c1958. (LITTLE GOLDEN ACTIVITY BOOK A21).

390. <u>Let's visit the dentist</u> by Patricia M. Scarry, ill. by Dagmar Wilson; NY: GP, c1970. Copyright A209019 dated 2 Nov 70. (LITTLE GOLDEN BOOK 599).

391. <u>Life and legend of Wyatt Earp, The</u> by Monica Hill, ill. by Mel Crawford; NY: S&S, c1958. LC# 65-43911. (LITTLE GOLDEN BOOK 315).

392. <u>Linda and her little sister</u> by Esther Wilkin, ill. by Eloise Wilkin; NY: S&S, c1954. LC# 55-1002. Copyright A179210 dated 3 Jan 55 (54 in notice), renewal RE-148-056 dated 13 Dec 82. (LITTLE GOLDEN BOOK 214).

393. <u>Lion's paw: a tale of African animals, The</u> by Jane Werner Watson, ill. by Gustaf Tenggren; NY: GP, c1959. Copyright A415429 dated 21 Sept 59. (LITTLE GOLDEN BOOK 367).

394. <u>Lippy the Lion and Hardy Har Har, Hanna-Barbera</u> by Gina Ingoglia Weiner, ill. by Hawley Pratt and Norm McGary; NY: GP, c1963. (LITTLE GOLDEN BOOK 508).

395. Lisa and the eleven swans by Hans Christian Andersen, ill. by Gordon Laite; NY: GP, c1963. (LITTLE GOLDEN BOOK 515).

396. Little Benny wanted a pony by Oliver O'Connor Barrett, ill. by Richard Scarry; NY: S&S, c1950. LC# 50-11910. Copyright A49558 dated 26 Oct 50. With real mask on last page. (LITTLE GOLDEN BOOK 97).

397. Little black puppy, The by Charlotte Zolotow, ill. by Lilian Obligado; NY: GP, c1974. (LITTLE GOLDEN BOOK 804); (EAGER READER).

398. Little black Sambo by Helen Bannerman, ill. by Gustaf Tenggren; NY: S&S, c1948. LC# 49-940. Copyright A29300 dated 13 Dec 48; renewal R623881 dated 8 Jan 76. (LITTLE GOLDEN BOOK 57).

399. Little book, The by Sherl Horvath, ill. by Eloise Wilkin; NY: GP, c1969. (LITTLE GOLDEN BOOK 583).

399a. --- reissued (LITTLE GOLDEN BOOK 209-23).

400. Little boy and the giant, The by David L. Harrison, ill. by ROFry; NY: GP, c1973. Copyright A435415 dated 22 Mar 73. (LITTLE GOLDEN BOOK 536).

401. Little boy with a big horn by Jack Bechdolt, ill. by Aurelius Battaglia; NY: S&S, c1950. LC# 51-9574. Copyright A52312 dated 22 Jan 51; renewal RE-21-289 dated 14 Feb 79. (LITTLE GOLDEN BOOK 100).

401SR. ---- [sound recording] NY: Golden Record, [197-]. 1 disc (45 rpm, mono., 7 in.) + book, c1950. Narrated by Alan Cole with Kay Lande. Song: "I want to blow my horn" by The Sandpipers. Title on record: Little boy, big horn. (READ AND HEAR GR 00183).

401SR. ---- [sound recording] Burbank, CA: Disneyland Records / Buena Vista, 1976. 1 disc (33 1/3 rpm, mono., 7 in.) + book. Song: "I want to blow my horn" by The Sandpipers. (LITTLE GOLDEN BOOK AND RECORD).

402. Little Cottontail by Carl Memling, ill. by Lilian Obligado; NY: GP, c1960. LC# 73-5228/AC. Copyright A491704 dated 10 Jan 61. (LITTLE GOLDEN BOOK 414).

403. Little Crow by Caroline McDermott, ill. by Andy Aldrich; NY: GP, c1974. (LITTLE GOLDEN BOOK 113X).

404. Little engine that could, The retold by Watty Piper, ill. by George and Doris Hauman; NY: GP, c1964. (LITTLE GOLDEN BOOK 548).

404SR. ---- [sound recording]; c1976. (DISNEYLAND STORYTELLER CASSETTE 216B).

405. <u>Little Eskimo, The</u> by Kathryn Jackson, ill. by Leonard Weisgard; NY: S&S, c1952. LC# 52-10807. Copyright A68610 dated 8 May 52; renewal RE-68-195 dated 20 Oct 80. (LITTLE GOLDEN BOOK 155).

406. <u>Little fat policeman, The</u> by Margaret Wise Brown and Edith Thacher Hurd, ill. by Alice and Martin Provensen; NY: S&S, c1950. LC# 50-13023. Copyright A45301 dated 8 Jun 50. (LITTLE GOLDEN BOOK 91).

406SR. ---- [sound recording] NY: Golden Record, [197-]. 1 disc (45 rpm, mono., 7 in.) + book, c1950. Narrated by Dave Teig. (READ AND HEAR GR 00246).

406SR. ---- [sound recording] Burbank, CA: Disneyland Records, c1976. 1 disc (33 1/3 rpm, 7 in.) + book. Song: "I'm a policeman" by Larry Groce. (LITTLE GOLDEN BOOK AND RECORD).

406SR. ---- [sound recording]; c1976. (DISNEYLAND STORYTELLER CASSETTE 224B).

407. <u>Little galoshes</u> by Kathryn and Byron Jackson, ill. by J.P. Miller; NY: S&S, c1949. LC# 49-11453. Copyright A36998 dated 12 Sept 49. (LITTLE GOLDEN BOOK 68).

408. <u>Little golden ABC, The</u> ill. by Cornelius DeWitt; NY: S&S, c1951. LC# 51-1777. Copyright A52308 dated 22 Jan 51; renewal RE-21-291 dated 14 Feb 79. With jigsaw puzzle in back cover. (LITTLE GOLDEN BOOK 101).

408B. ---- [braille] Tarzana, CA: American Brotherhood for the Blind, Twin Vision Publication Division; reprint of the c1951 ed. Opposite pages in braille. (TWIN VISION BOOK).

408a. ---- reissued (LITTLE GOLDEN BOOK 200-21).

409. <u>Little golden book about colors, A</u> by Kathleen N. Daly, ill. by Richard Scarry; NY: GP, c1959. (LITTLE GOLDEN ACTIVITY BOOK A28).

410. <u>Little golden book about the seashore, A</u> by Kathleen N. Daly, ill. by Tibor Gergely; NY: S&S, c1957. LC# 60-2220. Copyright AA295626 dated 27 May 57. (LITTLE GOLDEN BOOK 284).

411. <u>Little golden book of dogs, The</u> by Nita Jonas, ill. by Tibor Gergely; NY: S&S, c1952. LC# 52-11752. Copyright A68951 dated 9 Jun 52; renewal RE-68-199 dated 20 Oct 80. (LITTLE GOLDEN BOOK 131).

411a. ---- reissued in 1956 (LITTLE GOLDEN BOOK 260).

411b. ---- reissued in 1959 (LITTLE GOLDEN BOOK 391).

411c. ---- reissued (LITTLE GOLDEN BOOK 202-3).

412. <u>Little golden book of helicopters, The</u> by Carl Memling,
ill. by Mel Crawford; NY: GP, c1959. Copyright A416369 dated
16 Jul 59. (LITTLE GOLDEN BOOK 357).

413. <u>Little golden book of holidays, The</u> by Jean Lewis, ill.
by Kathy Wilburn; NY: GB, c1985. LC# 83-82199. (LITTLE
GOLDEN BOOK 209-58).

414. <u>Little golden book of hymns, The</u> compiled by Miss Elsa
Jane Werner, ill. by Corinne Malvern; NY: S&S, c1947. LC#
47-6320rev. Copyright A14578 dated 10 Jul 47; renewal
R581866 dated 15 Jul 74. (LITTLE GOLDEN BOOK 34).

414a. ---- reissued in 1960 (LITTLE GOLDEN BOOK 392).

414b. ---- reissued (LITTLE GOLDEN BOOK 403-1).

414c. ---- compiled by Elsa Jane Werner and E.D. Ebsun, ill.
by Frances Score Mitchell; NY: GB, c1985. LC# 84-46030.
(LITTLE GOLDEN BOOK 211-57).

415. <u>Little golden book of jokes & riddles, The</u> compiled by
E.D. Ebsun, ill. by John O'Brien; NY: GP, c1983. LC#
82-83069. (LITTLE GOLDEN BOOK 211-45).

416. <u>Little golden book of poetry, The</u> ill. by Corinne
Malvern; NY: S&S, c1947. LC# 47-5528. Copyright A14579 dated
10 Jul 47. (LITTLE GOLDEN BOOK 38).

417. <u>Little golden book of singing games, The</u> selected and
arranged by Katharine Tyler Wessells, ill. by Corinne
Malvern; NY: S&S, c1947. LC# 47-11993. Copyright A19679
dated 15 Oct 47. With piano accompaniment. (LITTLE GOLDEN
BOOK 40).

418. <u>Little golden book of Uncle Wiggly, The</u> by Howard R.
Garis, ill. by Mel Crawford, based on Uncle Wiggly and the
alligator; NY: S&S, c1953. LC# 53-8197. (LITTLE GOLDEN BOOK
148).

419. <u>Little golden book of words, The</u> by Selma Lola
Chambers, ill. by Gertrude Elliott; NY: S&S, c1948. LC#
49-7120. Copyright A28613 dated 13 Dec 48. (LITTLE GOLDEN
BOOK 45).

419B. ---- [braille] Tarzana, CA: American Brotherhood for
the Blind, Twin Vision Publishing Division; reprint of the
c1948 ed. Opposite pages in braille. (TWIN VISION BOOK).

419a. ---- NY: GP, c1955. LC# 56-13515. (LITTLE GOLDEN
ACTIVITY BOOK A1).

419b. ---- NY: GP, c1955. (LITTLE GOLDEN ACTIVITY BOOK A30).

419c. ---- NY: GP, c1961. (LITTLE GOLDEN ACTIVITY BOOK A45).

420. Little golden Christmas manger, The by Jane Werner
Watson, ill. by Steffie Lerch; NY: S&S, c1953. LC#
54-1175rev. Copyright A105651 dated 27 Jul 53; renewal
RE-109-110 dated 29 Oct 81. Cover title: The little golden
cut-out Christmas manger. Has cut-outs. (LITTLE GOLDEN BOOK
176).

Little golden cut-out Christmas manger. See Little golden
Christmas manger (420).

421. Little golden funny book, The by Gertrude Crampton,
ill. by J.P. Miller; NY: S&S, c1950. LC# 50-7513. Copyright
A42927 dated 13 Mar 50. (LITTLE GOLDEN BOOK 74).

422. Little golden holiday book, The by Marion Conger, ill.
by Eloise Wilkin; NY: S&S, c1951. LC# 51-39069. Copyright
A60573 dated 4 Jul 51; renewal RE-46-374 dated 7 Nov 79.
(LITTLE GOLDEN BOOK 109).

423. Little golden Mother Goose, A ill. by Feodor
Rojankovsky; NY: S&S, c1957. LC# 57-1223. Copyright AA283235
dated 22 Feb 57. (LITTLE GOLDEN BOOK 283).

423a. ---- reissued in 1959 (LITTLE GOLDEN BOOK 390).

423b. ---- reissued in 1962 (LITTLE GOLDEN BOOK 472).

423c. ---- reissued (LITTLE GOLDEN BOOK 300-21).

424. Little golden paper dolls, The by Hilda Miloche and
Wilma Kane; NY: S&S, c1951. LC# 52-368. Copyright A62294
dated 27 Mar 51; renewal RE-38-497 dated 7 Nov 79. Has
punch-out dolls. (LITTLE GOLDEN BOOK 113).

424a. ---- NY: S&S, c1955; LC# 56-13520. (LITTLE GOLDEN
ACTIVITY BOOK A3).

424b. ---- (LITTLE GOLDEN ACTIVITY BOOK A47).

424c. ---- reissued in 1956 (LITTLE GOLDEN BOOK 280).

425. Little golden picture dictionary, The by Nancy Fielding
Hulick, ill. by Tibor Gergely; NY: GP, c1959. Copyright
A404076 dated 17 Jul 59. (LITTLE GOLDEN BOOK 369).

425B. ---- [braille] Tarzana, CA: American Brotherhood for
the Blind, Twin Vision Publishing Division; reprint of the
c1959 ed. Opposite pages in braille. (TWIN VISION BOOK).

425a. ---- reissued (LITTLE GOLDEN BOOK 205-32).

425b. ---- ill. by Marie DeJohn; NY: GP, c1981. LC#
80-85026. (LITTLE GOLDEN BOOK 202-41).

426. <u>Little gray donkey</u> by Alice Lunt, ill. by Tibor Gergely; NY: S&S, c1954. LC# 54-14960. Copyright A175277 dated 20 Oct 54; renewal RE-148-057 dated 13 Dec 82. (LITTLE GOLDEN BOOK 206).

427. <u>Little Indian</u> by Margaret Wise Brown, ill. by Richard Scarry; NY: S&S, c1954. LC# 54-3675. Copyright A146457 dated 31 May 54; renewal RE-143-931 dated 15 Nov 82. (LITTLE GOLDEN BOOK 202).

428. <u>Little Lulu, Marge's</u> adapted by Gina Ingoglia Weiner, ill. by Woody Kimbrell and Al White; NY: GP, c1962. Based on the character created by Marjorie Henderson Buell. (LITTLE GOLDEN BOOK 476).

429. <u>Little Lulu and her magic tricks, Marge's</u> [written and ill. by Marge]; NY: S&S, c1954. Contains a packet of Kleenex tissues and instructions for making a doll, carnation, and bunny. (LITTLE GOLDEN BOOK 203).

430. <u>Little man of Disneyland, Walt Disney's</u> adapted by Annie North Bedford, ill. by the Walt Disney Studio, adapted by Dick Kelsey; NY: S&S, c1955. (WALT DISNEY BOOK D46); (MICKEY MOUSE CLUB BOOK D46).

431. <u>Little Mommy</u> written and ill. by Sharon Kane; NY: GP, c1967. (LITTLE GOLDEN BOOK 569).

432. <u>Little Peewee: or, Now open the box</u> by Dorothy Kunhardt, ill. by J.P. Miller; NY: S&S, c1948. LC# 48-6657rev. Copyright A23292 dated 5 Apr 48. Cover title: Little Peewee, the circus dog. (LITTLE GOLDEN BOOK 52).

432SR. ---- [sound recording] Copyright KK38749 dated 1 Sep 48 (LITTLE GOLDEN RECORD 9).

433. <u>Little pond in the woods, The</u> by Muriel Ward, ill. by Tibor Gergely; NY: S&S, c1948. LC# 48-1918. Copyright A16556 dated 13 Feb 48. (LITTLE GOLDEN BOOK 43).

434. <u>Little pussycat</u> by Margaret Wise Brown, ill. by Leonard Weisgard; NY: GB, c1951. (LITTLE GOLDEN BOOK 302-51).
    Originally issued with title <u>Pussy Willow</u> (611).

435. <u>Little red caboose, The</u> by Marian Potter, ill. by Tibor Gergely; NY: S&S, c1953. LC# 53-2328. Copyright A92981 dated 10 Apr 53; renewal RE-107-446 dated 5 Oct 81. (LITTLE GOLDEN BOOK 162).

435SR. ---- [sound recording] NY: Golden Record. 1 disc (45 rpm, mono., 7 in.) + book, c1953. Sung by Kari. (READ AND HEAR GR 00159).

435a. ---- reissued in 1958 (LITTLE GOLDEN BOOK 319).

435b. ---- reissued (LITTLE GOLDEN BOOK 306-22).

436. <u>Little red hen: a favorite folk-tale, The</u> ill. by
Rudolf [Freund]; NY: S&S, c1942. LC# 42-50765. Copyright
A169131 dated 1 Oct 42. First printing Sept 42. (LITTLE
GOLDEN BOOK 6).

436a. ---- ill. by J.P. Miller, cover by Rudolf; NY: S&S,
c1954. LC# 54-14959. Copyright A175275 dated 20 Nov 54;
renewal RE-148-058 dated 13 Dec 82. (LITTLE GOLDEN BOOK
209).

436aSR. ---- [sound recording] NY: Golden Record, [197-]. 1
disc (45 rpm, mono., 7 in.) + book, c1954. Narrated by Rita.
(READ AND HEAR GR 00166).

436b. ---- reissued in 1957 (LITTLE GOLDEN BOOK 296).

436c. ---- reissued in 1963 (LITTLE GOLDEN BOOK 519).

436d. ---- as told by Evelyn M. Begley, ill. by Carl and
Mary Hauge; NY: GP, c1966. (LITTLE GOLDEN BOOK 438).

437. <u>Little Red Riding Hood</u> told and ill. by Elizabeth Orton
Jones; NY: S&S, c1948. LC# 48-1942. Copyright A16558 dated
13 Feb 48. (LITTLE GOLDEN BOOK 42).

437B. ---- [braille] Tarzana, CA: American Brotherhood for
the Blind, Twin Vision Publication Division; reprint of the
c1948 ed. Opposite pages in braille. (TWIN VISION BOOK).

437SR. ---- [sound recording] NY: Golden Record. 1 disc (45
rpm, mono., 7 in.) + book, c1948. Narrated by Anne Lloyd and
Jack Lazare. Musical director, Mitch Miller. (READ AND HEAR
GR 00156).

437a. ---- as told by Mabel Watts, ill. by Les Gray; NY: GP,
c1972. Copyright A340568 dated 8 May 72. (LITTLE GOLDEN BOOK
232).

437b. ---- reissued (LITTLE GOLDEN BOOK 309-21).

438. <u>Little trapper, The</u> by Kathryn and Byron Jackson, ill.
by Gustaf Tenggren; NY: S&S, c1950. LC# 50-6271. Copyright
A41543 dated 18 Jan 50. (LITTLE GOLDEN BOOK 79).

439. <u>Little Yip Yip and his bark</u> by Kathryn and Byron
Jackson, ill. by Tibor Gergely; NY: S&S, c1950. LC# 50-7825.
Copyright A43472 dated 19 Apr 50. (LITTLE GOLDEN BOOK 73).

440. <u>Littlest raccoon</u> by Peggy Parish, ill. by Claude
Humbert; NY: GP, c1961. Copyright A533452 dated 18 Sept 61.
(LITTLE GOLDEN BOOK 457).

441. <u>Lively little rabbit, The</u> by Ariane, ill. by Gustaf
Tenggren; NY: S&S, c1943. LC# 43-14466. Copyright A175686
dated 15 Jul 43. First printing Apr 43. Issued with dust
jacket. (LITTLE GOLDEN BOOK 15).

441SR. ---- [sound recording] Copyright KK38742 dated 1 Sep 48 (LITTLE GOLDEN RECORD 2).

441SR. ---- [sound recording] Burbank, CA: Disneyland Records, c1976. 1 disc (33 1/3 rpm, 7 in.) + book. Songs: "Friends lullaby" and "Hurray for the dragon" by Larry Groce. (LITTLE GOLDEN BOOK AND RECORD).

441SR. ---- [sound recording] NY: Golden Records. 1 disc (45 rpm, mono., 7 in.) + book, c1943. Narrated by Kay Lande. (READ AND HEAR GR 00243).

441a. ---- reissued in 1965 (LITTLE GOLDEN BOOK 551).

441b. ---- reissued (LITTLE GOLDEN BOOK 201-44).

442. Lone Ranger, The by Steffi Fletcher, ill. by E. Joseph Dreany; NY: S&S, c1956. LC# 56-4681. (LITTLE GOLDEN BOOK 263).

443. Lone Ranger and the talking pony, The by Emily Broun, ill. by Frank Bolle; NY: GP, c1958. (LITTLE GOLDEN BOOK 310).

444. Lone Ranger and Tonto, The by Charles Spain Verral, ill. by Edwin Schmidt; NY: S&S, c1957. (LITTLE GOLDEN BOOK 297).

445. Loopy de Loop goes West by Kathryn Hitte, ill. by George Santos; NY: GP, c1960. (LITTLE GOLDEN BOOK 417).

446. Love bug: Herbie's special friend, Walt Disney Productions The NY: GP, c1974. (WALT DISNEY BOOK D130).

447. Lucky Mrs. Ticklefeather by Dorothy Kunhardt, ill. by J.P. Miller; NY: S&S, c1951. LC# 51-13830. Copyright A60570 dated 30 Sept 51; renewal RE-46-371 dated 7 Nov 79. (LITTLE GOLDEN BOOK 122).

448. Lucky puppy, Walt Disney's adapted from the Walt Disney motion picture "One hundred and one dalmations" told by Jane Werner Watson, ill. by Allen Hubbard and Don Bestor; NY: GP, c1960. (WALT DISNEY BOOK D89).

449. Lucky rabbit by Dr. Frances R. Horwich, ill. by Ruth Bendel; NY:GP, c1960. (DING DONG SCHOOL BOOK Din7).

450. Ludwig Von Drake, Walt Disney presents by Gina Ingoglia and George Sherman, ill. by the Walt Disney Studio, adapted by Hawley Pratt and Herbert Stott; NY: GP, c1961. (WALT DISNEY BOOK D98).

451. Machines written and ill. by William Dugan; NY: GP, c1961. Copyright A543645 dated 6 Dec 61. (LITTLE GOLDEN BOOK 455).

452. <u>Mad Hatter's tea party, Walt Disney's</u> from Walt
Disney's "Alice in Wonderland" retold by Jane Werner, ill.
by the Walt Disney Studio, adapted by Richmond I. Kelsey and
Don Griffith, based on the story by Lewis Carroll; NY: S&S,
c1951. LC# 51-13856. (WALT DISNEY BOOK D23).

453. <u>Madeline</u> written and ill. by Ludwig Bemelmans; NY: S&S,
c1954. LC# 54-2640. (LITTLE GOLDEN BOOK 186).

454. <u>Magic compass: a story from "Mary Poppins", The</u> by
Pamela L. Travers, ill. by Gertrude Elliott; NY: S&S, c1953.
Authorized ed. LC# 53-8215. Copyright A92985 dated 2 Feb 53.
(LITTLE GOLDEN BOOK 146).

455. <u>Magic friend-maker, The</u> by Gladys Baker Bond, ill. by
Stina Nagel; NY: GP, c1966. (LITTLE GOLDEN BOOK 137X).

455SR. ---- [sound recording] Racine: Western, [1977]. 1
cassette (8 min. 30 sec., 2 track, mono.) + text and
teacher's guide by Joanne Wylie. (LITTLE GOLDEN READ ALONG
3504).

456. <u>Magic next door, The</u> by Evelyn Swetnam, ill. by Judy
Stang; NY: GP, c1971. (LITTLE GOLDEN BOOK 106).

457. <u>Magic wagon</u> by Dr. Frances R. Horwich, ill. by
Elizabeth Webbe; NY: GP, c1960. (DING DONG SCHOOL BOOK
Din6).

458. <u>Magilla Gorilla</u> by Bruce Carrick, ill. by Hawley Pratt
and Al White; NY: GP, c1964. (LITTLE GOLDEN BOOK 547).

459. <u>Make way for the highway</u> by Caroline Emerson, ill. by
Tibor Gergely; NY: GP, c1961. LC# 82-83089. (LITTLE GOLDEN
BOOK 439).
    Also issued with title <u>Make way for the thruway</u> (460).

460. <u>Make way for the thruway</u> by Caroline Emerson, ill. by
Tibor Gergely; NY: GP, c1961. Copyright A533453 dated 6 Sept
61. (LITTLE GOLDEN BOOK 439V).
    Also issued with title <u>Make way for the highway</u> (459).

Manners. See <u>My little golden book of manners</u> (315).

461. <u>Manni the donkey</u> adapted by Emily Broun from A forest
world by Felix Salten, with pictures by the Walt Disney
Studio; NY: GP, c1959. (WALT DISNEY BOOK D75).

462. <u>Many faces of Ernie, The</u> by Judy Freudberg, ill. by
Normand Chartier, from a Sesame Street script written by
Judy Freudberg, Tony Geiss, and Herbert Hartig. Racine:
Western, in conjunction with Children's Television Workshop,
c1971. (LITTLE GOLDEN BOOK 109-24; 109-4); (SESAME STREET
BOOK).

463. <u>Marvelous merry-go-round, The</u> by Jane Werner Watson, ill. by J.P. Miller; NY: S&S, c1950. LC# 50-13053rev. Copyright A45305 dated 8 Jun 50. (LITTLE GOLDEN BOOK 87).

464. <u>Mary Poppins, Walt Disney's</u> based on the Walt Disney motion picture, story adapted by Annie North Bedford, ill. by Al White; NY: GP, c1964. (WALT DISNEY BOOK D113).

465. <u>Mary Poppins : A jolly holiday</u> by Jane Werner Watson, ill. by Jason Art Studios; NY: GP, c1964. (WALT DISNEY BOOK D112).

466. <u>Maverick</u> by Carl Memling, ill. by John Leone; NY: GP, c1959. Authorized ed. (LITTLE GOLDEN BOOK 354).

467. <u>Merry shipwreck, The</u> by Georges Duplaix, ill. by Tibor Gergely; NY: S&S, c1953. LC# 53-3480. Copyright A108168 dated 6 Jul 53; renewal RE-109-114 dated 29 Oct 81. (LITTLE GOLDEN BOOK 170).

Mickey Mouse. See <u>Surprise for Mickey Mouse</u> (701).

468. <u>Mickey Mouse and Goofy: the big bear scare, Walt Disney's</u> NY: GP, c1978. (WALT DISNEY BOOK D138).

468a. ---- reissued (LITTLE GOLDEN BOOK 100-44).

469. <u>Mickey Mouse and his space ship, Walt Disney's</u> told by Jane Werner, pictures by the Walt Disney Studio, adapted by Milton Banta and John Ushler; NY: S&S, c1952. (WALT DISNEY BOOK D29).

469a. ---- reissued in 1963 (WALT DISNEY BOOK D108).

470. <u>Mickey Mouse and Pluto Pup, Walt Disney's</u> told by Elizabeth Beecher, ill. by the Walt Disney Studio, adapted by Campbell Grant; NY: S&S, c1953. LC# 53-2894. (WALT DISNEY BOOK D32).

470a. ---- adapted by Annie North Bedford, ill. by the Walt Disney Studio, adapted by Yale Gracey; NY: GP, c1959. (WALT DISNEY BOOK D76).

471. <u>Mickey Mouse and the best-neighbor contest, Walt Disney's</u> illustrations by the Walt Disney Studio; NY: GP, c1977. (WALT DISNEY BOOK D134).

472. <u>Mickey Mouse and the great lot plot, Walt Disney's</u> [story by Russell K. Schroeder]; NY: GP, c1974. (WALT DISNEY BOOK D129).

473. <u>Mickey Mouse and the missing Mouseketeers, Walt Disney's</u> told by Annie North Bedford, ill. by the Walt Disney Studio, adapted by Julius Svendsen and Bob Totten; NY: S&S, c1956. LC# 56-59185. (WALT DISNEY BOOK D57); (MICKEY MOUSE CLUB BOOK D57).

474. Mickey Mouse and the Mouseketeers, ghost town adventure, Walt Disney's by Walt Disney Productions; NY: GP, c1977. (WALT DISNEY BOOK D135).

475. Mickey Mouse Club stamp book by Kathleen N. Daly, pictures adapted by Julius Svendsen; NY: S&S, c1956. (LITTLE GOLDEN ACTIVITY BOOK A10).

476. Mickey Mouse flies the Christmas mail, Walt Disney's told by Annie North Bedford, ill. by the Walt Disney Studio, adapted by Julius Svendsen and Neil Boyle; NY: S&S, c1956. LC# 56-58195. (WALT DISNEY BOOK D53); (MICKEY MOUSE CLUB BOOK D53).

477. Mickey Mouse goes Christmas shopping, Walt Disney's told by Annie North Bedford, pictures by the Walt Disney Studio, adapted by Bob Moore and Xavier Atencio; NY: S&S, c1953. LC# 53-3525. (WALT DISNEY BOOK D33); (MICKEY MOUSE CLUB BOOK D33).

478. Mickey Mouse: the kitten sitters, Walt Disney's illustrations by Walt Disney Studio; NY: GP, c1976. (WALT DISNEY BOOK D133).

479. Mickey Mouse's picnic, Walt Disney's story by Jane Werner, ill. by the Walt Disney Studio; NY: S&S, c1950. LC# 50-12283. (WALT DISNEY BOOK D15).

479a. ---- reissued (LITTLE GOLDEN BOOK 100-46).

480. Mickey's Christmas carol, Walt Disney's Productions' [artwork by Ron Dias]; NY: GP, c1983. LC# 82-84522. (LITTLE GOLDEN BOOK 459-9).

480SR. ---- [sound recording] Burbank, CA: Walt Disney Productions, c1982. 1 disc (33 1/3 rpm, 7 in.) + book.

481. Mike and Melissa and their magic mumbo jumbo by Jane Werner Watson; NY: GP, c1959. (LITTLE GOLDEN ACTIVITY BOOK A31).

Mister. See also Mr.

482. Mister Dog: the dog who belonged to himself by Margaret Wise Brown, ill. by Garth Williams; NY: S&S, c1952. LC# 52-13616. Copyright A71868 dated 10 Sept 52; renewal RE-68-204 dated 20 Oct 80. (LITTLE GOLDEN BOOK 128).

482SR. ---- [sound recording] NY: Golden Record, [197-]. 1 disc (45 rpm, mono., 7 in.) + book, c1952. Narrated by Dave Teig. (READ AND HEAR GR 00250).

482a. ---- reissued (LITTLE GOLDEN BOOK 204-27; 204-37).

483. Mister Ed by Barbara Hazen, ill. by Mel Crawford; NY: GP, c1962. (LITTLE GOLDEN BOOK 483).

484. Monster at the end of this book, The featuring Grover, a Jim Henson Muppet by Jon Stone, ill. by Mike Smollin; Racine: Western, in conjunction with Children's Television Workshop, c1971. (LITTLE GOLDEN BOOK 316); (SESAME STREET BOOK).

484a. ---- reissued (LITTLE GOLDEN BOOK 109-21; 109-31).

485. Monster! Monster! by David L. Harrison, ill. by Rosalind Fry; NY: GP, c1975. (LITTLE GOLDEN BOOK 808); (EAGER READER).

486. More Mother Goose rhymes ill. by Feodor Rojankovsky; NY: S&S, c1958. Copyright AA345949 dated 17 Mar 58. (LITTLE GOLDEN BOOK 317).

487. Mother Goose selected by Phyllis Fraser, ill. by Miss [Gertrude] Elliott; NY: S&S, c1942. LC# 42-50764. Copyright A169130 dated 1 Oct 42. First printing Sept 42. (LITTLE GOLDEN BOOK 4).

487a. ---- reissued in 1955 (LITTLE GOLDEN BOOK 240).

Mother Goose. See also Baby's Mother Goose (048); Little golden Mother Goose (413).

488. Mother Goose, Eloise Wilkin's [ill. by Eloise Wilkin]; NY: GP, c1961. (LITTLE GOLDEN BOOK 589).

488a. ---- reissued (LITTLE GOLDEN BOOK 300-22).

489. Mother Goose. Sixty-seven favorite rhymes ill. by Violet LaMont; NY: S&S, c1957. Copyright AA324812 dated 18 Nov 57. (GIANT LITTLE GOLDEN BOOK 5007).

490. Mother Goose, Walt Disney's ill. by the Walt Disney Studio, adapted by Al Dempster; NY: S&S, c1952. (WALT DISNEY BOOK D36).

490a. ---- reissued in 1956 (WALT DISNEY BOOK D51); (MICKEY MOUSE CLUB BOOK D51).

490b. ---- reissued in 1959 (WALT DISNEY BOOK D79).

491. Mother Goose in the city ill. by Dora Leder; NY: GP, c1974. Copyright A506806 dated 11 Jan 74. (LITTLE GOLDEN BOOK 336).

491a. ---- reissued (LITTLE GOLDEN BOOK 300-3).

492. Mother Goose rhymes. 154 childhood favorites ill. by Feodor Rojankovsky; NY: S&S, c1958. Copyright AA369641 dated 15 Sept 58. (GIANT LITTLE GOLDEN BOOK 5016).

Mr. See also Mister.

493. Mr. Bell's fixit shop by Ronne Peltzman, ill. by
Aurelius Battaglia; NY: GP, c1981. LC# 80-85031/AC. (LITTLE
GOLDEN BOOK 210-34).

494. Mr. Meyer's cow by Dr. Frances R. Horwich, ill. by
William Neebe; NY: GP, c1959. (DING DONG SCHOOL BOOK Din2).

495. Mr. Noah and his family by Jane Werner, ill. by Alice
and Martin Provensen; NY: S&S, c1948. LC# 48-7806rev.
Copyright A26682 dated 30 Jun 48. (LITTLE GOLDEN BOOK 49).

496. Mr. Puffer-Bill, train engineer by Leone Arlandson,
ill. by Tibor Gergely; NY: GP, c1965. (LITTLE GOLDEN BOOK
563).

496B. ---- [braille] Tarzana, CA: American Brotherhood for
the Blind, Twin Vision Publication Division; reprint of the
c1965 ed. Opposite pages in braille. (TWIN VISION BOOK).

497. Mr. Rogers' Neighborhood - Henrietta meets someone new
by Fred M. Rogers, ill. by Jason Art Studios; NY: GP, c1974.
(LITTLE GOLDEN BOOK 133X).

498. Mr. Wigg's birthday party, a story from Mary Poppins by
Pamela L. Travers, ill. by Gertrude Elliott; NY: S&S, c1952.
LC# 52-10821. Copyright A68613 dated 8 May 52. (LITTLE
GOLDEN BOOK 140).

499. Mrs. Brisby and the magic stone adapted by Gina
Ingoglia, ill. by Carol Nicklaus; NY: GP, c1982. LC#
81-86144. (LITTLE GOLDEN BOOK 110-38).

500. Musicians of Bremen, The adapted from Jacob and Wilhelm
Grimm, ill. by J.P. Miller; NY: S&S, c1954. LC# 54-2630.
Copyright A138907 dated 29 Mar 54; renewal RE-143-925 dated
15 Nov 82. (LITTLE GOLDEN BOOK 189).

500SR. ---- [sound recording] NY: Golden Record, [197-]. 1
disc (45 rpm, mono., 7 in.) + book, c1954. Narrated by Danny
Kaye. (READ AND HEAR GR 00177).

500a. ---- retold by Ben Cruise, ill. by Ann Schweninger;
NY: GP, c1983. LC# 82-83377. (LITTLE GOLDEN BOOK 307-47).

501. My baby brother by Patsy Scarry, ill. by Eloise Wilkin;
NY: S&S, c1956. LC# 57-1020. Copyright AA273109 dated 18 Dec
56; renewal RE-223-582 dated 21 Nov 84. (LITTLE GOLDEN BOOK
279).

502. My baby sister by Patsy Scarry, ill. by Sharon Koester;
NY: S&S, c1958. LC# 68-7849. Copyright AA358153 dated 22 Aug
58. (LITTLE GOLDEN BOOK 340).

502a. ---- reissued in 1963 (LITTLE GOLDEN BOOK 513).

My Christmas book. See My little golden Christmas book
(521).

503. My Christmas treasury compiled by Gale Wiersum, ill. by
Sylvia Emrich; NY: GP, c1976. (LITTLE GOLDEN BOOK 144X).

503a. ---- reissued (LITTLE GOLDEN BOOK 455-1).

504. My Christmas treasury: a collection of Christmas
stories, poems and songs ill. by Lowell Hess; NY: S&S,
c1957. LC# 62-5122/LA. Copyright AA313057 dated 12 Sept 57.
(GIANT LITTLE GOLDEN BOOK 5003).

505. My daddy is a policeman by Dr. Frances R. Horwich, ill.
by Helen Prickett; NY: GP, c1959. (DING DONG SCHOOL BOOK
Din3).

506. My dolly and me by Patricia Scarry, ill. by Eloise
Wilkin; NY: GP, c1960. Copyright A481099 dated 23 Sept 60.
(LITTLE GOLDEN BOOK 418).

507. My first book ill. by Bob Smith; NY: GP, c1942. (LITTLE
GOLDEN BOOK 10V).
     Originally issued with title Baby's book (044).

508. My first book of Bible stories by Mary Ann Walton, ill.
by Emmy Ferand; NY: Artists & Writers Guild, dist. by S&S,
c1943. LC# 44-4301. Copyright A179737 dated 13 Dec 43.
(LITTLE GOLDEN BOOK 19).

509. My first book of the planets by Elizabeth Winthrop,
ill. by John Nez; NY: GB, c1985. LC# 84-72869. (LITTLE
GOLDEN BOOK 308-56).

510. My first counting book by Lilian Moore, ill. by Garth
Williams; NY: S&S, c1956. LC# 56-13805. Copyright A244056
dated 2 Mar 56; renewal RE-222-977 dated 21 Nov 84. (LITTLE
GOLDEN BOOK 434).

510a. ---- reissued (LITTLE GOLDEN BOOK 445X).

510b. ---- reissued (LITTLE GOLDEN BOOK 201-1; 203-41).

511. My first little golden library. [Library of 12 little
golden books in box with book-end Poky Little Puppy popping
out]. Contents: What if?(788) -- Animal friends (021) --
Three bears (722) -- Fix it, please (246) -- Little golden
ABC (408) -- I can fly (343) -- Busy Timmy (118) -- What am
I? (787) -- Day at the zoo (185) -- Here comes the parade
(312) -- Mr. Noah (495) -- Animals of Farmer Jones (030);
NY: S&S, c1954.

512. My home by Renee Bartkowski, ill. by ROFry; NY: GP,
c1976. Copyright A282218 dated 14 Oct 71; renewal A827400
dated 21 Dec 76. (LITTLE GOLDEN BOOK 115).

512a. ---- reissued (LITTLE GOLDEN BOOK 206-21; 305-44).

513. **My kitten** by Patsy Scarry, ill. by Eloise Wilkin; NY:
S&S, c1953. LC# 53-2379. Copyright A92980 dated 16 Apr 53;
renewal RE-109-091 dated 29 Oct 81. (LITTLE GOLDEN BOOK
163).
See also **Giant little golden book of kittens** (273); **My
pets** (524).

513a. ---- reissued (LITTLE GOLDEN BOOK 300).

513b. --- reissued in 1963 (LITTLE GOLDEN BOOK 528).

514. **My little dinosaur** written and ill. by Ilse-Margret
Vogel; NY: GP, c1971. Copyright A262974 dated 23 Jul 71.
(LITTLE GOLDEN BOOK 571).

514a. ---- reissued (LITTLE GOLDEN BOOK 304-2).

515. **My little golden animal book** by Elizabeth MacPherson,
ill. by Moritz Kennel; NY: GP, c1962. Copyright A578227
dated 5 Jul 62. (LITTLE GOLDEN BOOK 441X).

515a. ---- reissued (LITTLE GOLDEN BOOK 465).

516. **My little golden book about God** by Jane Werner Watson,
ill. by Eloise Wilkin; NY: S&S, c1956. LC# 56-58148.
Copyright A254300 dated 16 Aug 56; renewal RE-223-046 dated
21 Nov 84. (LITTLE GOLDEN BOOK 268).

517. **My little golden book about the sky** by Rose Wyler, ill.
by Tibor Gergely; NY: S&S, c1956. LC# 56-4680. Copyright
A251967 dated 31 Jul 56; renewal RE-222-985 dated 21 Nov 84.
(LITTLE GOLDEN BOOK 270).

518. **My little golden book about travel** by Kathleen N. Daly,
ill. by Tibor Gergely; NY: S&S, c1956. LC# 56-4678.
Copyright A252971 dated 31 Jul 56; renewal RE-222-988 dated
21 Nov 84. (LITTLE GOLDEN BOOK 269).

519. **My little golden book of jokes** by George [Wolfson],
ill. by Tibor Gergely; NY: GP, c1961. Copyright A508040
dated 18 Apr 61. (LITTLE GOLDEN BOOK 424).

520. **My little golden book of manners** by Peggy Parish, ill.
by Richard Scarry; consultation by the third grade at Dalton
School, NY; NY: GP, c1962. Copyright A560032 dated 15 Mar
62. (LITTLE GOLDEN BOOK 460).

521. **My little golden Christmas book. Favorite Christmas
rhymes and stories** with pictures by Sheilah Beckett, cover
by Richard Scarry; NY: S&S, c1957. Copyright AA313050 dated
9 Aug 57. Cover title: My Christmas book. (LITTLE GOLDEN
BOOK 298).

522. **My little golden dictionary** by Mary Reed and Edith
Osswald, ill. by Richard Scarry; NY: S&S, c1949. LC#
49-48392. Copyright A37021 dated 15 Jul 49. (LITTLE GOLDEN
BOOK 90).

522a. ---- Copyright AA313055 dated 9 Sept 57. (GIANT LITTLE
GOLDEN BOOK 5001).

523. My magic slate book by Carl Memling, ill. by Bill
Dugan; NY: GP, c1959. Copyright A430114 dated 11 Dec 59.
(GIANT LITTLE GOLDEN BOOK 5025).

524. My pets: three stories about my puppy, my kitten, my
snuggly bunny by Patsy Scarry, ill. by Eloise Wilkin; NY:
GP, c1959. LC# a63-5161/L. Copyright A430111 dated 11 Dec
59. (GIANT LITTLE GOLDEN BOOK 5027).

525. My puppy by Patsy Scarry, ill. by Eloise Wilkin; NY:
S&S, c1955. LC# 55-12768. Copyright A224340 dated 8 Nov 55;
renewal RE-187-873 dated 5 Dec 83. (LITTLE GOLDEN BOOK 233).
    See also My pets (524).

525a. ---- reissued in 1962 (LITTLE GOLDEN BOOK 469).

526. My snuggly bunny by Patsy Scarry, ill. by Eloise
Wilkin; NY: S&S, c1956. LC# 56-1862. Copyright AA237064
dated 24 Feb 56; renewal RE-223-017 dated 21 Nov 84. (LITTLE
GOLDEN BOOK 250).
    See also My pets (524).

527. My teddy bear by Patsy Scarry, ill. by Eloise Wilkin;
NY: S&S, c1953. LC# 54-1146. Copyright A126760 dated 31 Dec
53. (LITTLE GOLDEN BOOK 168).

527a. ---- reissued in 1961 (LITTLE GOLDEN BOOK 448).

528. My word book by Roberta Miller, ill. by Claude Humbert;
NY: GP, c1963. Copyright A655063 dated 6 Sept 63. (LITTLE
GOLDEN BOOK 525).

529. Name for kitty, A by Phyllis McGinley, ill. by Feodor
Rojankovsky; NY: S&S, c1948. LC# 49-7138. Copyright A33514
dated 3 Dec 48. (LITTLE GOLDEN BOOK 55).

530. National Velvet adapted by Kathryn Hitte, ill. by Mel
Crawford; NY: GP, c1961. (LITTLE GOLDEN BOOK 431).

531. Naughty bunny written and ill. by Richard Scarry; NY:
GP, c1959. Copyright A430121 dated 19 Jan 60. (LITTLE GOLDEN
BOOK 377).

531SR. ---- [sound recording] NY: Golden Record, [197-]. 1
disc (45 rpm, mono., 7 in.) + book, c1959. Narrated by
Cecelia Scott. (READ AND HEAR GR 00251).

532. Neatos and the litterbugs in the mystery of the missing
ticket, The by Norah Smaridge, ill. by Charles Bracke; NY:
GP, c1973. Copyright A502197 dated 10 Dec 73. (LITTLE GOLDEN
BOOK 515X).

532FS. ---- [filmstrip] NY: Miller-Brody Productions, 1974.
1 filmstrip (46 fr., col., 35 mm) + disc (6 min., 33 1/3
rpm, 10 in.). LC# 74-735747/F. Adaptation of The Neatos and
the litterbugs by Norah Smaridge. (LITTLE GOLDEN BOOKS
FILMSTRIPS AND BOOKS).

532FS. ---- [filmstrip] NY: Miller-Brody Productions, 1974.
1 filmstrip (46 fr., col., 35 mm) + cassette. Adaptation of
The Neatos and the litterbugs by Norah Smaridge.

532MP. ---- [motion picture] Racine: Western Publishing Co.,
Education Division, made and released by Sandler
Institutional Films, 1974. (6 min., sd., col., 16 mm) +
study guide. LC# 75-700396/F. Based on book by Norah
Smaridge. Voices by June Foray and Les Tremayne. LC#
75-700396/F.

532MP. ---- [motion picture] Pasadena, CA: Barr, produced by
Sandler Institutional Films, 1974. An animated cartoon.

532SR. ---- [sound recording] Racine: Western, [1977]. 1
casette (8 min., 2 track, mono.) + text and teacher's guide
by Joanne Wylie. (LITTLE GOLDEN READ ALONG 3505).

533. Never pat a bear: a book about signs by Mabel Watts,
ill. by Art Seiden; NY: GP, c1971. Copyright A281591 dated
14 Oct 71. (LITTLE GOLDEN BOOK 105).

534. New baby, The by Ruth and Harold Shane, ill. by Eloise
Wilkin; NY: S&S, c1948. LC# 48-6215. Copyright A16555 dated
8 Mar 48; renewal R601947 dated 28 Mar 75. (LITTLE GOLDEN
BOOK 41).

534a. ---- reissued in 1957 (LITTLE GOLDEN BOOK 291).

534b. ---- reissued (LITTLE GOLDEN BOOK 541).

534c. ---- reissued (LITTLE GOLDEN BOOK 209-1).

535. New brother, new sister by Jean Fiedler, ill. by Joan
Esley; NY: GP, c1966. LC# 72-4898/AC. (LITTLE GOLDEN BOOK
564).

536. New friends for the saggy baggy elephant by Adelaide
Holl, ill. by Jan Neely and Peter Alvarado; NY: GP, c1975.
Copyright A676791 dated 11 Sept 75. (LITTLE GOLDEN BOOK
131X).

536SR. ---- [sound recording] Racine: Western, [1977]. 1
cassette (2 track, mono.) + text and teacher's guide by
Joanne Wylie. (LITTLE GOLDEN READ ALONG 3506).

537. New home for Snow Ball, A by Joan Bowden, ill. by Jan
Pyk; NY: GP, c1974. (LITTLE GOLDEN BOOK 800); (EAGER
READER).

538. <u>New house in the forest,</u> The by Lucy Sprague Mitchell, ill. by Eloise Wilkin; NY: S&S, c1946. LC# 46-3223. Copyright A1876 dated 16 Mar 46. (LITTLE GOLDEN BOOK 24); (BANK STREET BOOK).

539. <u>New kittens,</u> The story and photos by William Gottlieb; NY: S&S, c1957. Copyright AA326571 dated 26 Sept 57. (LITTLE GOLDEN BOOK 302).

540. <u>New pony,</u> The by Blanche Chenery Perrin, ill. by Dagmar Wilson; NY: GP, c1961. Copyright A499739 dated 24 Feb 61. (LITTLE GOLDEN BOOK 410).

541. <u>New puppy,</u> The by Kathleen N. Daly, ill. by Lilian Obligado; NY: GP, c1959. Copyright A430122 dated 29 Oct 59. (LITTLE GOLDEN BOOK 370).

541a. ---- reissued (LITTLE GOLDEN BOOK 202-5).

542. <u>Night before Christmas,</u> The by Clement C. Moore, ill. by Cornelius DeWitt; NY: S&S, c1946. Copyright A9346 dated 29 Nov 46. (LITTLE GOLDEN BOOK 20).

542a. ---- ill. by Corinne Malvern; NY: S&S, c1949. LC# 49-48153. Copyright A37022 dated 12 Sept 49. (LITTLE GOLDEN BOOK 20).

542b. ---- ill. by Eloise Wilkin; NY: S&S, c1955. LC# 55-4128. Copyright A201876 dated 28 Jul 55; renewal RE-186-012 dated 5 Dec 83. (LITTLE GOLDEN BOOK 241).

543. <u>Noah's ark</u> by Barbara Shook Hazen, ill. by Tibor Gergely; NY: GP, c1969. (LITTLE GOLDEN BOOK 109X).

543SR. ---- [sound recording] Burbank, CA: Disneyland Vista Records, c1976. 1 disc (33 1/3 rpm, 7 in.) + book. Song: "The will of God" by Larry Groce.

543a. ---- reissued (LITTLE GOLDEN BOOK 307-41; 400-1).

544. <u>Noah's ark, Walt Disney's</u> told by Annie North Bedford, ill. by the Walt Disney Studio, adapted by Campbell Grant; NY: S&S, c1952. LC# 52-10799. (WALT DISNEY BOOK D28).

545. <u>Noises and Mr. Flibberty-Jib</u> by Gertrude Crampton, ill. by Eloise Wilkin; NY: S&S, c1947. LC# 48-2210. Copyright AA73622 dated 26 Dec 47. (LITTLE GOLDEN BOOK 29).

546. <u>Numbers, what they look like and what they do</u> by Mary Reed and Edith Osswald, ill. by Violet LaMont; NY: S&S, c1955. LC# 55-3179. Copyright A201874 dated 14 Jul 55; renewal RE-186-010 dated 5 Dec 83. (LITTLE GOLDEN BOOK 243).

546SR. ---- [sound recording] NY: Golden Record, [197-]. 1 disc (45 rpm, mono., 7 in.) + book, c1955. Narrated by Rita (READ AND HEAR GR 00167).

546a. ---- reissued in 1959 (LITTLE GOLDEN BOOK 337).

546b. ---- reissued (LITTLE GOLDEN BOOK 201-23).

547. Nurse Nancy by Kathryn Jackson, ill. by Corinne
Malvern; NY: S&S, c1952. LC# 53-815. Copyright A76448 dated
10 Dec 52; renewal RE-68-210 dated 20 Oct 80. Has Band-aids
in three shapes. (LITTLE GOLDEN BOOK 154).

547a. ---- reissued in 1959 (LITTLE GOLDEN BOOK 346).

547b. ---- reissued in 1962 (LITTLE GOLDEN BOOK 473).

548. Nursery rhymes ill. by Gertrude Elliott; NY: S&S,
c1948. LC# 49-4192. Copyright A31738 dated 10 Feb 49.
(LITTLE GOLDEN BOOK 59).

549. Nursery songs arranged by Leah Gale, ill. by Corinne
Malvern; NY: S&S, c1942. LC# 42-24379. Copyright E109279
dated 1 Oct 42. First printing Sept 42. (LITTLE GOLDEN BOOK
7).

549a. ---- ill. by Adriana Mazza Saviozzi; NY: GP, c1959.
Copyright A380771 dated 17 Feb 59. (LITTLE GOLDEN BOOK 348).

549b. ---- reissued in 1963 (LITTLE GOLDEN BOOK 529).

550. Nursery tales ill. by Masha; NY: S&S, c1942. LC#
43-13842. Copyright A175687 dated 15 Jul 43. First printing
Apr 43. (LITTLE GOLDEN BOOK 14).

Nursery tales. See also Favorite nursery tales (233).

551. Nursery tales: six stories with pictures by Richard
Scarry; NY: S&S, c1958. Copyright AA333445 dated 10 Feb 58.
(GIANT LITTLE GOLDEN BOOK 5009).

552. Off to school by Kathryn Jackson and others, ill. by
Corinne Malvern and Violet LaMont; NY: S&S, c1958. Copyright
AA370529 dated 15 Sept 58. (GIANT LITTLE GOLDEN BOOK 5015).

553. Old MacDonald had a farm adapted by Jane Werner Watson,
ill. by Gustaf Tenggren; NY: GP, c1960. Copyright A458298
dated 22 Jun 60. (LITTLE GOLDEN BOOK 400).

553a. ---- ill. by Moritz Kennel; NY: GP, c1960.

553aSR. ---- [sound recording] NY: Golden Record, [197-]. 1
disc (45 rpm, mono., 7 in.) + book, c1960. Narrated by Alan
Cole. (READ AND HEAR GR 00182).

553b. ---- reissued (LITTLE GOLDEN BOOK 303-21).

554. Old Mother Hubbard by Sarah Catherine Martin, ill. by
Aurelius Battaglia; NY: GP, c1970. LC# 82-83096. (LITTLE
GOLDEN BOOK 591).

554a. ---- reissued (LITTLE GOLDEN BOOK 300-42).

555. Old Yeller, Walt Disney's from the Walt Disney motion picture "Old Yeller" based on the novel of the same title by Fred Gipson. Told by Willis Lindquist, ill. by Edwin Schmidt and E. Joseph Dreany; NY: S&S, c1957. (WALT DISNEY BOOK D65).

556. Once upon a wintertime, Walt Disney's ill. adapted by Tom Oreb from the Walt Disney motion picture "Melody time". NY: S&S, c1950. LC# 50-3121. (WALT DISNEY BOOK D12).

557. One of the family by Peggy Archer, ill. by Ruth Sanderson; NY: GP, c1983. LC# 82-82289. (LITTLE GOLDEN BOOK 208-42).

558. 1,2,3, Juggle with me! A counting book written and ill. by Ilse-Margret Vogel; NY: GP, c1970. (LITTLE GOLDEN BOOK 594).

558a. ---- reissued (LITTLE GOLDEN BOOK 201-2; 203-42).

559. Ookpik, the Arctic owl by Barbara Shook Hazen, ill. by Beverley Edwards; NY: GP, c1963. (LITTLE GOLDEN BOOK 579).

560. Open up my suitcase by Alice Low, ill. by Corinne Malvern; NY: S&S, c1954. LC# 54-3746. Copyright A146456 dated 27 May 54; renewal RE-143-930 dated 15 Nov 82. (LITTLE GOLDEN BOOK 207).

561. Oscar's book by Jeffrey Moss, ill. by Michael Gross, featuring Oscar the Grouch and other Jim Henson Muppets. Racine: Western, in conjunction with Children's Television Workshop, c1971. (LITTLE GOLDEN BOOK 120X); (SESAME STREET BOOK).

561a. ---- reissued (LITTLE GOLDEN BOOK 108-21; 108-41).

562. Our baby by Dr. Frances R. Horwich, ill. by Priscilla Pointer; NY: GP, c1960. (DING DONG SCHOOL BOOK Din8).

563. Our flag by Carl Memling, ill. by Stephen Cook; NY: GP, c1960. Copyright A444243 dated 17 Feb 60. (LITTLE GOLDEN BOOK 388).

564. Our puppy by Elsa Ruth Nast, ill. by Feodor Rojankovsky; NY: S&S, c1948. LC# 49-8169rev. Copyright A31739 dated 10 Feb 49. (LITTLE GOLDEN BOOK 56).

564a. ---- reissued; copyright AA295628 dated 18 Apr 57. LC# 60-26339. (LITTLE GOLDEN BOOK 292).

565. Our world: a beginner's introduction to geography by Jane Werner Watson, ill. by William Sayles; NY: S&S, c1955. LC# 55-3191. Copyright A201875 dated 14 Jul 55; renewal RE-186-011 dated 5 Dec 83. (LITTLE GOLDEN BOOK 242).
    Later issued with title First golden geography (241).

566. Out of my window by Alice Low, ill. by Polly Jackson; NY: S&S, c1955. LC# 55-13903. Copyright A224341 dated 12 Dec 55. (LITTLE GOLDEN BOOK 245).

567. Owl and the pussycat, The by Edward Lear, ill. by Ruth Sanderson; NY: GP, c1982. LC# 82-80525. (LITTLE GOLDEN BOOK 300-41).

568. Pal and Peter story and photos by William P. Gottlieb; NY: S&S, c1956. LC# 56-4679. Copyright A252968 dated 31 Jul 56; renewal RE-222-987 dated 31 Jul 56. (LITTLE GOLDEN BOOK 265).

569. Pano the train by Sharon Holaves, ill. by Giannini; NY: GP, c1975. Copyright A661784 dated 17 Jul 75. (LITTLE GOLDEN BOOK 117X).

569SR. ---- [sound recording] Racine: Western, [1977]. 1 cassette (7 min., 2 track, mono.) + text and teacher's guide by Joanne Wylie. (LITTLE GOLDEN READ ALONG 3507).

569a. ---- reissued (LITTLE GOLDEN BOOK 210-1).

570. Pantaloon by Kathryn Jackson, ill. by Leonard Weisgard; NY: S&S, c1951. LC# 51-11263. Copyright A60563 dated 10 Apr 51; renewal RE-46-365 dated 7 Nov 79. (LITTLE GOLDEN BOOK 114).

571. Paper doll wedding by Hilda Miloche and Wilma Kane; NY: S&S, c1954. Copyright A159057 dated 11 Aug 54; renewal RE-143-628 dated 15 Nov 82. (LITTLE GOLDEN BOOK 193).

Paper dolls. See Little golden paper dolls (424).

572. Party in Shariland by Ann McGovern, ill. by Doris and Marion Henderson; NY: GP, c1959. (LITTLE GOLDEN BOOK 360).

573. Party pig, The by Kathryn and Byron Jackson, ill. by Richard Scarry; NY: S&S, c1954. LC# 54-2629. Copyright A138909 dated 23 Apr 54; renewal RE-143-927 dated 15 Nov 82. (LITTLE GOLDEN BOOK 191).

574. Pat-a-cake: A baby's Mother Goose ill. by Aurelius Battaglia; NY: S&S, c1948. LGB 54. LC# 49-4193. Copyright A31735 dated 3 Dec 48. (LITTLE GOLDEN BOOK 54).
    Later reissued with title Baby's Mother Goose (048).

574SR. ---- [sound recording] NY: Golden Record. 1 disc (45 rpm, mono., 7 in.) + book, c1948. Narrated by Kari. (READ AND HEAR GR 00158).

575. Paul Revere, Walt Disney's by Irwin Shapiro, ill. by the Walt Disney Studio, adapted by Paul Luhrs; NY: S&S, c1957. (WALT DISNEY BOOK D64).

576. Pebbles Flintstone by Jean Lewis, ill. by Mel Crawford; NY: GP, c1963. (LITTLE GOLDEN BOOK 531).

577. <u>Pepper plays nurse</u> by Gina Ingoglia Weiner, ill. by
John Fernie; NY: GP, c1964. (LITTLE GOLDEN BOOK 555).

577B. ---- [braille] Tarzana, CA: American Brotherhood for
the Blind, Twin Vision Publication Division; reprint of the
c1964 ed. Opposite pages in braille. (TWIN VISION BOOK).

578. <u>Perri and her friends, Walt Disney's</u> based on the book
Perri by Felix Salten, ill. with kodachromes from the Walt
Disney motion picture, story adapted by Annie North Bedford.
NY: S&S, c1956. LC# 57-13501. (WALT DISNEY BOOK D54);
(MICKEY MOUSE CLUB BOOK D54).

579. <u>Pet in the jar, The</u> written and ill. by Judy Stang; NY:
GP, c1974. (LITTLE GOLDEN BOOK 801); (EAGER READER).

580. <u>Peter and the wolf, Walt Disney's</u> a fairy tale adapted
from Serge Prokofieff's musical theme, pictures by Richmond
Kelsey for the Walt Disney Studio, based on the animated
cartoon sequence in Walt Disney's "Make mine music." NY:
S&S, c1946. LC# 47-11901. (WALT DISNEY BOOK D5).

580a. ---- reissued in 1956 (WALT DISNEY BOOK D56); (MICKEY
MOUSE CLUB BOOK D56).

581. <u>Peter Pan and the Indians, Walt Disney's</u> told by Annie
North Bedford, pictures by the Walt Disney Studio, adapted
by Brice Mack and Dick Kinney, based on the story by Sir
James M. Barrie; NY: S&S, c1952. LC# 52-4578. (WALT DISNEY
BOOK D26).

581a. ---- reissued in 1958 (WALT DISNEY BOOK D74).

582. <u>Peter Pan and the pirates, Walt Disney's</u> from the
motion picture "Peter Pan" based on the story by Sir James
M. Barrie, illustrations by the Walt Disney Studio, adapted
by Bob Moore; NY: S&S, c1952. LC# 52-4579. (WALT DISNEY BOOK
D25).

582a. ---- reissued in 1958 (WALT DISNEY BOOK D73).

583. <u>Peter Pan and Wendy, Walt Disney's</u> told by Annie North
Bedford, ill. by the Walt Disney Studio, adapted by Eyvind
Earle; based on the story by Sir James M. Barrie; NY: S&S,
c1952. LC# 52-4580. (WALT DISNEY BOOK D24).

583B. ---- [braille] Tarzana, CA: American Brotherhood for
the Blind, Twin Vision Publication Division; reprint of the
c1952 ed. Opposite pages in braille. (TWIN VISION BOOK).

583a. ---- reissued in 1958 (WALT DISNEY BOOK D72).

583b. ---- reissued (WALT DISNEY BOOK D110).

583c. ---- reissued (LITTLE GOLDEN BOOK 104-41).

584. Peter Potamus by Carl Memling, ill. by Hawley Pratt; NY: GP, c1964. (LITTLE GOLDEN BOOK 556).

Peter Rabbit. See Tale of Peter Rabbit (707).

585. Pete's dragon, Walt Disney Productions NY: GP, c1977. (WALT DISNEY BOOK D137).

586. Petey and I: a story about being a friend by Martha Orr Conn, ill. by Fred Irvin; NY: GP, c1973. (LITTLE GOLDEN BOOK 186X).

587. Pets for Peter by Jane Werner Watson, ill. by Aurelius Battaglia; NY: S&S, c1950. LC# 50-10653rev. Copyright A49618 dated 6 Oct 50. With jig-saw puzzle. (LITTLE GOLDEN BOOK 82).

588. Pick up sticks by Pauline Wilkins, ill. by Piet Pfloog; NY: GP, c1962. Copyright A578152 dated 5 Jul 62. (LITTLE GOLDEN BOOK 461).

Picture dictionary. See Little golden picture dictionary (425).

589. Pierre Bear by Patsy Scarry, ill. by Richard Scarry; NY: S&S, c1954. LC# 55-1020. Copyright A176969 dated 6 Dec 54; renewal RE-149-957 dated 30 Dec 82. (LITTLE GOLDEN BOOK 212).

590. Pink Panther and sons: Fun at the picnic by Sandra Beris, ill. by David Gantz; NY: GB, c1985. LC# 85-70339. (LITTLE GOLDEN BOOK 111-60).

591. Pink Panther in the haunted house, The by Kennon Graham, ill. by Darrell Baker and Jason Art Studios; NY: GP, c1975. (LITTLE GOLDEN BOOK 140X).

591a. ---- reissued (LITTLE GOLDEN BOOK 115-5).

592. Pinocchio, Walt Disney's ill. by the Walt Disney Studio, adapted by Campbell Grant from the Walt Disney motion picture "Pinocchio." Based on the story by Carlo Collodi. NY: S&S, c1948. LC# 48-6665. (WALT DISNEY BOOK D8); (MICKEY MOUSE CLUB BOOK D8).

592a. ---- reissued in 1961 (WALT DISNEY BOOK D100).

593. Pinocchio and the whale, Walt Disney's based on the story by Carlo Collodi, adapted by Gina Ingoglia, illustrated by the Walt Disney Studio, adapted by Al White; NY: GP, c1961. (WALT DISNEY BOOK D101).

Pippi Longstocking. See Remarkably strong Pippi Longstocking (628).

594. Pixie and Dixie and Mr. Jinks, Hanna-Barbera's by Carl Buettner, ill. by Carl Buettner and Sylvia and Burnett Mattinson; NY: GP, c1961. (LITTLE GOLDEN BOOK 454).

Planets. See My first book of the planets (509).

Plants and animals. See Giant little golden book about plants and animals (269).

595. Play ball by Charles Spain Verral, ill. by Gerald McCann; NY: S&S, c1958. Copyright AA357020 dated 21 May 58. (LITTLE GOLDEN BOOK 325).

596. Play Street by Esther Wilkin, ill. by Joan Esley; NY: GP, c1962. Copyright A621129 dated 15 Sept 62. (LITTLE GOLDEN BOOK 484).

597. Play with me by Esther Wilkin, ill. by Eloise Wilkin; NY: GP, c1967. (LITTLE GOLDEN BOOK 567).

598. Pluto and the adventure of the golden scepter, Walt Disney's NY: GP, c1972. (WALT DISNEY BOOK D124).

599. Pluto Pup goes to sea, Walt Disney's told by Annie North Bedford, ill. by the Walt Disney Studio, adapted by Yale Gracey; NY: S&S, c1952. LC# 52-12317. (WALT DISNEY BOOK D30).

Poetry. See Little golden book of poetry (416).

600. Poky little puppy, The by Janette Sebring Lowrey, ill. by Gustaf Tenggren; NY: S&S, c1942. LC# 42-24234/AC. Copyright A169133 dated 1 Oct 42. First printing Sept 42. Issued with dust jacket. (LITTLE GOLDEN BOOK 8).

600FS. ---- [filmstrip] NY: Miller-Brody Productions, 1974. 1 filmstrip (67 fr., col., 35 mm) + cassette (7 min., 2 track, mono.). Based on the book by Janette Sebring Lowrey. (LITTLE GOLDEN BOOKS FILMSTRIPS AND BOOKS).

600MP. ---- [motion picture] Racine : Western Publishing Co., Educational Division, made and released by Sandler Institutional Films, 1974. 1 film (8 min., sd., col., 16 mm) + study guide. Animated cartoon based on book by Janette Sebring Lowrey. Voices by June Foray, Les Tremayne, and Kerry Maclane.

600SR. ---- [sound recording] NY: Golden Record, [197-]. 1 disc (45 rpm, mono., 7 in.) + book, c1942. Narrated by Frank Milano; music director: Mitch Miller. (READ AND HEAR GR 00154).

600SR. ---- [sound recording] Racine: Western, [1977]. 1 cassette (2 track, mono.) + text and teacher's guide by Joanne Wylie. (LITTLE GOLDEN READ ALONG 3508).

600SR. ---- [sound recording] Copyright KK38745 dated 1 Sep 48 (LITTLE GOLDEN RECORD 5).

600a. ---- reissued in 1956 (LITTLE GOLDEN BOOK 271).

600b. ---- reissued in 1963 (LITTLE GOLDEN BOOK 506).

600c. ---- reissued (LITTLE GOLDEN BOOK 301-2).

600cSR. ---- [sound recording] Burbank, CA: Disneyland, 1976. 1 cassette (30 min., 1 7/8 ips, mono., 3 7/8 x 2 1/2 in, 1/8 in. tape) + book, c1970. Song: "That poky little puppy" by Larry Groce. (LITTLE GOLDEN BOOK AND CASSETTE); (DISNEYLAND STORYTELLER CASSETTE 203B).

600cSR. ---- [sound recording] Burbank, CA: Disneyland, 1976. 1 disc (8 min., 33 1/3 rpm, mono., 7 in.) + book, c1970. Song: "That poky little puppy" by Larry Groce. (LITTLE GOLDEN BOOK AND RECORD).

601. Poky little puppy follows his nose home, The by Adelaide Holl, ill. by Alex C. Miclat; NY: GP, c1975. Copyright A676790 dated 11 Sept 75. (LITTLE GOLDEN BOOK 130X).

601a. ---- reissued (LITTLE GOLDEN BOOK 301-21).

602. Poky little puppy's naughty day, The by Jean Chandler; NY: GP, c1984. LC# 82-82286. (LITTLE GOLDEN BOOK ---).

603. Polly's pet by Lucille Hammond, ill. by Amye Rosenberg; NY: GP, c1984. LC# 83-82198. (LITTLE GOLDEN BOOK 302-55).

604. Pollyanna, Walt Disney's based on the story by Eleanor H. Porter, adapted by Elizabeth Beecher, ill. by Karen Hedstrom; NY: GP, c1960. (WALT DISNEY BOOK D91).

605. Pony for Tony, A story and photos by William P. Gottlieb; NY: S&S, c1955. LC# 55-14337. Copyright A180488 dated 18 Feb 55; renewal RE-185-988 dated 5 Dec 83. (LITTLE GOLDEN BOOK 220).

606. Porky Pig and Bugs Bunny. Just like magic! by Stella Williams Nathan, ill. by Bob Totten and Tom McKimson; NY: GP, c1976. (LITTLE GOLDEN BOOK 146X).

606a. ---- reissued (LITTLE GOLDEN BOOK 110-22).

607. Prayers for children [additions by Leah Gale], ill. by Rachel Taft Dixon; NY: S&S, c1942. LC# 42-24405. Copyright A169134 dated 1 Oct 42. First printing Sept 42. (LITTLE GOLDEN BOOK 5).

607a. ---- ill. by Eloise Wilkin; NY: S&S, c1952. LC# 52-4401. Copyright A70777 dated 15 Aug 52; renewal RE-68-201 dated 20 Oct 80. (LITTLE GOLDEN BOOK 205).

607aB. ---- [braille] Tarzana, CA: American Brotherhood for the Blind, Twin Vision Publication Division; reprint of the c1952 ed. Opposite pages in braille. (TWIN VISION BOOK).

607b. ---- reissued (LITTLE GOLDEN BOOK 405-1).

Princess and the pea. See Rumpelstiltskin (658).

608. Puff the blue kitten written and ill. by Pierre Probst; NY: GP, c1961. Copyright A513330 dated 19 Jun 61. (LITTLE GOLDEN BOOK 443).

609. Puppy love by Madeline Sunshine, ill. by Carol Nicklaus, featuring the Muppets by Jim Henson; Racine: Western, in conjunction with Children's Television Workshop, c1983. LC# 82-83330. (LITTLE GOLDEN BOOK 109-46); (SESAME STREET BOOK).

610. Puss in Boots, Charles Perrault's retold by Kathryn Jackson, ill. by J.P. Miller; NY: S&S, c1952. LC# 53-816. Copyright A76449 dated 22 Dec 52; renewal RE-68-211 dated 20 Oct 80. (LITTLE GOLDEN BOOK 137).

610a. ---- reissued; copyright A395440 dated 20 Mar 59 (LITTLE GOLDEN BOOK 359).

610aSR. ---- [sound recording] NY: Golden Record. 1 disc (45 rpm, mono., 7 in.) + book, c1959. Narrated by Kay Lande and Ed Powell. (READ AND HEAR GR 00175).

611. Pussy Willow by Margaret Wise Brown, ill. by Leonard Weisgard; NY: S&S, c1951. (LITTLE GOLDEN BOOK 314).
    Later issued with title Little pussycat (434).

611a. ---- reissued (LITTLE GOLDEN BOOK 302-24; 302-41).

612. Pussycat tiger, The by Joan Chase Bacon, ill. by Lilian Obligado; NY: GP, c1972. Copyright A377977 dated 30 Aug 72. (LITTLE GOLDEN BOOK 362).

612SR. ---- [sound recording] Racine: Western, [1977]. 1 cassette (8 min. 30 sec., 2 track, mono.) + text and teacher's guide by Joanne Wylie. (LITTLE GOLDEN READ ALONG 3509).

612SR. ---- [sound recording] Burbank, CA: Disneyland, c1976. 1 disc (33 1/3 rpm, 7 in.) + book. (LITTLE GOLDEN BOOK AND RECORD).

613. Quick Draw McGraw by Carl Memling, ill. by Hawley Pratt and Al White; NY: GP, c1960. (LITTLE GOLDEN BOOK 398).

614. Quiz fun: hundreds of questions and answers by Horace Elmo and Nancy Fielding Hulick, ill. by Tibor Gergely; NY: GP, c1959. Copyright A395420 dated 30 Mar 59. (GIANT LITTLE GOLDEN BOOK 5024).

615. Rabbit and his friends written and ill. by Richard Scarry; NY: S&S, c1953. LC# 53-3030. Copyright A92979 dated 16 Apr 53; renewal RE-109-090 dated 29 Oct 81. (LITTLE GOLDEN BOOK 169).

615a. ---- reissued (LITTLE GOLDEN BOOK 472-21).

616. Rabbit is next, The by Gladys Leithauser and Lois Breitmeyer, ill. by Linda Powell; NY: GP, c1978. (LITTLE GOLDEN BOOK 173X).

616a. ---- reissued (LITTLE GOLDEN BOOK 474-1).

617. Rabbit's adventure, The by Betty Ren Wright, ill. by Maggie Swanson; NY: GP, c1977. (LITTLE GOLDEN BOOK 164X).

617a. ---- reissued (LITTLE GOLDEN BOOK 471-21).

618. Raggedy Ann and Andy: Five birthday parties in a row by Eileen Daly, ill. by Mary S. McClain; NY: GP, c1979. (LITTLE GOLDEN BOOK 107-4).

619. Raggedy Ann and Andy and the rainy-day circus by Barbara Shook Hazen, ill. by June Goldsborough; NY: GP, c1973. (LITTLE GOLDEN BOOK 401).

619a. ---- reissued (LITTLE GOLDEN BOOK 107-22).

620. Raggedy Ann and Andy help Santa Claus by Polly Curren, ill. by June Goldsborough; NY: GP, c1977. (LITTLE GOLDEN BOOK 156X).

620a. ---- reissued (LITTLE GOLDEN BOOK 457-1).

621. Raggedy Ann and Andy: the little gray kitten by Polly Curren, ill. by June Goldsborough; NY: GP, c1975. (LITTLE GOLDEN BOOK 139X).

621a. ---- reissued (LITTLE GOLDEN BOOK 107-21; 107-41).

622. Raggedy Ann and Fido by Barbara Shook Hazen, ill. by Rochelle Boonshaft; NY: GP, c1969. (LITTLE GOLDEN BOOK 585).

622FS. ---- [filmstrip] Chicago: Society for Visual Education, 1979. 1 filmstrip (38 fr., col., 35 mm) + cassette (8 min. 10 sec., 4 track, mono.) + script.

622SR. ---- [sound recording] Chicago: Society for Visual Education, 1978. 1 cassette (9 min., 1 7/8 ips, 2 track, mono.) + book.

623. Raggedy Ann and the cookie snatcher by Barbara Shook Hazen, ill. by June Goldsborough; NY: GP, c1972. (LITTLE GOLDEN BOOK 262).

623a. ---- reissued (LITTLE GOLDEN BOOK 107-3).

624. Rags by Patricia Scarry, ill. by J.P. Miller; NY: GP, c1983. LC# 82-83094 (LITTLE GOLDEN BOOK 586).

624SR. ---- [sound recording] Racine: Western, [1977]. 1 cassette (8 min., 2 track, mono.) + text and teacher's guide by Joanne Wylie. (LITTLE GOLDEN READ ALONG 3510).

624a. ---- reissued (LITTLE GOLDEN BOOK 303-44).

625. Rainbow Brite and the brook meadow deer by Sarah Leslie, ill. by Roy Wilson; NY: GB, c1984. (LITTLE GOLDEN BOOK 107-48).

625SR. ---- [sound recording] Burbank, CA: Buena Vista, c1984. 1 cassette.

625SR. ---- [sound recording] Burbank, CA: Buena Vista Records, c1984. 1 disc (33 1/3 rpm, 7 in.) + book.

626. Rainy day play book, The by Marion Conger and Natalie Young, ill. by Corinne Malvern; NY: S&S, c1951. LC# 51-13906. Copyright A62295 dated 9 Oct 51; renewal RE-46-390 dated 7 Nov 79. (LITTLE GOLDEN BOOK 133).

626a. ---- by Susan Young with Marion Conger and Natalie Young, ill. by Ib Ohlsson; NY: GP, c1981. LC# 80-85032. (LITTLE GOLDEN BOOK 211-51).

627. Reading, writing and spelling stamps by Carol Kaufman, ill. by Lilian Obligado; NY: GP, c1959. (LITTLE GOLDEN ACTIVITY BOOK A24).

Red little golden book of fairy tales. See Rumpelstiltskin (658).

628. Remarkably strong Pippi Longstocking, The retold by Cecily Hogan, ill. by Don Turner, based on the motion picture "Pippi Longstocking" suggested by the original story Pippi Longstocking by Astrid Lindgren; NY: GP, c1974. (LITTLE GOLDEN BOOK 123X).

629. Rescuers, Authorized Walt Disney Productions' edition The from the Disney film suggested by the book by Margery Sharp; NY: GP, c1977. (WALT DISNEY BOOK D136).

629a. ---- reissued (LITTLE GOLDEN BOOK 105-43).

630. Return to Oz: Dorothy saves the Emerald City, Walt Disney Pictures based on the motion picture from the Walt Disney Studios; NY: GB, c1985. LC# 84-72880. (LITTLE GOLDEN BOOK 103-55).

631. Return to Oz: escape from the witch's castle, Walt Disney Pictures based on the motion picture from Walt Disney Studios; NY: GB, c1985. LC# 84-72881. (LITTLE GOLDEN BOOK 105-56).

632. Riddles, riddles, from A to Z by Carl Memling, ill. by
Trina Schart; NY: GP, c1962. Copyright A609559 dated 22 Nov
62. (LITTLE GOLDEN BOOK 490).

632SR. ---- [sound recording] NY: Golden Record, [197-]. 1
disc (45 rpm, mono., 7 in.) + book, c1962. Narrated by Joan
Wile. (READ AND HEAR GR 00234).

633. Right's animal farm story and pictures by Joan
Elizabeth Goodman; NY: GP, c1983. LC# 82-83067/AC. (LITTLE
GOLDEN BOOK 200-9).

634. Rin Tin Tin and Rusty by Monica Hill, ill. by Mel
Crawford; NY: S&S, c1955. Authorized ed. LC# 55-13909.
(LITTLE GOLDEN BOOK 246).

635. Rin Tin Tin and the lost Indian by Monica Hill, ill. by
Hamilton Greene; NY: S&S, c1956. Authorized ed. LC#
57-13506. (LITTLE GOLDEN BOOK 276).

636. Rin Tin Tin and the outlaw by Charles Spain Verral,
ill. by Mel Crawford; NY: S&S, c1957. Authorized ed. (LITTLE
GOLDEN BOOK 304).

637. Road Runner: a very scary lesson, The by Russell K.
Schroeder, ill. by Phil DeLara and Bob Totten; NY: GP,
c1974. (LITTLE GOLDEN BOOK 122X).

637a. ---- reissued (LITTLE GOLDEN BOOK 111-25).

638. Road runner: mid-mesa marathon by Teddy Slater, ill. by
John Costanza; NY: GB, c1985. LC# 84-72882. (LITTLE GOLDEN
BOOK 110-57).

639. Road to Oz, The by Lyman Frank Baum, adapted by Peter
Archer, ill. by Harry McNaught; NY: S&S, c1951. LC# 52-6566.
(LITTLE GOLDEN BOOK 144).

640. Robert and his new friends by Nina Schneider, ill. by
Corinne Malvern; NY: S&S, c1951. LC# 51-13060. Copyright
A60565 dated 5 Sept 51; renewal RE-46-366 dated 7 Nov 79.
(LITTLE GOLDEN BOOK 124).

641. Robin Hood, Walt Disney's retold by Annie North Bedford
with scenes from the motion picture; NY: S&S, c1955. LGB
D48. (WALT DISNEY BOOK D48); (MICKEY MOUSE CLUB BOOK D48).

641a. ---- reissued (WALT DISNEY BOOK D126).

642. Robin Hood and the daring mouse, Walt Disney's NY: GP,
c1974. (WALT DISNEY BOOK D128).

643. Robotman & friends at school by Justine Korman, ill. by
John Costanza; NY: GB, c1985. LC# 85-70310. (LITTLE GOLDEN
BOOK 110-58).

644. Rocky and his friends by Ann McGovern, ill. by Ben De Nunez and Al White; NY: GP, c1960. (LITTLE GOLDEN BOOK 408).

645. Romper Room do bees: a book of manners by Nancy Claster, ill. by Eleanor Dart; NY: S&S, c1956. LC# 56-14399. Copyright A273108 dated 8 Nov 56; renewal RE-222-969 dated 21 Nov 84. (LITTLE GOLDEN BOOK 273).

646. Romper Room exercise book: physical fitness for boys and girls by Nancy Claster, ill. by Sergio Leone; NY: GP, c1964. (LITTLE GOLDEN BOOK 527).

647. Ronald McDonald and the tale of the talking plant by John Albano, ill. by John Costanza; NY: GB, c1984. LC# 83-83357. (LITTLE GOLDEN BOOK 111-50).

648. Rootie Kazootie, baseball star by Steve Carlin, ill. by Mel Crawford; NY: S&S, c1954. LC# 54-2763. (LITTLE GOLDEN BOOK 190).

649. Rootie Kazootie, detective by Steve Carlin, ill. by Mel Crawford; NY: S&S, c1953. LC# 53-2329. (LITTLE GOLDEN BOOK 150).

650. Rootie Kazootie joins the circus by Steve Carlin, ill. by Mel Crawford; NY: S&S, c1955. LC# 55-2054. (LITTLE GOLDEN BOOK 226).

651. Roy Rogers and Cowboy Toby by Elizabeth Beecher, ill. by Mel Crawford; NY: S&S, c1954. LC# 54-3676. (LITTLE GOLDEN BOOK 195).

652. Roy Rogers and the Indian sign by Gladys Wyatt, ill. by Mel Crawford; NY: S&S, c1956. LC# 56-3057. (LITTLE GOLDEN BOOK 259).

653. Roy Rogers and the mountain lion by Ann McGovern, ill. by Mel Crawford; NY: S&S, c1955. LC# 55-3190. (LITTLE GOLDEN BOOK 231).

654. Roy Rogers and the new cowboy by A. N. Bedford, ill. by Hans Helweg and Mel Crawford; NY: S&S, c1953. LC# 53-4351rev. (LITTLE GOLDEN BOOK 177).

655. Rudolph the red-nosed reindeer by Barbara Shook Hazen, adapted from the story by Robert L. May, ill. by Richard Scarry; NY: GP, c1958. (LITTLE GOLDEN BOOK 331).

655SR. ---- [sound recording] Paramount, CA: Disneyland Records, 1976. 1 disc (20 min., 33 1/3 rpm, mono., 7 in.) + book, c1958. (LITTLE GOLDEN BOOK AND RECORD).

655a. ---- reissued (LITTLE GOLDEN BOOK 452-1).

656. Rudolph the red-nosed reindeer shines again adapted from the story by Robert L. May, ill. by Darrell Baker; NY: GP, c1982. LC# 80-85028/AC. (LITTLE GOLDEN BOOK 452-42).

657. Ruff and Reddy by Ann McGovern, ill. by Harvey
Eisenberg and Al White; NY: GP, c1959. (LITTLE GOLDEN BOOK
378).

657a. ---- reissued in 1962 (LITTLE GOLDEN BOOK 477).

658. Rumpelstiltskin by the Brothers Grimm and The princess
and the pea by Hans Christian Andersen, ill. by William J.
Dugan. [The red little golden book of fairy tales]. NY: S&S,
c1957. Copyright AA328888 dated 20 Dec 57. (LITTLE GOLDEN
BOOK 306).

658SR. ---- [sound recording] c1976. (DISNEYLAND STORYTELLER
CASSETTE 204B).

658a. ---- reissued in 1962 (LITTLE GOLDEN BOOK 498).

659. Runaway squash: an American folktale retold by Gale
Wiersum, ill. by Bunky; NY: GP, c1976. Adapted from "Big
blue marble." (LITTLE GOLDEN BOOK 143X).

660. Rupert the rhinoceros by Carl Memling, ill. by Tibor
Gergely; NY: GP, c1960. LC# 82-83091. Copyright A498321
dated 14 Dec 60. (LITTLE GOLDEN BOOK 419).

661. Rusty goes to school written and ill. by Pierre Probst;
NY: GP, c1962. Copyright A591303 dated 6 Aug 62. (LITTLE
GOLDEN BOOK 479).

662. Saggy baggy elephant, The by K[athryn] and B[yron]
Jackson, ill. by Gustaf Tenggren; NY: S&S, c1947. LC#
47-5467. Copyright A14580 dated 10 Jul 47. (LITTLE GOLDEN
BOOK 36).

662FS. ---- [filmstrip] NY: Miller-Brody Productions, 1978.
1 filmstrip (53 fr., col., 35 mm) + cassette (8 min., 1/2
track, mono.). (LITTLE GOLDEN BOOK FILMSTRIPS AND BOOKS).

662SR. ---- [sound recording] Burbank, CA: Disneyland
Records, c1976. 1 disc (33 1/3 rpm, 7 in.) + book. Songs:
"The saggy baggy elephant" and "Smile-drops" by Larry Groce.
(LITTLE GOLDEN BOOK AND RECORD).

662SR. ---- [sound recording] c1976. (DISNEYLAND STORYTELLER
CASSETTE 201B).

662a. ---- reissued in 1959 (LITTLE GOLDEN BOOK 385).

662b. ---- reissued (LITTLE GOLDEN BOOK 201-42; 304-4).

663. Sailor dog, The by Margaret Wise Brown, ill. by Garth
Williams; NY: S&S, c1953. LC# 53-2327. Copyright A92987
dated 5 Mar 53; renewal RE-109-094 dated 29 Oct 81. (LITTLE
GOLDEN BOOK 156).

663VC. ---- [videocassette] Racine: Western, c1985. 3 best-loved Golden stories [including The sailor dog]. 1 videocassette (30 min., sd., col., 1/2 in.) VHS (GOLDEN BOOK VIDEO) #13822.

664. Sam the firehouse cat written and ill. by Virginia Parsons; NY: GP, c1968. (LITTLE GOLDEN BOOK 580).

665. Santa's surprise book by Joan Potter Elwart, ill. by Florence Sarah Winship; NY, GP, c1966. (LITTLE GOLDEN BOOK 121X).

665a. ---- reissued (LITTLE GOLDEN BOOK 459-1).

666. Santa's toy shop, Walt Disney's ill. by the Walt Disney Studio, adapted by Al Dempster; NY: S&S, c1950. LC# 50-14111. (WALT DISNEY BOOK D16).

667. Savage Sam, Walt Disney's based on the novel Savage Sam by Fred Gipson, told by Carl Memling, ill. by Hamilton Greene; NY: GP, c1963. (WALT DISNEY BOOK D104).

668. Scamp, Walt Disney's told by Annie North Bedford, pictures by the Walt Disney Studio, adapted by Norm McGary and Joe Rinaldi; NY: S&S, c1957. (WALT DISNEY BOOK D63).

669. Scamp's adventure, Walt Disney's told by Annie North Bedford, ill. by the Walt Disney Studio, adapted by Joe Rinaldi and Neil Boyle; NY: GP, c1958. (WALT DISNEY BOOK D70).

669a. ---- reissued in 1960 (WALT DISNEY BOOK D88).

670. Scooby Doo and the pirate treasure by Jean Lewis, ill. by William Lorencz and Michael Arens; NY: GP, c1974. (LITTLE GOLDEN BOOK 126X).

671. Scuffy the tugboat and his adventures down the river by Gertrude Crampton, ill. by Tibor Gergely; NY: S&S, c1946. LC# 47-260. Copyright A9015 dated 29 Nov 46. (LITTLE GOLDEN BOOK 30).

671SR. ---- [sound recording] Copyright KK38741 dated 1 Sep 48 (LITTLE GOLDEN RECORD 1).

671SR. ---- [sound recording] Burbank, CA: Disneyland, c1976. 1 disc (33 1/3 rpm, stereo., 7 in.) + book. Songs: "I was meant for bigger things" and "It's a great big world out there" by Larry Groce. (LITTLE GOLDEN BOOK AND RECORD).

671SR. ---- [sound recording] Burbank, CA: Disneyland, c1976. 1 cassette (1 7/8 ips, mono., 3 7/8 x 2 1/2 in., 1/8 in. tape)
"It's a great big world out there" by Larry Groce.
(DISNEYLAND STORYTELLER CASSETTE 205B).

671a. ---- reissued; copyright A195914 dated 30 May 55; renewal RE-186-002 dated 5 Dec 83. LC# 55-3422. (LITTLE GOLDEN BOOK 244).

671aSR. ---- [sound recording] NY: Golden Record, [197-]. 1 disc (45 rpm, mono., 7 in.) + book, c1955. Narrated by Alan Cole. Songs: "Scuffy song" performed by Gil Mack and the Sandpipers. (READ AND HEAR GR 00181).

671b. ---- reissued in 1959 (LITTLE GOLDEN BOOK 363).

671bVC. ---- [videocassette] Racine: Western, c1985. 3 favorite Golden stories [including Scuffy the tugboat]. 1 videocassette (30 min., sd., col., 1/2 in.) VHS (GOLDEN BOOK VIDEO) #13821.

671c. ---- reissued (LITTLE GOLDEN BOOK 305-21; 310-44).

Seashore. See Little golden book about the seashore (410).

Sesame Street together book. See Together book (736).

672. Seven dwarfs find a house adapted by Annie North Bedford, ill. by Julius Svendsen; NY: S&S, c1953. (WALT DISNEY BOOK D35); (MICKEY MOUSE CLUB BOOK D35).

672a. ---- reissued in 1958 (WALT DISNEY BOOK D67).

673. Seven little postmen by Margaret Wise Brown and Edith Thacher Hurd, ill. by Tibor Gergely; NY: S&S, c1952. LC# 52-8667. Copyright A65902 dated 6 Mar 52; renewal RE-68-191 dated 20 Oct 80. (LITTLE GOLDEN BOOK 134).

673SR. ---- [sound recording] NY: Golden Record, [197-]. 1 disc (45 rpm, mono., 7 in.) + book, c1952. Narrated by Kay Lande. (READ AND HEAR GR 00214).

673SR. ---- [sound recording] Burbank, CA: Disneyland, c1976. 1 cassette (1 7/8 ips, mono., 3 7/8 x 2 1/2 in., 1/8 in. tape) + book. Song: "The mail must go through" by Larry Groce. (DISNEYLAND STORYTELLER CASSETTE 222B).

673a. ---- reissued in 1963 (LITTLE GOLDEN BOOK 504).

674. Seven sneezes, The by Olga Cabral, ill. by Tibor Gergely; NY: S&S, c1948. LC# 48-6667. Copyright A31736 dated 5 Apr 48. (LITTLE GOLDEN BOOK 51).

674FS. ---- [filmstrip] NY: S&S, released by Young America Films, 1951. 1 filmstrip (38 fr., col., 35 mm) + teacher's guide. LC# fia52-1742. (GOLDEN BOOK SERIES. SET NO. 3).

675. Shaggy dog, Walt Disney's The story adapted by Charles Spain Verral, ill. by Joe Cellini; NY: GP, c1959. (WALT DISNEY BOOK D82).

676. Shazam! A circus adventure by Bob Ottum, ill. by Kurt
Shafenburger [sic Schaffenberger]; NY: GP, c1977. (LITTLE
GOLDEN BOOK 155X).

677. Shoelace box, The by Elizabeth Winthrop, ill. by Kathy
Wilburn; NY: GB, c1984. LC# 83-82197. (LITTLE GOLDEN BOOK
211-56).

678. Shy little kitten, The by Cathleen Schurr, ill. by
Gustaf Tenggren; NY: S&S, c1946. LC# 46-3067. Copyright
A1878 dated 16 Mar 46; renewal R548208 dated 23 Mar 73.
Issued with dust jacket. (LITTLE GOLDEN BOOK 23).
    See also Giant little golden book of kittens (273).

678FS. ---- [filmstrip] NY: Miller-Brody Productions, 1978.
1 filmstrip (53 fr., col., 35 mm) + cassette (7 min., 1/2
track, mono.). LC# 78-730646/F. (LITTLE GOLDEN BOOKS
FILMSTRIPS AND BOOKS).

678SR. ---- [sound recording] Copyright KK38743 dated 1 Sep
48 (LITTLE GOLDEN RECORD 3).

678SR. ---- [sound recording] NY: Golden Record. 1 disc (45
rpm, mono., 7 in.) + book. Narrated by Kay Lande. (READ AND
HEAR GR 00242).

678a. ---- reissued (LITTLE GOLDEN BOOK 248).

678b. ---- reissued in 1962 (LITTLE GOLDEN BOOK 494).

678c. ---- reissued (LITTLE GOLDEN BOOK 302-22; 302-32).

Singing games. See Little golden book of singing games
(417).

Sky. See My little golden book about the sky (517).

679. Sleeping Beauty, Walt Disney's based on the Walt Disney
motion picture "Sleeping Beauty" told by Annie North
Bedford, ill. by the Walt Disney Studio, ill. adapted by
Julius Svendsen, Frank Armitage, Walt Peregoy; NY: S&S,
c1957. (WALT DISNEY BOOK D61).

680. Sleeping Beauty and the good fairies, Walt Disney's by
Dorothy Strebe and Annie North Bedford, ill. by the Walt
Disney Studio, adapted by Julius Svendsen and C.W.
Satterfield; NY: GP, c1958. (WALT DISNEY BOOK D71).

681. Sleeping Beauty paper dolls, Walt Disney's illustrated
by Walt Disney Studio, adapted by Julius Svendsen, Frank
Armitage, Walt Peregoy, C.W. Satterfield and Thelma Witmar;
NY: GP, c1959. (LITTLE GOLDEN ACTIVITY BOOK A33).

682. Sleepy book, The by Margaret Wise Brown, ill. by Garth
Williams; NY: GP, c1948, 1975. (LITTLE GOLDEN BOOK 301-41).
    Originally issued with title The golden sleepy book.

683. Sly little bear and other bears by Kathryn Jackson, ill. by Scott Johnston, NY: GP, c1960. (LITTLE GOLDEN BOOK 411).

684. Smokey and his animal friends by Charles Spain Verral, ill. by Mel Crawford; NY: GP, c1960. Copyright A430125 dated 20 Jan 60. (LITTLE GOLDEN BOOK 387).

685. Smokey Bear and the campers by S. Quentin Hyatt, ill. by Mel Crawford; NY: GP, c1961. Copyright A498389 dated 26 Jan 61. (LITTLE GOLDEN BOOK 423).

686. Smokey Bear finds a helper by Eileen Daly, ill. by Al Andersen; NY: GP, c1972. (LITTLE GOLDEN BOOK 345).

687. Smokey, the bear by Jane Werner, ill. by Richard Scarry; NY: S&S, c1955. LC# 55-14368. Copyright A186510 dated 1 Mar 55; renewal RE-185-993 dated 5 Dec 83. (LITTLE GOLDEN BOOK 224).

687SR. ---- [sound recording] NY: Golden Record, [197-]. 1 disc (45 rpm, mono., 7 in.) + book, c1955. Narrated by Kay Lande. (READ AND HEAR GR 00170).

687SR. ---- [sound recording] Burbank, CA: Disneyland Vista Records, c1976. 1 disc (33 1/3 rpm, 7 in.) + book. Song: "Listen to Smokey the Bear" by Larry Groce.

687a. ---- reissued in 1962 (LITTLE GOLDEN BOOK 481).

687b. ---- reissued (LITTLE GOLDEN BOOK 111-21).

688. Snow White and Rose Red: a favorite fairy tale [from Grimm] ill. by Gustaf Tenggren; NY: S&S, c1955. LC# 55-2055. Copyright A193398 dated 28 Apr 55; renewal RE 185-998 dated 5 Dec 83. (LITTLE GOLDEN BOOK 228).

688SR. ---- [sound recording] NY: Golden Record, [197-]. 1 disc (45 rpm, mono., 7 in.) + book, c1955. Narrated by Danny Kaye. (READ AND HEAR GR 00176).

689. Snow White and the seven dwarfs, Walt Disney's adapted from Grimm's fairy tales, ill. by the Walt Disney Studio, adapted by Ken O'Brien and Al Dempster from the Walt Disney motion picture "Snow White and the seven dwarfs;" NY: S&S, c1948. (WALT DISNEY BOOK D4); (MICKEY MOUSE CLUB BOOK D4).

689a. ---- reissued in 1957 (WALT DISNEY BOOK D66).

690. So big by Esther Wilkin, ill. by Eloise Wilkin; NY: GP, c1968. LC# 71-4895. (LITTLE GOLDEN BOOK 574).

690a. ---- reissued (LITTLE GOLDEN BOOK 209-26).

691. Sport Goofy and the racing robot, Disney's ill. by the Walt Disney Studio; NY: GB, c1984. LC# 83-83356. (LITTLE GOLDEN BOOK 100-57; 105-47).

692. Steve Canyon, Milton Caniff's by Carl Memling. ill. by Tom Gill; NY: GP, c1959. (LITTLE GOLDEN BOOK 356).

693. Sticks by Pauline Wilkins, ill. by Scott Johnston; NY: GP, c1961. (LITTLE GOLDEN BOOK 453).

694. Stop and go: a safety book by Loyta Higgins, ill. by Joan Walsh Anglund; NY: S&S, c1957. (LITTLE GOLDEN ACTIVITY BOOK A17).

695. Store-bought doll, The by Lois Meyer, ill. by Ruth Sanderson; NY: GP, c1983. LC# 82-83070. (LITTLE GOLDEN BOOK 204-54).

696. Stories of Jesus by Jean H. Richards, ill. by Ati Forberg; NY: GP, c1974. Contents: The boy in the temple -- Food for all -- The good neighbor -- Saved from the storm -- Children were always welcome. Copyright A528527 dated 29 Apr 74. (LITTLE GOLDEN BOOK 114X).

696a. ---- reissued (LITTLE GOLDEN BOOK 402-1).

697. Story of Jesus, The by Beatrice Alexander, ill. by Steffie Lerch; NY: S&S, c1946. LC# 47-1316rev. Copyright A10192 dated 15 Jan 47. (LITTLE GOLDEN BOOK 27).

698. Storytime book, Walt Disney's ill. by the Walt Disney Studio, adapted by Bob Grant and Campbell Grant; NY: S&S, c1958. Contents: Bambi (049) -- Pinocchio (592) -- Bongo (087). (GIANT LITTLE GOLDEN BOOK 5014).

699. Supercar by George Sherman, ill. by Mel Crawford; NY: GP, c1962. (LITTLE GOLDEN BOOK 492).

700. Superstar Barbie, the fairy princess by Anne Foster, ill. by Jim Robison and Fred Irvin; NY: GP, c1977. (LITTLE GOLDEN BOOK 162X).

700a. ---- reissued (LITTLE GOLDEN BOOK 111-8).

701. Surprise for Mickey Mouse, Walt Disney's NY: GP, c1971. (WALT DISNEY BOOK D105).

702. Surprise for Sally and other stories by Ethel Crowninshield, ill. by Corinne Malvern; NY: S&S, c1950. Contents: Marianna's baby carriage -- Surprise for Sally -- Sally-Sally-snow-shoes (song) -- Ketty's secret -- A secret (poem) -- Ketty's secret (song) -- Who lives in the little red house? -- Cookie (song). LC# 50-7817. Copyright A43471 dated 31 Mar 50. (LITTLE GOLDEN BOOK 84).

703. Susan in the driver's seat by Kathi Gibeault, ill. by Jane Ike; NY: GP, c1973. Copyright A502199 dated 10 Dec 73. (LITTLE GOLDEN BOOK 600).

704. Susie's new stove, the little chef's cookbook by Annie North Bedford, ill. by Corinne Malvern; NY: S&S, c1950. LC# 50-7511rev. Copyright A42928 dated 13 Mar 50. (LITTLE GOLDEN BOOK 85).

705. Swiss family Robinson, Walt Disney's adapted by Jean Lewis from the book by Johann Wyss, ill. by the Walt Disney Studio, adapted by Paul Granger; NY: GP, c1961. (WALT DISNEY BOOK D95).

706. Sword in the stone, Walt Disney's The told by Carl Memling, ill. by Norm McGary; NY: GP, c1963. (WALT DISNEY BOOK D106).

707. Tale of Peter Rabbit, The by Beatrix Potter, ill. by Adriana Saviozzi; NY: S&S, c1958. Copyright AA345954 dated 6 Feb 58. (LITTLE GOLDEN BOOK 313).

707a. ---- reissued in 1963; Copyright A224150 dated 2 Nov 70. (LITTLE GOLDEN BOOK 505).

707b. ---- reissued (LITTLE GOLDEN BOOK 307-42; 479-21).

708. Tales of Wells Fargo: Danger at Mesa Flats by Leon Lazarus, ill. by John Leone; NY: GP, c1958. (LITTLE GOLDEN BOOK 328).

709. Tammy by Kathleen N. Daly, ill. by Ada Salva; NY: GP, c1963. (LITTLE GOLDEN ACTIVITY BOOK A52).

Taran finds a friend. See Black cauldron (081).

710. Tarzan, Edgar Rice Burroughs' by Gina Ingoglia Weiner, ill. by Mel Crawford; NY: GP, c1964. (LITTLE GOLDEN BOOK 549).

711. Tawny scrawny lion, Tenggren's by Kathryn Jackson, ill. by Gustaf Tenggren; NY: S&S, c1952. LC# 52-8697. Copyright A65051 dated 11 Feb 52; renewal RE-68-188 dated 20 Oct 80. (LITTLE GOLDEN BOOK 138).

711FS. ---- [filmstrip] NY: Miller-Brody Productions, 1974. 1 filmstrip (67 fr., col., 35 mm) + disc (7 min., 33 1/3 rpm, 10 in.) LC# 75-732548/F. (LITTLE GOLDEN BOOKS FILMSTRIPS AND BOOKS).

711FS. ---- [filmstrip] Racine: Western Publishing Co., Education Division, 1972. 1 filmstrip (55 fr., col., 35 mm) + disc (6 min., 33 1/3 rpm, 7 in.) + teacher's guide by Adelaide Holl. LC# 72-733480/F. (EDUCATIONAL EXPERIENCES SOUND FILMSTRIPS: ABOUT MAKE-BELIEVE ANIMALS).

711MP. ---- [motion picture] Racine: Western Publishing Co.,Education Division, made and released by Sandler Institutional Films, 1974. Animated cartoon (7 min., sd., col., 16 mm) + study guide. LC# 75-700397/F. Based on book by Kathryn Jackson. Voices by June Foray, Les Tremayne and Kerry Maclane.

711MP. ---- [motion picture] Pasadena, CA: Barr Films, made and released by Sandler Institutional Films, [197-?]. 1 film (7 min., sd., col., 16 mm). Voices by June Foray, Les Tremayne and Kerry Maclane.

711SR. ---- [sound recording] Burbank, CA: Disneyland, 1976. 1 disc (33 1/3 rpm, mono., 7 in.) + book. Songs: "I'm hungry" and "Carrot stew" by Larry Groce. (LITTLE GOLDEN BOOK AND RECORD).

711SR. ---- [sound recording] Burbank, CA: Disneyland, c1976. 1 sound cassette (1 7/8 ips, mono., 3 7/8 x 2 1/2 in., 1/8 in. tape) + book. Songs: "I'm hungry" and "Carrot stew" by Larry Groce. (DISNEYLAND STORYTELLER CASSETTE 202B).

711a. ---- reissued in 1963 (LITTLE GOLDEN BOOK 532).

711b. ---- reissued (LITTLE GOLDEN BOOK 201-43; 304-23).

712. Tawny scrawny lion and the clever monkey, The by Mary Carey, ill. by Milli Jancar; NY: GP, c1974. (LITTLE GOLDEN BOOK 128X).

712SR. ---- [sound recording] Racine: Western, [1977]. 1 cassette (12 min., 2 track, mono.) + text and teacher's guide by Joanne Wylie. (LITTLE GOLDEN READ ALONG 3511).

713. Taxi that hurried, The by Lucy Sprague Mitchell, Irma Simonton Black and Jessie Stanton, ill. by Tibor Gergely; NY: S&S, c1946. LC# 46-3222. Copyright A1877 dated 16 Mar 46. (LITTLE GOLDEN BOOK 25); (BANK STREET BOOK).

713B. ---- [braille] Tarzana, CA: American Brotherhood for the Blind, Twin Vision Publication Division; reprint of the c1946 ed. Opposite pages in braille. (TWIN VISION BOOK).

713SR. ---- [sound recording] Burbank, CA: Disneyland, c1976. 1 cassette (1 7/8 ips, mono., 3 7/8 x 2 1/2 in., 1/8 in. tape) + book. Song: "The taxi song" by Larry Groce. (DISNEYLAND STORYTELLER CASSETTE 214B).

713SR. ---- [sound recording] Burbank, CA: Disneyland Records, c1976. 1 disc (33 1/3 rpm, 7 in.) + book. (LITTLE GOLDEN BOOK AND RECORD).

714. Ten items or less: a counting book by Stephanie Calmenson, ill. by Terri Super; NY: GB, c1985. LC# 84-72873. (LITTLE GOLDEN BOOK 203-54).

715. 10 little animals by Carl Memling, ill. by Feodor Rojankovsky; NY: GP, c1961. Copyright A543668 dated 6 Dec 61. (LITTLE GOLDEN BOOK 451).

716. <u>Tex and his toys</u> by Elsa Ruth Nast, ill. by Corinne Malvern; NY: S&S, c1952. LC# 52-8416rev. Copyright A65050 dated 5 Feb 52; renewal RE-68-187 dated 20 Oct 80. A Little Golden make-it book. This book contains a genuine roll of TEXCEL Cellophane tape. (LITTLE GOLDEN BOOK 129).

717. <u>Theodore Mouse goes to sea</u> by Michaela Muntean, ill. by Lucinda McQueen; NY: GP, c1983. LC# 82-82290/AC. (LITTLE GOLDEN BOOK 201-45; 211-45).

717VC. ---- [videocassette] Racine: Western, c1985. <u>3 favorite Golden stories</u> [including <u>Theodore Mouse goes to sea</u>]. 1 videocassette (30 min., sd., col., 1/2 in.) VHS (GOLDEN BOOK VIDEO) #13821.

718. <u>There's no such thing as a dragon</u> story and pictures by Jack Kent; NY: GP, c1975. LC# 73-93309/AC. (LITTLE GOLDEN BOOK ---).

718SR. ---- [sound recording] Burbank, CA: Disneyland Vista Records, c1976. 1 cassette (1 7/8 ips) + book, c1975. Songs: "Little orange dragon" by Larry Groce and "Everybody likes to be noticed" by Larry Groce and Jymn Magon. (DISNEYLAND STORYTELLER CASSETTE 223B).

718SR. ---- [sound recording] Burbank, CA: Disneyland Vista Records, c1976. 1 disc (33 1/3 rpm, 7 in.) + book. Songs: "Little orange dragon" by Larry Groce and "Everybody likes to be noticed" by Larry Groce and Jymn Magon.

719. <u>Things in my house</u> written and ill. by Joe Kaufman; NY: GP, c1972. Copyright A359563 dated 23 Jun 72. (LITTLE GOLDEN BOOK 570).

719a. ---- reissued (LITTLE GOLDEN BOOK 206-22).

720. <u>This little piggy and other counting rhymes</u> selected by Phyllis Fraser, ill. by Roberta Paflin; NY: Artists & Writers Guild, dist. by S&S, c1942. LC# 42-50766rev2. Copyright A168876 dated 1 Oct 42. First printing Sept 42. Issued with dust jacket. (LITTLE GOLDEN BOOK 12).
    Also issued with title <u>Counting rhymes</u> (164).

721. <u>This world of ours</u> by Jane Werner Watson, ill. by Eloise Wilkin; NY: GP, c1959. LC# A63-5166. Copyright A430093 dated 11 Dec 59. (GIANT LITTLE GOLDEN BOOK 5026).

722. <u>Three bears, The</u> ill. by Feodor Rojankovsky; NY: S&S, c1948. LC# 48-7825. Copyright A28131 dated 30 Jun 48. (LITTLE GOLDEN BOOK 47).

722SR. ---- [sound recording] NY: Golden Record. 1 disc (45 rpm, mono., 7 in.) + book, c1948. Narrated by Anne Lloyd; music director, Mitch Miller. (READ AND HEAR GR 00155).

722a. ---- reissued (LITTLE GOLDEN BOOK 307-1).

722b. ---- by Mabel Watts, ill. by June Goldsborough; NY:
GP, c1965. (LITTLE GOLDEN BOOK 204X).

722c. ---- reissued (LITTLE GOLDEN BOOK 307-22).

723. Three bedtime stories ill. by Garth Williams; NY: S&S,
c1958. Copyright AA333444 dated 17 Jan 58. Contents: The
three bears -- The three kittens -- The three little pigs.
(LITTLE GOLDEN BOOK 309).

723a. ---- reissued (LITTLE GOLDEN BOOK 311-23).

3 best-loved Golden stories [videocassette]. See The sailor
dog (663VC).

724. Three billy goats gruff and The wolf and the kids by
Peter Christian Asbjornsen, ill. by Richard Scarry; NY: S&S,
c1953. LC# 53-3218. Copyright A99471 dated 10 Jun 53;
renewal RE-109-105 dated 29 Oct 81. (LITTLE GOLDEN BOOK
173).

3 favorite Golden stories [videocassette]. See Scuffy the
tugboat (671VC) and Theodore Mouse goes to sea (717VC).

725. Three little kittens ill. by Masha; NY: S&S, c1942. LC#
42-24236. Copyright A169132 dated 1 Oct 42. (LITTLE GOLDEN
BOOK 1).
    See also Giant little golden book of kittens (273).

725SR. ---- [sound recording] NY: Golden Record, [197-]. 1
disc (45 rpm, mono., 7 in.) + book, c1942. Narrated by Kay
Lande with Anne Lloyd and the Golden Orchestra. (READ AND
HEAR GR 00213).

725a. ---- reissued (LITTLE GOLDEN BOOK 225).

725b. ---- reissued in 1957 (LITTLE GOLDEN BOOK 288).

725c. ---- reissued in 1959 (LITTLE GOLDEN BOOK 381).

725d. ---- reissued (LITTLE GOLDEN BOOK 302-3).

726. Three little pigs, The as told by Elizabeth Ross, ill.
by ROFry; NY: GP, c1973. Copyright A435416 dated 18 Apr 73.
(LITTLE GOLDEN BOOK 544).

726SR. ---- [sound recording] NY: Golden Record, [197-]. 1
disc (45 rpm, mono., 7 in.) + book, c1966. Narrated by Kay
Lande. (READ AND HEAR GR 00209).

726a. ---- reissued (LITTLE GOLDEN BOOK 309-22).

727. Three little pigs, Walt Disney's The ill. by the Walt
Disney Studio, adapted by Milt Banta and Al Dempster from
the Walt Disney movie "The three little pigs;" NY: S&S,
c1948. LC# 48-10774. (WALT DISNEY BOOK D10); (MICKEY MOUSE
CLUB BOOK D10).
    See also Favorite stories, Walt Disney's (234).

727a. ---- reissued in 1959 (LITTLE GOLDEN BOOK D78).

3 Richard Scarry animal nursery tales [videocassette]. See
The gingerbread man. (276aVC).

728. Through the picture frame, Walt Disney's adapted by
Robert Edmunds, from the Hans Christian Andersen story, Ole
Lukoie ill. by the Walt Disney Studio; NY: S&S, c1944. LC#
44-51049. First printing Sept 44. Issued with dust jacket.
(WALT DISNEY BOOK D1).

729. Thumbelina, Tenggren's by Hans Christian Andersen, ill.
by Gustaf Tenggren; NY: S&S, c1953. LC# 53-2330. Copyright
A92976 dated 10 Apr 53; renewal RE-109-089 dated 20 Oct 81.
(LITTLE GOLDEN BOOK 153).

729SR. ---- [sound recording] Burbank, CA: Buena Vista
Distribution Co., 1976. 1 cassette (1 7/8 ips, mono., 3 7/8
x 2 1/2 in., 1/8 in. tape) + book. Song: "Thumbelina" by
Larry Groce. (LITTLE GOLDEN BOOK AND CASSETTE); (DISNEYLAND
STORYTELLER CASSETTE 206B).

729a. ---- reissued in 1963 (LITTLE GOLDEN BOOK 514).

730. Thumper, Walt Disney's based on the character created
by Walt Disney for the motion picture "Bambi;" NY: GP,
c1968. (WALT DISNEY BOOK D119).

731. Tiger's adventure story and pictures by William P.
Gottlieb; NY: S&S, c1954. LC# 54-14964. Copyright A179975
dated 20 Nov 54; renewal RE-149-964 dated 30 Dec 82. (LITTLE
GOLDEN BOOK 208).

731SR. ---- [sound recording] NY: Golden Record. 1 disc (45
rpm, mono., 7 in.) + book, c1954. Narrated by Cecelia Scott.
(READ AND HEAR GR 00253).

731a. ---- reissued in 1959 (LITTLE GOLDEN BOOK 351).

732. Tin woodman of Oz, The by Lyman Frank Baum, adapted by
Peter Archer, ill. by Harry McNaught; NY: S&S, c1952. LC#
53-235. (LITTLE GOLDEN BOOK 159).

733. Tiny, tawny kitten, The by Barbara Hazen, ill. by Jan
Pfloog; NY: GP, c1969. (LITTLE GOLDEN BOOK 590).

734. Toad flies high, Walt Disney's with characters from the
Walt Disney motion picture "The adventures of Ichabod and
Mr. Toad." Adapted from The wind in the willows by Kenneth
Grahame; NY: GP, c1982. LC# 80-85426. (LITTLE GOLDEN BOOK
103-44).

735. Toby Tyler, Walt Disney's story adapted by Carl
Memling, ill. by Sam McKim; NY: GP, c1960. LC# 61-4929.
Adapted from the book by James Otis Kaler. (WALT DISNEY BOOK
D87).

736. Together book, The by Ravena Dwight, ill. by Roger
Bradfield, featuring Jim Henson's Muppets. Racine: Western,
in conjunction with Children's Television Workshop, c1971.
(LITTLE GOLDEN BOOK 315X); (SESAME STREET BOOK).

736a. ---- reissued (LITTLE GOLDEN BOOK 108-3; 108-23).

737. Tom and Jerry, MGM's story and pictures by MGM
Cartoons, pictures adapted by Don MacLaughlin and Harvey
Eisenberg; NY: S&S, c1951. LC# 51-39074. (LITTLE GOLDEN BOOK
117).

737a. ---- reissued (LITTLE GOLDEN BOOK 561).

738. Tom and Jerry meet Little Quack, MGM's story and
pictures by MGM Cartoons, pictures adapted by Don
MacLaughlin and Harvey Eisenberg; NY: S&S, c1953. LC#
53-3482. (LITTLE GOLDEN BOOK 181).

738B. ---- [braille] Tarzana, CA: American Brotherhood for
the Blind, Twin Vision Publication Division; reprint of the
c1953 ed. Opposite pages in braille. (TWIN VISION BOOK).

738a. ---- reissued in 1958 (LITTLE GOLDEN BOOK 311).

739. Tom and Jerry's merry Christmas, MGM's told by Peter
Archer, pictures by MGM Cartoons, adapted by Harvey
Eisenberg and Samuel Armstrong; NY: S&S, c1954. LC#
54-14443. (LITTLE GOLDEN BOOK 197).

740. Tom and Jerry's party, MGM's told by Steffi Fletcher,
ill. by MGM Cartoons, adapted by Harvey Eisenberg and Samuel
Armstrong; NY: S&S, c1955. LC# 55-3188. (LITTLE GOLDEN BOOK
235).

741. Tom and Jerry's photo finish by Jean Lewis, ill. by Al
Andersen; NY: GP, c1974. (LITTLE GOLDEN BOOK 124X).

742. Tom Thumb, M-G-M presents the George Pal Production of
adapted by Carl Memling, ill. by William Dugan; NY: GP,
c1959. (LITTLE GOLDEN BOOK 353).

743. Tommy visits the doctor by Jean H. Seligman and Milton
I. Levine, M.D., ill. by Richard Scarry; NY: GP, c1962.
Copyright AA591222 dated 19 Sept 62. (LITTLE GOLDEN BOOK
480).

744. Tommy's camping adventure by Gladys Saxon, ill. by Mel
Crawford; NY: GP, c1962. Copyright A569103 dated 18 May 62.
(LITTLE GOLDEN BOOK 471).

745. Tommy's wonderful rides by Helen Palmer, ill. by J.P.
Miller; NY: S&S, c1948. LC# 49-7107. Copyright A28612 dated
13 Dec 48. (LITTLE GOLDEN BOOK 63).

746. Tonka, Walt Disney's adapted by Elizabeth Beecher, ill.
with kodachromes; NY; GP, c1959. (WALT DISNEY BOOK D80).

747. <u>Tootle</u> by Gertrude Crampton, ill. by Tibor Gergely; NY:
S&S, c1945. LC# 48-3538. Copyright A191212 dated 26 Sept 45.
First printing Jun 45. Issued with dust jacket. (LITTLE
GOLDEN BOOK 21).

747B. ---- [braille] Tarzana, CA: American Brotherhood for
the Blind, Twin Vision Publication Division; reprint of the
c1945 ed. Opposite pages in braille. (TWIN VISION BOOK).

747FS. ---- [filmstrip] NY: Miller-Brody Productions, 1977.
1 filmstrip (77 fr., col., 35 mm) + cassette (12 min., 2
track, mono.). Based on the book by Gertrude Crampton.
(LITTLE GOLDEN BOOKS FILMSTRIPS AND BOOKS).

747FS. ---- [filmstrip] NY: Miller-Brody Productions, 1978.
1 filmstrip (84 fr., col., 35 mm) + cassette (12 min., 1/2
track, mono.). LC# 78-730647/F. (LITTLE GOLDEN BOOKS
FILMSTRIPS AND BOOKS).

747SR. ---- [sound recording] NY: Golden Record, [197-]. 1
disc (45 rpm, mono., 7 in.) + book, c1946. Narrated by Larry
Harmon. (READ AND HEAR GR 00208).

747SR. ---- [sound recording] Copyright KK38744 dated 1 Sep
48 (LITTLE GOLDEN RECORD 4).

747SR. ---- [sound recording] Burbank, CA: Disneyland Vista
Records, c1976. 1 disc (33 1/3 rpm, 7 in.) + book. Song:
"You must stay on the rails" by Larry Groce.

747a. ---- reissued (LITTLE GOLDEN BOOK 306-21).

748. <u>Top Cat, Hanna-Barbera's</u> by Carl Memling, ill. by
Hawley Pratt; NY: GP, c1962. (LITTLE GOLDEN BOOK 453X).

749. <u>Topsy turvy circus</u> by Georges Duplaix, ill. by Gustaf
Tenggren; NY: S&S, c1953. LC# 53-2332. Copyright A92982
dated 18 Mar 53; renewal RE-109-092 dated 29 Oct 81. (LITTLE
GOLDEN BOOK 161).

750. <u>Touche turtle, Hanna-Barbera</u> by Carl Memling, ill. by
Al White, Norm McGary, and Bill Lorencz; NY: GP, c1962.
(LITTLE GOLDEN BOOK 474).

751. <u>Toy soldiers, Walt Disney's The</u> retold by Barbara Shook
Hazen, ill. by the Walt Disney Studio, adapted by Robert
Thompson; NY: GP, c1961. (WALT DISNEY BOOK D99).

752. <u>Toys</u> by Edith Osswald, ill. by Masha; NY: S&S, c1945.
LC# 48-4728. Copyright A1226 dated 1 Feb 46. First printing
Oct 45. (LITTLE GOLDEN BOOK 22).

753. <u>Train stories</u> NY: S&S, c1958. Contents: <u>Tootle</u> /
Gertrude Crampton, ill. Tibor Gergely (747) -- <u>The train to
Timbuctoo</u> / Margaret Wise Brown, ill. by Art Seiden (754) --
<u>The little red caboose</u> / Marian Potter, ill. by Tibor
Gergely (435). Copyright AA369645 dated 6 Oct 58. (GIANT
LITTLE GOLDEN BOOK 5018).

754. Train to Timbuctoo, The by Margaret Wise Brown, ill. by
Art Seiden; NY: S&S, c1951. LC# 51-39071. Copyright A60562
dated 6 Jul 51; renewal RE-46-364 dated 7 Nov 79. (LITTLE
GOLDEN BOOK 118).

755. Trains: a little golden stamp book by Kathleen N. Daly,
ill. by E. Joseph Dreany; NY: S&S, c1958. (LITTLE GOLDEN
ACTIVITY BOOK A26).

Travel. See My little golden book about travel (518).

756. Treasury of Disney little golden books: 22 best-loved
Disney favorites, A NY: GP, c1978.

757. Treasury of little golden books: 48 of the best-loved
stories for the very young, A selected and edited by Ellen
Lewis Buell, cover and end papers designed by Feodor
Rojankovsky; NY: GP, c1960. LC# 60-14883. A collection of 48
stories and poems originally published in separate editions
of Little Golden Books.

757a. ---- reissued in 1972. LC# 72-178994.

758. Treasury of little golden books: 30 best-loved stories,
A selected and edited by Ellen Lewis Buell; NY: GP, c1982.
LC# 82-80361.

759. Trim the Christmas tree by Elsa Ruth Nast, ill. by
Doris and Marion Henderson; NY: S&S, c1957. (LITTLE GOLDEN
ACTIVITY BOOK A15).

759a. ---- reissued in 1963 (LITTLE GOLDEN ACTIVITY BOOK
A50).

760. Trucks by Kathryn Jackson, ill. by Ray Quigley; NY:
S&S, c1955. LC# 56-13517. With two authentic International
trucks to make. (LITTLE GOLDEN ACTIVITY BOOK A6).

761. Tweety plays catch the puddy tat by Eileen Daly, ill.
by Peter Alvarado and William Lorencz; NY: GP, c1975.
(LITTLE GOLDEN BOOK 141X).

761a. ---- reissued (LITTLE GOLDEN BOOK 111-24; 111-44).

762. Twelve dancing princesses, The a story by Jakob and
Wilhelm Grimm, retold by Jane Werner, ill. by Sheilah
Beckett; NY: S&S, c1954. Copyright A172863 dated 7 Sept 54;
renewal RE-143-614 dated 15 Nov 82. (LITTLE GOLDEN BOOK
194).

763. Twelve days of Christmas: a Christmas carol, The ill.
by Tony deLuna; NY: GP, c1963. Copyright A655072 dated 6
Sept 63. (LITTLE GOLDEN BOOK 526).

763SR. ---- [sound recording] NY: Golden Record. 1 disc (45
rpm, mono., 7 in.) + book, c1963. Narrated by Kay Lande with
the Sandpiper chorus and orchestra. (READ AND HEAR).

763a. ---- ill. by Mike Eagle; NY: GP, c1983. LC#
82-83504/AC. (LITTLE GOLDEN BOOK 454-42).

764. Twins: the story of two little girls who look alike,
The by Ruth and Harold Shane, ill. by Eloise Wilkin; NY:
S&S, c1955. LC# 55-14362. Copyright A186511 dated 30 Mar 55;
renewal RE-185-994 dated 5 Dec 83. (LITTLE GOLDEN BOOK 227).

765. Two little gardeners by Margaret Wise Brown and Edith
Thacher Hurd, ill. by Gertrude Elliott; NY: S&S, c1951. LC#
51-1257. Copyright A60575 dated 17 Apr 51; renewal RE-38-495
dated 7 Nov 79. Song: "Full as a fiddle" words by Margaret
Wise Brown, music by Dorothy Cadzow. (LITTLE GOLDEN BOOK
108).

766. Two little miners by Margaret Wise Brown and Edith
Thacher Hurd, ill. by Richard Scarry; NY: S&S, c1949. LC#
49-9957. Copyright A37026 dated 7 Jun 49. (LITTLE GOLDEN
BOOK 66).

767. Ugly dachshund, Walt Disney presents The adapted by
Carl Memling, ill. by Mel Crawford; NY: GP, c1966. (WALT
DISNEY BOOK D118).

768. Ugly duckling, Walt Disney's The told by Annie North
Bedford, pictures by the Walt Disney Studio, adapted by Don
MacLaughlin from the motion picture "The ugly duckling;" NY:
S&S, c1952. LC# 52-2383. (WALT DISNEY BOOK D22).

768SR. ---- [sound recording] NY: Golden Press/A.A. Records,
1966. 1 disc (45 rpm, mono., 7 in.) + book. Narrated by
Danny Kaye. (READ AND HEAR GR 00211).

769. Ukelele and her new doll by Clara Louise Grant, ill. by
Campbell Grant; NY: S&S, c1951. LC# 51-1838. Copyright
A52307 dated 22 Jan 51; renewal RE-21-292 dated 14 Feb 79.
With jigsaw puzzle in back cover. (LITTLE GOLDEN BOOK 102).

769SR. ---- [sound recording] NY: Golden Record, [197-]. 1
disc (45 rpm, mono., 7 in.) + book, c1951. Narrated by
Cecelia Scott. (READ AND HEAR GR 00249).

770. Uncle Mistletoe told by Jane Werner, ill. by Corinne
Malvern; NY: S&S, c1953. LC# 53-3514rev. Copyright A105647
dated 6 Jul 53; renewal RE-109-108 dated 29 Oct 81. (LITTLE
GOLDEN BOOK 175).

771. Uncle Remus, Walt Disney's pictures by Bob Grant for
the Walt Disney Studio adapted from the characters and
backgrounds created for Walt Disney's "Song of the South"
retold by Marion Palmer, from the original Uncle Remus
stories by Joel Chandler Harris; NY: S&S, c1947, 1946. LC#
47-11931. (WALT DISNEY BOOK D6); (MICKEY MOUSE CLUB BOOK
D6).
    See also Favorite stories, Walt Disney's (234).

771a. ---- reissued in 1959 (WALT DISNEY BOOK D85).

Uncle Wiggly. See Little golden book of Uncle Wiggly (418).

772. Underdog and the disappearing ice cream by Mary Jane Fern, ill. by Jason Art Studio; NY: GP, c1975. (LITTLE GOLDEN BOOK 135X).

773. Up in the attic: a story ABC by Hilda K. Williams, ill. by Corinne Malvern; NY: S&S, c1948. LC# 48-8166. Copyright A26683 dated 10 Aug 48. (LITTLE GOLDEN BOOK 53).

774. Very best home for me, The by Jane Werner Watson, ill. by Garth Williams; NY: GP, c1953, 1982. (LITTLE GOLDEN BOOK 206-52).
    Originally issued with title Animal friends (021).

775. Visit to the children's zoo, A by Barbara Shook Hazen, ill. by Mel Crawford; NY: GP, c1963. Copyright A634180 dated 25 Apr 63. (LITTLE GOLDEN BOOK 511).

775SR. ---- [sound recording] NY: Golden Record, [197-]. 1 disc (45 rpm, mono., 7 in.) + book, c1963. Narrated by Patricia Hall. (READ AND HEAR GR 00232).

775a. ---- reissued (LITTLE GOLDEN BOOK 204-1).

776. Wacky witch and the mystery of the king's gold by Jean Lewis, ill. by Peter Alvarado, A.J. Specter, and Bob Totten; NY: GP, c1973. (LITTLE GOLDEN BOOK 416).

776SR. ---- [sound recording] NY: Golden Record, c1973. 1 disc (45 rpm, mono., 7 in.) + book, c1973. Narrated by Pat Lordier. (READ AND HEAR GR 00261).

777. Wagon train by Emily Broun, ill. by Frank Bolle; NY: S&S, c1958. (LITTLE GOLDEN BOOK 326).

778. Wait-for-me kitten, The by Patricia Scarry, ill. by Lilian Obligado; NY: GP, c1962. Copyright A569102 dated 11 Apr 62. (LITTLE GOLDEN BOOK 463).

779. Wally Gator by Tom Golberg, ill. by Hawley Pratt and Bill Lorencz; NY: GP, c1963. (LITTLE GOLDEN BOOK 502).

Walt Disney's favorite nursery tales. See Favorite nursery tales (233).

Walt Disney's storytime book. See Storytime book (698).

780. Waltons and the birthday present, The by Jane Godfrey; NY: GP, c1975. (LITTLE GOLDEN BOOK 134X).

781. We help Daddy by Mini Stein, ill. by Eloise Wilkin; NY: GP, c1962. Copyright A569216 dated 24 Apr 62. (LITTLE GOLDEN BOOK 468).

781a. ---- reissued (LITTLE GOLDEN BOOK 208-1; 305-41).

782. We help Mommy by Jean Cushman, ill. by Eloise Wilkin; NY: GP, c1959. Copyright A380767 dated 20 Jan 59. (LITTLE GOLDEN BOOK 352).

782a. ---- reissued (LITTLE GOLDEN BOOK 208-2).

783. We like kindergarten by Clara Cassidy, ill. by Eloise Wilkin; NY: GP, c1965. (LITTLE GOLDEN BOOK 552).

783a. ---- reissued (LITTLE GOLDEN BOOK 207-22).

784. We like to do things by Walter M. Mason, ill. by Steffie Lerch; NY: S&S, c1949. LC# 50-5802. Copyright A40466 dated 29 Nov 49. (LITTLE GOLDEN BOOK 62).

784FS. ---- [filmstrip] NY: S&S, released by Young America Films, 1951. 1 filmstrip (40 fr., col., 35 mm) + teacher's guide. LC# fia52-1747. (GOLDEN BOOK SERIES. SET NO. 3).

785. We love Grandpa by Dr. Frances R. Horwich, ill. by Dorothy Grider; NY: GP, c1959. (DING DONG SCHOOL BOOK Din4).

Wells Fargo. See Tales of Wells Fargo (708).

786. Whales by Jane Werner Watson, ill. by Rod Ruth; NY: GP, c1978. (LITTLE GOLDEN BOOK 171X).

786a. ---- reissued (LITTLE GOLDEN BOOK 204-4; 308-41).

787. What am I? a picture quiz book by Ruth Leon, ill. by Cornelius DeWitt; NY: S&S, c1949. Copyright A31737 dated 10 Feb 49. (LITTLE GOLDEN BOOK 58).

787a. ---- reissued in 1963 (LITTLE GOLDEN BOOK 509).

788. What if? by Helen and Henry Tanous, ill. by J.P. Miller; NY: S&S, c1951. LC# 51-13063. Copyright A60569 dated 5 Sept 51; renewal RE-46-370 dated 7 Nov 79. (LITTLE GOLDEN BOOK 130).

789. What Lily Goose found by Annabelle Sumera, ill. by Lorinda Bryan Cauley; NY: GP, c1977. (LITTLE GOLDEN BOOK 163X).

790. What will I be? A wish book by Kathleen Krull Cowles, ill. by Eulala Conner, NY: GP, c1979. (LITTLE GOLDEN BOOK 205-42; 206-3).

791. Wheels by Kathryn Jackson, ill. by Leonard Weisgard; NY: S&S, c1952. LC# 52-8698. Copyright A65052 dated 11 Feb 52; renewal RE-68-189 dated 20 Oct 80. (LITTLE GOLDEN BOOK 141).

792. When I grow up by Kay and Harry Mace, ill. by Corinne Malvern; NY: S&S, c1950. LC# 50-58103. Copyright A49616 dated 31 Aug 50. With jigsaw puzzle in back cover. (LITTLE GOLDEN BOOK 96).

792a. ----story and pictures by Ilse-Margret Vogel; NY: GP, c1968. (LITTLE GOLDEN BOOK 578).

792aSR. ---- [sound recording] NY: Golden Record, [197-]. 1 disc (45 rpm, mono., 7 in.) + book, c1968. Narrated by Cecelia Scott. (READ AND HEAR GR 00244).

793. When you were a baby by Rita Eng, ill. by Corinne Malvern; NY: S&S, c1949. Copyright A37025 dated 19 Jul 49. (LITTLE GOLDEN BOOK 70).

793a. ---- reissued in 1961 (LITTLE GOLDEN BOOK 435).

793b. ---- by Linda Hayward, ill. by Ruth Sanderson; NY: GP, c1982. LC# 80-85029/AC. (LITTLE GOLDEN BOOK 306-51).

794. Where did the baby go? by Sheila Hayes, ill. by Eloise Wilkin; NY: GP, c1974. (LITTLE GOLDEN BOOK 116X).

794a. ---- reissued (LITTLE GOLDEN BOOK 209-2; 306-44).

795. Where is the bear? by Betty Hubka, ill. by Mel Crawford; NY: GP, c1967. LC# 79-4933/AC. (LITTLE GOLDEN BOOK 568).

795a. ---- reissued (LITTLE GOLDEN BOOK 204-3; 206-44).

796. Where is the poky little puppy? by Janette Sebring Lowrey, ill. by Gustaf Tenggren; NY: GP, c1962. Copyright A569411 dated 18 May 62. (LITTLE GOLDEN BOOK 467).

797. Where Jesus lived by Jane Werner Watson, ill. by Ronald Lettew; NY: GP, c1977. (LITTLE GOLDEN BOOK 147X).

797a. ---- reissued (LITTLE GOLDEN BOOK 408-1).

798. Where will all the animals go? by Sharon Holaves, ill. by Leigh Grant; NY: GP, c1978. (LITTLE GOLDEN BOOK 175X).

798a. ---- reissued (LITTLE GOLDEN BOOK 204-5).

799. Whistling Wizard, Bil Baird's story by Alan Stern and Rupert Pray, ill. by Mel Crawford; NY: S&S, c1952. LC# 53-2324. (LITTLE GOLDEN BOOK 132).

800. White bunny and his magic nose, The by Lily Duplaix, ill. by Feodor Rojankovsky; NY: S&S, c1957. LC# 60-26340. Copyright AA324808 dated 26 Nov 57. (LITTLE GOLDEN BOOK 305).

800SR. ---- [sound recording] NY: Golden Record. 1 disc (45 rpm, mono., 7 in.) + book, c1957. Read by Jim Dukas, music director, Ralph Stein. (READ AND HEAR GR 00217).

801. Who comes to your house? by Margaret Hillert, ill. by Tom O'Sullivan; NY: GP, c1973. (LITTLE GOLDEN BOOK 575).

801SR. ---- [sound recording] NY: Golden Record. 1 disc (45 rpm, mono., 7 in.) + book, c1973. Narrated by Laine Roberts; produced by Ralph Stein. (READ AND HEAR).

802. Who needs a cat? by Clara Cassidy, ill. by Audean Johnson; NY: GP, c1963. Copyright A621127 dated 1 Mar 63. (LITTLE GOLDEN BOOK 507).

803. Who took the top hat trick? by Joan Bowden, ill. by Jim Cummins; NY: GP, c1974. (LITTLE GOLDEN BOOK 805); (EAGER READER).

804. Wiggles by Louise Woodcock, ill. by Eloise Wilkin; NY: S&S, c1953. LC# 53-2863. Copyright A99466 dated 10 Jun 53; renewal RE-109-102 dated 29 Oct 81. (LITTLE GOLDEN BOOK 166).

805. Wild animal babies by Kathleen Daly, ill. by Feodor Rojankovsky; NY: S&S, c1958. Copyright AA369644 dated 23 Sept 58. (LITTLE GOLDEN BOOK 332).

806. Wild animals text and photos by W[olfgang] Suschitzky; NY: S&S, c1958. LC# 60-4126. Copyright AA333442 dated 10 Feb 58. (GIANT LITTLE GOLDEN BOOK 5010).

807. Wild animals written and ill. by Feodor Rojankovsky; NY: GP, c1960. Copyright A445014 dated 13 Apr 60. (LITTLE GOLDEN BOOK 394).

807a. ---- reissued in 1962 (LITTLE GOLDEN BOOK 499).

808. Wild kingdom: a can you guess book by Esta Meier, ill. by James Seward and Creative Studios I, Inc.; NY: GP, c1976. (LITTLE GOLDEN BOOK 151X).

809. Willie found a wallet by Mary Beth Markham, ill. by Lilian Obligado; NY: GB, c1984. LC# 83-82195. (LITTLE GOLDEN BOOK 205-56).

810. Winky Dink, CBS Television's told by Ann McGovern, ill. by Richard Scarry; NY: S&S, c1956. LC# 56-58193. (LITTLE GOLDEN BOOK 266).

811. Winnie-the-Pooh and Tigger, Walt Disney presents a story by A.A. Milne, ill. by the Walt Disney Studio; NY: S&S, c1956. Adapted from The house at Pooh Corner. (WALT DISNEY BOOK D121).

811a. ---- reissued (LITTLE GOLDEN BOOK 101-41).

812. <u>Winnie-the-Pooh meets Gopher, Walt Disney presents</u> based on a story by A.A. Milne, ill. by the Walt Disney Studio, adapted by George DeSantis; NY: GP, c1965. (WALT DISNEY BOOK D117).

812a. ---- reissued (LITTLE GOLDEN BOOK 101-42).

813. <u>Winnie-the-Pooh: the honey tree, Walt Disney presents</u> story by A.A. Milne, pictures by the Walt Disney Studio, adapted by Bob Totten; NY: GP, c1964. (WALT DISNEY BOOK D116).

814. <u>Wizard of Oz, The</u> retold by Mary Carey, ill. by Don Turner / Jason Art Studios, based on the best-loved children's classic The wonderful Wizard of Oz by L. Frank Baum; NY: GP, c1975. (LITTLE GOLDEN BOOK 119X).

814a. ---- reissued (LITTLE GOLDEN BOOK 310-22).

815. <u>Wizard's duel, Walt Disney's The</u> by Carl Memling, ill. by Hawley Pratt and Al White; NY: GP, c1963. (WALT DISNEY BOOK D107).

<u>Wolf and the kids.</u> See <u>Three billy goats gruff</u> (723).

816. <u>Wonderful house, The</u> by Margaret Wise Brown, ill. by J.P. Miller; NY: S&S, c1950. LC# 50-7816. Copyright A43473 dated 19 Apr 50. (LITTLE GOLDEN BOOK 76).

817. <u>Wonderful school</u> by May Justus, ill. by Hilde Hoffmann; NY: GP, c1969. (LITTLE GOLDEN BOOK 582).

818. <u>Wonders of nature</u> by Jane Werner Watson, ill. by Eloise Wilkin; NY; S&S, c1957. LC# 57-13853. Copyright AA295629 dated 24 Apr 57. (LITTLE GOLDEN BOOK 293).

819. <u>Woodsy owl and the trail bikers</u> by Kennon Graham, ill. by Frank McSavage; NY: GP, c1974. (LITTLE GOLDEN BOOK 107X).

820. <u>Woody Woodpecker at the circus, Walter Lantz's</u> by Stella Williams Nathan, ill. by Frank McSavage; NY: GP, c1976. (LITTLE GOLDEN BOOK 149X).

820a. ---- reissued (LITTLE GOLDEN BOOK 111-3; 111-43).

821. <u>Woody Woodpecker drawing fun for beginners, Walter Lantz</u> by Carl Buettner, ill. by Harvey Eisenberg and Norman McGary; NY: GP, c1959. (LITTLE GOLDEN BOOK 372).

822. <u>Woody Woodpecker joins the circus</u> by Walter Lantz, pictures by the Walter Lantz Studio adapted by Riley Thomson, story by Annie North Bedford; NY: S&S, c1952. LC# 52-1579. (LITTLE GOLDEN BOOK 145).

822a. ---- reissued in 1959 (LITTLE GOLDEN BOOK 330).

823. Woody Woodpecker takes a trip, Walter Lantz's story by
Ann McGovern, ill. by Al White and Ben DeNunez; NY: GP,
c1961. (LITTLE GOLDEN BOOK 445).

823a. ---- reissued (LITTLE GOLDEN BOOK 111-2).

Words. See Little golden book of words (419).

824. Words by Selma Lola Chambers, ill. by Louis Cary; NY:
GP, c1974. (LITTLE GOLDEN BOOK 202-42; 205-4).

Wyatt Earp. See Life and legend of Wyatt Earp (391).

825. Yakky Doodle and Chopper, Hanna-Barbera's by Pat Cherr,
ill. by Al White and Hawley Pratt; NY: GP, c1962. (LITTLE
GOLDEN BOOK 449).

826. Year in the city, A by Lucy Sprague Mitchell, ill. by
Tibor Gergely; NY: S&S, c1948. LC# 48-8178. Copyright A25504
dated 10 Aug 48. (LITTLE GOLDEN BOOK 48); (BANK STREET
BOOK).

827. Year on the farm, A by Lucy Sprague Mitchell, ill. by
Richard Floethe; NY: S&S, c1948. LC# 48-6216. Copyright
A23293 dated 8 Mar 48. (LITTLE GOLDEN BOOK 37); (BANK STREET
BOOK).

827FS. ---- [filmstrip] NY: S&S, released by Young America
Films, 1951. 1 filmstrip (38 fr., col., 35 mm) + teacher's
guide. LC# fia52-1748. (GOLDEN BOOK SERIES. SET NO. 3).

828. Yogi Bear by S. Quentin Hyatt, ill. by M. Kawaguchi and
Bob Barritt; NY: GP, c1960. (LITTLE GOLDEN BOOK 395).

Yogi Bear. See also Hey there! - It's Yogi Bear! (314).

829. Yogi Bear, a Christmas visit by Stuart Hyatt, ill. by
Sylvia and Burnett Mattinson; NY: GP, c1961. (LITTLE GOLDEN
BOOK 433).

830. Zorro, Walt Disney's adapted from the Walt Disney
television series featuring the famous character created by
Johnston McCulley, adapted by Charles Spain Verral, ill. by
John Steel; NY: GP, c1958. (WALT DISNEY BOOK D68).

831. Zorro and the secret plan, Walt Disney's adapted from
the Walt Disney television series featuring the famous
character created by Johnston McCulley, told by Charles
Spain Verral, ill. by Hamilton Greene; NY: GP, c1958. (WALT
DISNEY BOOK D77).

Series List

The arrangement of titles in the SERIES LIST follows either
an alphabetical or numerical scheme. Titles in series that
do not have their own numbering system (i.e. BANK STREET
BOOK, LITTLE GOLDEN BOOK AND RECORD and TWIN VISION BOOK)
are arranged alphabetically. Titles in series such as the
LITTLE GOLDEN BOOK, WALT DISNEY BOOK and LITTLE GOLDEN READ
ALONG are arranged according to the original series numbering
system (1, D1, and 3500 respectively). The number in
parenthesis following the title refers to the entry number in
the main TITLE LIST.

BANK STREET BOOK

The Bank Street College of Education is recognized as an
innovative leader in educational research pertaining to the
education of young children. From 1946-1951, a number of
LITTLE GOLDEN BOOK titles were written by those associated
with the school. Rather than having a separate numbering
system, the BANK STREET BOOK titles were incorporated into
the existing LITTLE GOLDEN BOOK numbering system. They bear
the familiar binding.

Fix it, please! (246)
Guess who lives here? (299)
I can fly (343)
New house in the forest (538)
Taxi that hurried (713)
Year in the city (826)
Year on the farm (827)

DING DONG SCHOOL BOOK

All of the titles in this series were written by Miss Frances
(Dr. Frances R. Horwich) from the popular Ding Dong School
television program. The DING DONG SCHOOL BOOK series had a
unique numbering system (Din1-8), but was issued in the
familiar LITTLE GOLDEN BOOK binding.

Din1   Jingle bell Jack (365)
Din2   Mr. Meyer's cow (494)
Din3   My daddy is a policeman (505)
Din4   We love Grandpa (785)
Din5   Here comes the band (311)
Din6   Magic wagon (457)
Din7   Lucky rabbit (449)
Din8   Our baby (562)

DISNEYLAND STORYTELLER CASSETTE

This series was issued by Walt Disney Productions in 1976.
The set consists of a book accompanied by a cassette. This
list includes only those titles that were originally a part
of the LITTLE GOLDEN BOOK series. The numbering system is
unique to this series and the books were issued in a paperback
format.

201B   Saggy baggy elephant (662SR)
202B   Tawny scrawny lion (711SR)
203B   Poky little puppy (600cSR)
204B   Rumpelstiltskin (658SR)
205B   Scuffy the tugboat (671SR)
206B   Thumbelina (729SR)
213B   Happy man and his dump truck (308aSR)
214B   Taxi that hurried (713SR)
216B   Little engine that could (404SR)
222B   Seven little postmen (673SR)
223B   There's no such thing as a dragon (718SR)
224B   Little fat policeman (406SR)

EAGER READER

Published by the Golden Press, the EAGER READERS were design-
ed for children who were beginning to read by themselves.The
EAGER READER series was published as a subseries within the
LITTLE GOLDEN BOOK line, issued in the same format.

800   New home for Snow Ball (537)
801   Pet in the jar (579)
802   Hat for the queen (309)
803   Boo and the flying Flews (088)
804   Little black puppy (397)
805   Who took the top hat trick? (803)
806   Cat who stamped his feet (127)
807   Elephant on wheels (224)
808   Monster! Monster! (485)
809   Bear's surprise party (055)

The following two filmstrip series were issued by the Education
Division of Western Publishing Co. in 1972. The package
consisted of a color filmstrip, a record, and a teacher's
guide written by Adelaide Holl. This list includes only those

titles that were originally a part of the LITTLE GOLDEN BOOK series.

EDUCATIONAL EXPERIENCES SOUND FILMSTRIPS: ABOUT MAKE-BELIEVE
    ANIMALS

Golden egg book (283FS)
Large and growly bear (380FS)
Tawny scrawny lion (711FS)

EDUCATIONAL EXPERIENCES SOUND FILMSTRIPS: IMAGINATIVE PLAY

Dragon in a wagon (221FS)

GIANT LITTLE GOLDEN BOOK

From 1957-1959, Simon & Schuster (later Golden Press), issued a series of GIANT LITTLE GOLDEN BOOKS. This new series resulted mainly from the compilation of three existing LITTLE GOLDEN BOOK stories into one longer book. For example, My pets (524), a GIANT LITTLE GOLDEN BOOK, combines My puppy (525), My kitten (513) and My snuggly bunny (526), all previously issued as single titles. The GIANT LITTLE GOLDEN BOOK titles consisted of 56 pages, but otherwise followed the familiar binding format.

5001   My little golden dictionary (522a)
5002   Five bedtime stories (243)
5003   My Christmas treasury (504)
5004   Favorite stories (234)
5005   Donald Duck treasury (213)
5006   Giant little golden book of animal stories (270)
5007   Mother Goose. Sixty seven favorite rhymes (489)
5008   Giant little golden book of dogs (272)
5009   Nursery tales (551)
5010   Wild animals (806)
5011   Giant little golden book of birds (271)
5012   Adventures of Lassie (005)
5013   Giant little golden book of kittens (273)
5014   Storytime book (698)
5015   Off to school (552)
5016   Mother Goose rhymes (492)
5017   Giant little golden book about plants and animals (269)
5018   Train stories (753)
5019   Cowboys and Indians (171)
5020   Fairy tales (229)
5021   Captain Kangaroo (119)
5022   Cub scouts (172)
5023   Fish (242)
5024   Quiz fun (614)
5025   My magic slate book (523)
5026   This world of ours (721)
5027   My pets (524)

GOLDEN BOOK SERIES. SET NO. 3

Eight LITTLE GOLDEN BOOK titles were included in this
filmstrip series released by Young America Films in 1951.
Each color filmstrip has an accompanying teacher's guide.

Circus time (153FS)
Color kittens (156FS)
Fix it, please! (246FS)
Fuzzy duckling (263FS)
Katie the kitten (373FS)
Seven sneezes (674FS)
We like to do things (784FS)
Year on the farm (827FS)

GOLDEN BOOK VIDEO
One of the newest formats for the Little Golden Books is the
videocasette. Familiar Little Golden Book titles are included with titles from other Golden book series.

13821   3 favorite Golden stories (671bVC, 719VC)
13822   3 best-loved Golden stories (663VC)
13863   5 Sesame Street stories (069VC)
13871   3 Richard Scarry animal nursery tales (276aVC)

LITTLE GOLDEN ACTIVITY BOOK

This series was created by Simon & Schuster as an offshoot
of the popular LITTLE GOLDEN BOOK series. Many of the books
employed the use of stamps, paper doll cut-outs, and movable
pieces. Some LITTLE GOLDEN BOOK titles were reissued as part
of this new series. LITTLE GOLDEN ACTIVITY BOOKS had a unique
numbering system, but the format was identical to the LITTLE
GOLDEN BOOK line.

A1   Little golden book of words (419a)
A2   Circus time (153a)
A3   Little golden paper dolls (424a)
A6   Trucks (760)
A7   Animal stamps (026)
A8   Bird stamps (077)
A9   Dog stamps (200)
A10   Mickey Mouse Club stamp book (475)
A11   Cowboy stamps (170)
A12   Baby Jesus stamps (040)
A13   Indian stamps (351)
A15   Trim the Christmas tree (759)
A16   Count to ten (164)
A17   Stop and go (694)
A18   ABC around the house (001a)
A19   Farm stamps (231)
A20   Car and truck stamps (124)
A21   Let's save money (389)
A24   Reading, writing and spelling stamps (627)

```
A25   Insect stamps (352)
A26   Trains (757)
A27   Fireman and fire engine stamps (239)
A28   Little golden book about colors (409)
A29   Animals and their babies (027)
A30   Little golden book of words (419b)
A31   Mike and Melissa and their magic mumbo jumbo (481)
A33   Sleeping Beauty paper dolls (681)
A36   Cinderella paper dolls (147)
A41   Hansel and Gretel: a paper doll story book (303)
A43   Count to ten (164a)
A44   ABC around the house (001b)
A45   Little golden book of words (419c)
A47   Little golden paper dolls (424b)
A50   Trim the Christmas tree (759a)
A52   Tammy (709)
---   How to tell time (328a)
```

LITTLE GOLDEN BOOK

The titles in the LITTLE GOLDEN BOOK series are arranged according to the series number that appears in the upper right corner of the book's front cover. The original series of numbers began in 1942 with number 1 and continued through 1973 ending with number 600.

New titles issued from 1971-1978 were assigned numbers previously used in the series. For example, LITTLE GOLDEN BOOK 102 was assigned to Ukelele and her new doll in 1951. The same number was used in 1974 for Daisy Dog's wake-up book. For these "second-use" numbers, I have added an "X" to the title number to signify that it is a new title with a previously assigned number.

LITTLE GOLDEN BOOK titles issued after 1978 also have a number in the upper right corner. This number consists of three digits, a hyphen, and either one or two additional digits. According to Steve Santi in his work on the Little Golden Book series, the numbering system adheres to the following code: "for example 101-42: 1 indicates assortment, 01 indicates category and -42 indicates position in category."[1]   Book titles issued within this numbering system are listed in this section following numbers 1-600 of the original series. Some titles in the new numbering system have been issued with more than one number and all numbers have not been used. The author therefore doubts that this is a complete listing of all new numbers.

A "V" following the series number indicates that a variant title exists for the same story with the same number.

----

[1] Santi, Steven J. A Guide to Little Golden Books. By the Author, 1985.

```
1     Three little kittens (725)
2     Bedtime stories (058)
3     Alphabet from A to Z (013)
4     Mother Goose (487)
5     Prayers for children (607)
6     Little red hen (436)
7     Nursery songs (549)
8     Poky little puppy (600)
9     Golden book of fairy tales (280,281)
10    Baby's book (044)
10V   My first book (507)
11    Animals of Farmer Jones (030)
12    This little piggy and other counting rhymes (720)
13    Golden book of birds (279)
14    Nursery tales (550)
15    Lively little rabbit (441)
16    Golden book of flowers (282)
17    Hansel and Gretel (302)
18    Day in the jungle (186)
19    My first book of Bible stories (508)
20    Night before Christmas (542,542a)
21    Tootle (747)
22    Toys (752)
23    Shy little kitten (678)
24    New house in the forest (538)
25    Taxi that hurried (713)
26    Christmas carols (141)
27    Story of Jesus (697)
28    Chip Chip (136)
29    Noises and Mr. Flibberty Jib (545)
30    Scuffy the tugboat (671)
31    Circus time (153)
32    Fix it, please (246)
33    Let's go shopping with Peter and Penny (387)
34    Little golden book of hymns (414)
35    Happy family (305)
36    Saggy baggy elephant (662)
37    Year on the farm (827)
38    Little golden book of poetry (416)
39    Animal babies (017)
40    Little golden book of singing games (417)
41    New baby (534)
42    Little Red Riding Hood (437)
43    Little pond in the woods (433)
44    Come play house (158)
44V   Come play with me (159)
45    Little golden book of words (419)
46    Golden sleepy book (286)
47    Three bears (722)
48    Year in the city (826)
49    Mr. Noah and his family (495)
50    Busy Timmy (118)
51    Seven sneezes (674)
52    Little Peewee (432)
53    Up in the attic (773)
54    Pat-a-cake (574)
```

55   Name for kitty (527)
56   Our puppy (564)
57   Little Black Sambo (398)
58   What am I? (787)
59   Nursery rhymes (548)
60   Guess who lives here (299)
61   Good morning and good night (292)
62   We like to do things (784)
63   Tommy's wonderful rides (745)
64   Five little firemen (244)
65   Gaston and Josephine (264)
66   Two little miners (766)
67   Jolly barnyard (369)
68   Little galoshes (407)
69   Bobby and his airplanes (085)
70   When you were a baby (793)
71   Johnny's machines (368)
72   Bugs Bunny (104)
73   Little Yip Yip and his bark (439)
74   Little golden funny book (421)
75   Katie the kitten (373)
76   Wonderful house (816)
77   Happy man and his dump truck (308)
78   Fuzzy duckling (263)
79   Little trapper (438)
80   Baby's house (047)
81   Duck and his friends (222)
82   Pets for Peter (587)
83   How big? (325)
84   Surprise for Sally (702)
85   Susie's new stove (704)
86   Color kittens (156)
87   Marvelous merry-go-round (463)
88   Day at the zoo (185)
89   Big brown bear (072)
90   My little golden dictionary (522)
91   Little fat policeman (406)
92   I can fly (343)
93   Brave cowboy Bill (096)
94   Jerry at school (362)
95   Christmas in the country (143)
96   When I grow up (792)
97   Little Benny wanted a pony (396)
98   Bugs Bunny's birthday (112)
99   Howdy Doody's circus (336)
100   Little boy with a big horn (401)
101   Little golden ABC (408)
102   Ukelele and her new doll (769)
102X Daisy Dog's wake-up book (174)
103   Christopher and the Columbus (145)
103X Fritzie goes home (256)
104   Just watch me (372)
105   Never pat a bear (531)
106   Magic next door (456)
107   Kitten's surprise (375)
107X Woodsy owl and the trail bikers (819)

108   Two little gardeners (765)
108X ABC is for Christmas (002)
109   Little golden holiday book (422)
109X Noah's ark (543)
110   Day at the beach (183)
110X David and Goliath (180)
111   Doctor Dan the bandage man (198)
111X I think about God (346)
112   Albert's zoo (008)
112X Book of God's gifts (089)
113   Little golden paper dolls (424)
113X Little Crow (403)
114   Pantaloon (570)
114X Stories of Jesus (696)
115   My home (510)
116   Laddie and the little rabbit (376)
116X Where did the baby go (794)
117   Tom and Jerry (737)
117X Pano the train (569)
118   Train to Timbuctoo (754)
119   Day at the playground (184)
119X Wizard of Oz (814)
120   Bugs Bunny and the Indians (105)
120X Oscar's book (561)
121   Howdy Doody and Clarabell (329)
121X Santa's surprise book (665)
122   Lucky Mrs. Ticklefeather (447)
122X Road Runner: a very scary lesson (637)
123   How to have a happy birthday (327)
123X Remarkably strong Pippi Longstocking (628)
124   Robert and his new friends (640)
124X Tom and Jerry's photo finish (741)
125   Boats (084)
125X Barbie (052)
126   Gingerbread shop (277)
126X Scooby Doo and the pirate treasure (670)
127   Bugs Bunny's carrot machine (113)
128   Mister Dog (482)
128X Tawny scrawny lion and the clever monkey (712)
129   Tex and his toys (716)
129X Bouncy baby bunny finds his bed (090)
130   What if? (788)
130X Poky little puppy follows his nose home (601)
131   Little golden book of dogs (411)
131X New friends for the saggy baggy elephant (536)
132   Whistling Wizard (799)
133   Rainy day play book (626)
133X Mr. Rogers' neighborhood - Henrietta meets someone
         new (497)
134   Seven little postmen (673)
134X Waltons and the birthday present (780)
135   Howdy Doody and the Princess (333)
135X Underdog and the disappearing ice cream (772)
136   Bugs Bunny gets a job (108)
136X Land of the lost - the surprise guest (379)

137   Puss in boots (610)
137X Magic friend-maker (455)
138   Tawny scrawny lion (711)
139   Fun with decals (260)
139X Raggedy Ann and Andy - The little gray kitten (621)
140   Mr. Wigg's birthday party (498)
140X Pink Panther in the haunted house (591)
141   Wheels (791)
141X Tweety plays catch the puddy tat (761)
142   Frosty the snow man (258)
143   Here comes the parade (312)
143X Runaway squash (659)
144   Road to Oz (639)
144X My Christmas treasury (501)
145   Woody Woodpecker joins the circus (822)
145X Bugs Bunny - Too many carrots (111)
146   Magic compass (454)
146X Porky Pig and Bugs Bunny - Just like magic (606)
147   Hopalong Cassidy and Bar-20 Cowboy (321)
147X Where Jesus lived (797)
148   Little golden book of Uncle Wiggly (418)
148X Ginghams - The backward picnic (278)
149   Indian, Indian (350)
149X Woody Woodpecker at the circus (820)
150   Rootie Kazootie, detective (649)
150X Cats (128)
151   Emerald city of Oz (226)
151X Wild kingdom (808)
152   All aboard (012)
152X Big enough helper (073)
153   Thumbelina (729)
153X Bible stories from the Old Testament (067)
154   Nurse Nancy (547)
154X Animals' Christmas eve (028)
155   Little Eskimo (403)
155X Shazam! (676)
156   Sailor dog (663)
156X Raggedy Ann and Andy help Santa Claus (620)
157   Doctor Squash, the doll doctor (199)
157X Big Bird's red book (071)
158   Christmas story (144)
159   Tin Woodman of Oz (732)
159X Cookie Monster and the cookie tree (160)
160   Danny Beaver's secret (178)
160X Donny and Marie - The top secret project (220)
161   Topsy turvy circus (749)
161X Bugs Bunny, pioneer (110)
162   Little red caboose (435)
162X Superstar Barbie (700)
163   My kitten (513)
163X What Lily Goose found (789)
164   Bugs Bunny at the county fair (106)
164X Rabbit's adventure (617)
165   Gingerbread man (276)
165X Benji, fastest dog in the West (060)
166   Wiggles (804)

```
167  Animal friends (021)
168  My teddy bear (527)
168X Circus is in town (152)
169  Rabbit and his friends (615)
170  Merry shipwreck (467)
170X Best of all! (063)
171  Howdy Doody's lucky trip (337)
171X Whales (786)
172  Howdy Doody in funland (334)
173  Three billy goats gruff (724)
173X Rabbit is next (616)
174  Bible stories of boys and girls (068)
175  Uncle Mistletoe (770)
175X Where will all the animals go? (798)
176  Little golden Christmas manger (420)
176X ABC around the house (001)
177  Roy Rogers and the new cowboy (654)
178  Brave little tailor (098)
179  Jack and the beanstalk (357)
180  Airplanes (006)
181  Tom and Jerry meet Little Quack (738)
181X Jack and the beanstalk (357a)
182  Gingerbread man (276b)
183  Bugs Bunny at the Easter party (107)
184  Howdy Doody and his magic hat (330)
184X Birds (078)
185  Laddie the superdog (377)
185X Let's go, trucks! (388)
186  Madeline (453)
186X Petey and I (586)
187  Daddies (173)
188  Hi ho! Three in a row (315)
189  Musicians of Bremen (500)
190  Rootie Kazootie, baseball star (648)
191  Party pig (573)
192  Heidi (310)
193  Paper doll wedding (571)
194  Twelve dancing princesses (762)
195  Roy Rogers and Cowboy Toby (651)
196  Georgie finds a Grandpa (268)
197  Tom and Jerry's merry Christmas (739)
198  First Bible stories (240)
199  Friendly book (255)
200  Golden goose (285)
201  From then to now (257)
202  Little Indian (427)
203  Little Lulu and her magic tricks (429)
204  Howdy Doody and Mr. Bluster (331)
204X Three bears (722b)
205  Prayers for children (607a)
206  Little gray donkey (426)
207  Open up my suitcase (560)
208  Tiger's adventure (731)
209  Little red hen (436a)
210  Kitten who thought he was a mouse (374)
211  Animals of Farmer Jones (030a)
212  Pierre Bear (589)
```

213 Dale Evans and the lost gold mine (176)
214 Linda and her little sister (392)
215 Bunny book (115)
216 Happy family (305a)
217 Hansel and Gretel (302a)
218 House that Jack built (323)
219 Giant with the three golden hairs (275)
220 Pony for Tony (605)
221 Annie Oakley and the rustlers (032)
222 Circus ABC (150)
223 It's Howdy Doody time (354)
224 Smokey the bear (687)
225 Three little kittens (725a)
226 Rootie Kazootie joins the circus (650)
227 Twins (764)
228 Snow White and Rose Red (688)
229 Houses (324)
230 Gene Autry (266)
231 Roy Rogers and the mountain lion (653)
232 Little Red Riding Hood (437a)
233 My puppy (525)
234 J. Fred Muggs (355)
235 Tom and Jerry's party (740)
236 Heroes of the Bible (313)
237 Howdy Doody and Santa Claus (332)
238 5 pennies to spend (245)
239 Bedtime stories (058a)
240 Mother Goose (487a)
241 Night before Christmas (542b)
242 Our world (565)
243 Numbers (546)
244 Scuffy the tugboat (671a)
245 Out of my window (566)
246 Rin Tin Tin and Rusty (634)
247 Happy days (304)
248 Shy little kitten (678a)
249 Animal gym (022)
250 My snuggly bunny (526)
251 Cars (125)
252 Howdy Doody's animal friends (335)
253 Dale Evans and the coyote (175)
254 Buffalo Bill, Jr. and the Indian chief (103)
255 Lassie shows the way (385)
256 Daniel Boone (177)
257 Counting rhymes (165a)
258 Heidi (310a)
259 Roy Rogers and the Indian sign (652)
260 Little golden book of dogs (411a)
261 Captain Kangaroo (120)
262 Raggedy Ann and the cookie snatcher (623)
263 Lone Ranger (442)
264 Just for fun (371)
265 Pal and Peter (568)
266 Winky Dink (810)
267 Gene Autry and Champion (267)
268 My little golden book about God (516)

```
269   My little golden book about travel (518)
270   My little golden book about the sky (517)
271   Poky little puppy (600a)
272   Farmyard friends (232)
273   Romper Room do bees (645)
274   Baby animals (037)
275   Annie Oakley, sharpshooter (033)
276   Rin Tin Tin and the lost Indian (635)
277   Lassie and the daring rescue (383)
278   Captain Kangaroo and the panda (122)
279   My baby brother (501)
280   Little golden paper dolls (424c)
281   Jack and the beanstalk (357b)
282   Animals of Farmer Jones (030b)
283   Little golden Mother Goose (423)
284   Little golden book about the seashore (410)
285   How to tell time (328)
286   Fury (261)
287   Cleo (154)
288   Three little kittens (725b)
289   Child's garden of verses (134)
290   Circus boy (151)
291   New baby (534a)
292   Our puppy (564a)
293   Wonders of nature (818)
294   Brave Eagle (097)
295   Doctor Dan, the bandage man (198a)
296   Little red hen (436b)
297   Lone Ranger and Tonto (444)
298   My little golden Christmas book (521)
299   Broken arrow (100)
300   My kitten (513a)
301   Five little firemen (244a)
302   New kittens (539)
303   Baby's Mother Goose (048)
304   Rin Tin Tin and the outlaw (636)
305   White bunny and his magic nose (800)
306   Rumplestiltskin (658)
307   Lassie and her day in the sun (381)
308   Jack's adventure (358)
309   Three bedtime stories (723)
310   Lone Ranger and the talking pony (443)
311   Tom and Jerry meet Little Quack (738a)
312   Bugs Bunny (104a)
313   Tale of Peter Rabbit (707)
314   Pussy Willow (611)
315   Life and legend of Wyatt Earp (391)
315X  Together book (736)
316   Monsters at the end of this book (484)
317   More Mother Goose rhymes (486)
318   Cheyenne (132)
319   Little red caboose (435a)
320   Gunsmoke (301)
321   Bert's hall of great inventions (061)
322   Four little kittens (251)
323   Ali Baba and the forty thieves (009)
```

324 Day at the zoo (185a)
325 Play ball (595)
326 Wagon train (777)
327 Good-bye, tonsils (289)
328 Tales of Wells Fargo (708)
329 Animals' Merry Christmas (029)
330 Woody Woodpecker joins the circus (822a)
331 Rudolph the red-nosed reindeer (655)
332 Wild animal babies (805)
333 Baby farm animals (039)
334 Animal orchestra (023)
335 Big brown bear (072a)
336X Mother Goose in the city (489)
336 Fury takes the jump (262)
337 Numbers (546a)
338 Deep blue sea (189)
339 Boats (084a)
340 My baby sister (502)
341 Captain Kangaroo's surprise party (123)
342 Exploring space (228)
343 Lassie and the lost explorer (384)
344 Happy golden ABC (306)
345 Smokey Bear finds a helper (686)
346 Nurse Nancy (547a)
347 Leave it to Beaver (386)
348 Nursery songs (549a)
349 Animal alphabet from A to Z (016)
350 Forest hotel (250)
351 Tiger's adventure (731a)
352 We help Mommy (782)
353 Tom Thumb (742)
354 Maverick (466)
355 Dinosaurs (194)
356 Steve Canyon (692)
357 Little golden book of helicopters (412)
358 Baby's first book (045)
359 Puss in boots (610a)
360 Party in Shariland (572)
361 Counting rhymes (165b)
362X Pussycat Tiger (612)
363 Scuffy the tugboat (671b)
364 Bedtime stories (058b)
365 Animal friends (021a)
365X Baby's birthday (043)
366 Cars and trucks (126)
367 Lion's paw (393)
368 Baby's first Christmas (046)
369 Little golden picture dictionary (425)
370 New puppy (541)
371 Aladdin and his magic lamp (007)
372 Woody Woodpecker drawing fun for beginners (821)
373 Airplanes (006a)
374 Blue book of fairy tales (083)
375 Chipmunk's Merry Christmas (138)
376 Huckleberry Hound builds a house (340)
377 Naughty bunny (531)

378   Ruff and Reddy (657)
379   Animal dictionary (020)
380   Birds of all kinds (079)
381   Three little kittens (725c)
382   Fire engines (236)
383   Baby listens (041)
384   How to have a happy birthday (327a)
385   Saggy baggy elephant (662a)
386   Dennis the Menace and Ruff (191)
387   Smokey and his animal friends (684)
388   Our flag (563)
389   Cowboy ABC (169)
390   Little golden Mother Goose (423a)
391   Little golden book of dogs (411b)
392   Little golden book of hymns (414a)
393   Happy little whale (307)
394   Wild animals (807)
395   Yogi Bear (828)
396   Animal quiz (024)
397   Bear in the boat (054)
398   Quick Draw McGraw (613)
399   Doctor Dan at the circus (197)
400   Old MacDonald had a farm (553)
401   Raggedy Ann and Andy and the rainy day circus (619)
402   Bravest of all (099)
403   Huckleberry Hound and the Christmas sleigh (339)
404   Baby looks (042)
405   Four puppies (252)
406   Huckleberry Hound and his friends (338)
407   Day on the farm (187)
408   Rocky and his friends (644)
409   Brownie scouts (101)
410   New pony (540)
411   Sly little bear and other bears (683)
412   Dennis the Menace - A quiet afternoon (190)
413   Chicken Little (133)
414   Little Cottontail (402)
415   Lassie shows the way (385a)
416   Wacky Witch and the mystery of the king's gold (776)
417   Loopy De Loop goes West (445)
418   My dolly and me (506)
419   Rupert the rhinoceros (660)
420   Jack and the beanstalk (357c)
421   Captain Kangaroo and the panda (122a)
422   Baby's Mother Goose (048a)
423   Smokey Bear and the campers (685)
424   My little golden book of jokes (519)
425   I'm an Indian today (348)
426   Country mouse and the city mouse (166)
427   Captain Kangaroo and the beaver (121)
428   Home for a bunny (319)
429   Farmyard friends (232a)
430   Bugs Bunny and the Indians (105a)
431   National Velvet (530)
432   Dennis the Menace waits for Santa (192)
433   Yogi Bear - A Christmas visit (829)

```
434  My first counting book (510)
435  When you were a baby (793a)
436  Color kittens (156b)
437  Gingerbread man (276a)
438  Little red hen (436d)
439  Make way for the highway (459)
439V Make way for the thruway (460)
440  Bobby the dog (086)
441  Bunny's magic tricks (117)
441X My little golden animal book (515)
442  Cindy Bear (149)
443  Puff the blue kitten (608)
444  Hokey Wolf and Ding-a-Ling (318)
445  Woody Woodpecker takes a trip (823)
445X My first counting book (510a)
446  Bozo the clown (095)
447  Good night, Little Bear (294)
448  My teddy bear (527a)
449  Yakky Doodle and Chopper (825)
450  Flintstones (247)
451  10 little animals (715)
452  Busy Timmy (118a)
453  Sticks (693)
453X Top Cat (748)
454  Pixie and Dixie and Mr. Jinks (594)
455  Machines (451)
456  Golden egg book (283)
457  Littlest raccoon (440)
458  Huckleberry Hound safety signs (341)
459  Horses (322)
460  My little golden book of manners (520)
461  Pick up sticks (588)
462  Bullwinkle (114)
463  Wait-for-me kitten (778)
464  Baby farm animals (039a)
465  My little golden animal book (515a)
466  Baby dear (038)
467  Where is the poky little puppy? (796)
468  We help Daddy (781)
469  My puppy (525a)
470  Heidi (310b)
471  Tommy's camping adventure (744)
472  Little golden Mother Goose (423b)
473  Nurse Nancy (547b)
474  Touche turtle (750)
475  Bugs Bunny (104b)
476  Little Lulu (428)
477  Ruff and Reddy (657a)
478  Christmas ABC (140)
479  Rusty goes to school (661)
480  Tommy visits the doctor (743)
481  Smokey the bear (687a)
482  Big little book (074)
483  Mister Ed (483)
484  Play Street (596)
485  Bozo finds a friend (094)
```

486 Corky (161)
487 Golden goose (285a)
488 Gay purr-ee (265)
489 Baby's first book (045a)
489X Aren't you glad? (034)
490 Riddles, riddles A to Z (632)
491 Hansel and Gretel (302b)
492 Supercar (699)
493 Child's garden of verses (134a)
494 Shy little kitten (678b)
495 I have a secret (344)
496 Colors are nice (157)
497 Dick Tracy (193)
498 Rumplestiltskin (658a)
499 Wild animals (807a)
500 Jetsons (363)
500X Buck Rogers and the children of Hopetown (102)
501 Boats (084b)
501X Black hole (082)
502 Wally Gator (779)
503 Corky's hiccups (162)
504 Seven little postmen (673a)
505 Tale of Peter Rabbit (707a)
506 Poky little puppy (600b)
507 Who needs a cat? (802)
508 Lippy the Lion and Hardy Har Har (394)
509 What am I? (787a)
510 Large and growly bear (380)
511 Visit to the children's zoo (775)
512 Chipmunk's ABC (137)
513 My baby sister (502a)
514 Thumbelina (729a)
515 Lisa and the eleven swans (395)
515X Neatos and the litterbugs (532)
516 Cow went over the mountain (168)
517 Baby animals (037a)
518 Lassie and her day in the sun (381a)
519 Little red hen (436c)
520 Happy man and his dump truck (308a)
521 Fun for Hunky Dory (259)
522 Jamie looks (359)
523 Bow Wow! Meow! (091)
524 Baby's house (047a)
524X Chicken little (133a)
525 My word book (528)
526 Twelve days of Christmas (763)
527 Romper Room exercise book (646)
528 My kitten (513b)
529 Nursery songs (549b)
530 Four little kittens (251a)
531 Pebbles Flintstone (576)
532 Tawny scrawny lion (711a)
532X Dogs (201)
533 Fuzzy duckling (263a)
533X Animal dictionary (020a)
534 First golden geography (241)

535 Dennis the Menace and Ruff (191a)
536 Little boy and the giant (400)
537 Beaney goes to sea (053)
538 Bedtime stories (058c)
539 Cave kids (129)
540 Bamm-Bamm, with Pebbles Flintstone (051)
541 New baby (534b)
542 Hey there - It's Yogi Bear! (314)
543 ABC rhymes (003)
544 Three little pigs (726)
545 Jack and the beanstalk (356)
546 Fireball XL5 (238)
547 Magilla Gorilla (458)
548 Little engine that could (404)
549 Tarzan (710)
550 Good humor man (290)
551 Lively little rabbit (441a)
552 We like kindergarten (783)
553 Jingle bells (366)
554 Charmin' Chatty (131)
555 Pepper plays nurse (577)
556 Peter Potamus (584)
557 Fuzzy duckling (263b)
558 Hop little kangaroo (320)
559 Betsy McCall (064)
560 Animal friends (021b)
561 Tom and Jerry (737a)
562 Good little, bad little girl (291)
563 Mr. Puffer-Bill (496)
564 New brother, new sister (535)
565 Dragon in a wagon (221)
566 Cars (125a)
567 Play with me (597)
568 Where is the bear? (795)
569 Little Mommy (431)
570 Things in my house (719)
571 My little dinosaur (514)
572 Lassie and the big clean up day (382)
573 Animals on the farm (031)
574 So big (690)
575 Who comes to your house? (801)
576 Animal daddies and my daddy (019)
577 Hush, hush, it's sleepytime (342)
578 When I grow up (792a)
579 Ookpik, the Arctic owl (559)
580 Sam, the firehouse cat (664)
581 Chitty Chitty Bang Bang (139)
582 Wonderful school (817)
583 Little book (399)
584 Animal counting book (018)
585 Raggedy Ann and Fido (622)
586 Rags (624)
587 Charlie (130)
588 Boy with a drum (092)
589 Mother Goose, Eloise Wilkin's (488)
590 Tiny, tawny kitten (733)

591 Old Mother Hubbard (554)
592 Friendly book (255a)
593 I like to live in the city (345)
594 1-2-3 juggle with me (558)
595 Christmas carols (141a)
596 Jenny's new brother (360)
597 Fly high (248)
598 Bozo and the hide 'n' seek elephant (093)
599 Let's visit the dentist (390)
600 Susan in the driver's seat (703)

800 New home for Snow Ball (537)
801 Pet in the jar (579)
802 Hat for the queen (309)
803 Boo and the flying Flews (088)
804 Little black puppy (397)
805 Who took the top hat trick? (803)
806 Cat who stamped his feet (127)
807 Elephant on wheels (224)
808 Monster! Monster! (485)
809 Bear's surprise party (055)

100-44 Mickey Mouse and Goofy: the big bear scare (468a)
100-46 Mickey Mouse's picnic (479a)
100-57 Sport Goofy and the racing robot (691)
101-41 Winnie-the-Pooh and Tigger (811a)
101-42 Winnie-the-Pooh meets Gopher (812a)
102-44 Donald Duck, instant millionaire (209a)
103-41 Alice in Wonderland meets the white rabbit (011a)
103-43 Cinderella (146c)
103-44 Toad flies high (734)
103-55 Return to Oz: Dorothy saves the Emerald City (630)
104-34 Dumbo (223a)
104-41 Peter Pan and Wendy (583c)
104-44 Fox and the hound (254)
105-43 Rescuers (629a)
105-45 Lady (378b)
105-47 Sport Goofy and the racing robot (691)
105-54 Black cauldron (081)
105-56 Return to Oz: escape from the witch's castle (631)
106-4   Favorite nursery tales (233a)
106-9   Bambi (049b)
106-41 Bambi (049b)
106-42 Bambi, friends of the forest (050a)
107-3   Raggedy Ann and the cookie snatcher (623a)
107-4   Raggedy Ann and Andy: Five birthday parties ...(618)
107-21 Raggedy Ann and Andy: the little gray kitten (621a)
107-22 Raggedy Ann and Andy and the rainy-day circus (619a)
107-41 Raggedy Ann and Andy: the little gray kitten (621a)
107-47 Bisketts in double trouble (080)
107-48 Rainbow Brite and the brook meadow deer (625)
107-59 Inspector Gadget in Africa (353)
107-61 Big Bird's day on the farm (070)
108-3   Together book (736a)

```
108-21   Oscar's book (561a)
108-22   Big Bird's red book (071a)
108-23   Together book (736a)
108-24   Four seasons (253)
108-41   Oscar's book (561a)
108-44   Four seasons (253)
108-45   Amazing Mumford forgets the magic words (015)
108-46   Grover's own alphabet (298)
108-56   Grover's own alphabet (298)
108-57   Big Bird brings Spring to Sesame Street (069)
109-4    Many faces of Ernie (462)
109-5    Ernie's work of art (227)
109-9    I think that it is wonderful (347)
109-21   Monster at the end of this book (484a)
109-22   Cookie monster and the cookie tree (160a)
109-23   Bert's hall of great inventions (061a)
109-24   Many faces of Ernie (462)
109-25   Ernie's work of art (227)
109-31   Monster at the end of this book (484a)
109-46   Puppy love (609)
110-21   Bugs Bunny - too many carrots (111a)
110-22   Porky Pig and Bugs Bunny. Just like magic! (606a)
110-23   Bugs Bunny's carrot machine (113a)
110-38   Mrs. Brisby and the magic stone (499)
110-41   Bugs Bunny - too many carrots (111a)
110-44   Bugs Bunny pioneer (110a)
110-55   Bugs Bunny marooned! (109)
110-57   Road Runner: mid-mesa marathon (638)
110-58   Robotman & friends at school (643)
111-2    Woody Woodpecker takes a trip (823a)
111-3    Woody Woodpecker at the circus (820a)
111-6    Benji, fastest dog in the West (060a)
111-8    Superstar Barbie (700a)
111-21   Smokey the bear (687b)
111-24   Tweety plays catch the puddy tat (761a)
111-25   Road Runner: a very scary lesson (637a)
111-43   Woody Woodpecker at the circus (820a)
111-44   Tweety plays catch the puddy tat (761a)
111-50   Ronald McDonald and the tale of the talking ...(647)
111-60   Pink Panther and sons: Fun at the picnic (590)
115-5    Pink Panther in the haunted house (591a)
200-2    Happy golden ABC (306a)
200-3    ABC rhymes (003a)
200-6    Feelings from A to Z (235)
200-9    Right's animal farm (633)
200-21   Little golden ABC (408a)
200-25   ABC around the house (001c)
200-41   Animals on the farm (031a)
200-44   Jolly barnyard (369a)
201-1    My first counting book (510b)
201-2    1-2-3 juggle with me (558a)
201-4    Circus is in town (152a)
201-10   Animal quiz (024a)
201-10   Adventures of goat (004)
201-23   Numbers (546b)
201-25   Forest hotel (250a)
```

```
201-42   Saggy baggy elephant (662b)
201-43   Tawny scrawny lion (711b)
201-44   Lively little rabbit (441b)
201-45   Theodore Mouse goes to sea (717)
202-1    Birds (078a)
202-2    Horses (322a)
202-3    Little golden book of dogs (411c)
202-4    Four puppies (252a)
202-5    New puppy (541a)
202-7    Cats (128a)
202-26   Dinosaurs (194a)
202-28   Color kittens (156c)
202-41   Little golden picture dictionary (425b)
202-42   Words (824)
203-3    Animals on the farm (031a)
203-4    Best of all (063a)
203-21   Day on the farm (187a)
203-22   Baby farm animals (039b)
203-41   My first counting book (510b)
203-42   1-2-3 juggle with me (558a)
203-54   Ten items or less (714)
203-55   Fire fighters' counting book (237)
203-56   Count all the way to Sesame Street (163)
204-1    Visit to the children's zoo (775a)
204-3    Where is the bear? (795a)
204-4    Whales (786a)
204-5    Where will all the animals go? (798a)
204-22   Baby animals (037b)
204-27   Mister Dog (482a)
204-37   Mister Dog (482a)
204-43   Hiram's red shirt (317)
204-54   Store-bought doll (695)
204-55   Bialosky's special picnic (066)
204-56   Amanda's first day of school (014)
205-1    Animal dictionary (020b)
205-4    Words (824)
205-32   Little golden picture dictionary (425a)
205-41   Color kittens (156c)
205-42   What will I be? (790)
205-51   If I had a dog (349)
205-56   Willie found a wallet (809)
206-1    My home (512a)
206-3    What will I be? (790)
206-21   My home (512a)
206-22   Things in my house (719a)
206-24   Friendly book (255b)
206-44   Where is the bear (795a)
206-52   Very best home for me (774)
206-55   Gull that lost the sea (300)
207-3    Bow wow! Meow! (091a)
207-4    Giant who wanted company (274)
207-21   Colors are nice (157a)
207-22   We like kindergarten (783a)
207-41   Hansel and Gretel (302c)
208-1    We help Daddy (781a)
208-2    We help Mommy (782a)
```

```
208-4    Bravest of all (099a)
208-5    Big enough helper (073a)
208-41   Big enough helper (073a)
208-42   One of the family (557)
208-52   One of the family (557)
208-54   Good night, Aunt Lilly (293)
209-1    New baby (534c)
209-2    Where did the baby go? (794a)
209-4    Baby Dear (038a)
209-5    Baby's birthday (043a)
209-23   Little book   (399a)
209-26   So big (690a)
209-27   Golden sleepy book (286a)
209-41   Friendly book (255b)
209-56   Best friends (062)
209-57   Good-by day (288)
209-58   Little golden book of holidays (413)
210-1    Pano the train (569a)
210-2    Fire engines (236a)
210-34   Mr. Bell's fixit shop (493)
211-1    Let's go trucks (388a)
211-3    Cars (125b)
211-22   Cars and trucks (126a)
211-45   Theodore Mouse goes to sea (717)
211-45   Little golden book of jokes & riddles (415)
211-51   Rainy day play book (626a)
211-56   Shoelace box (677)
211-57   Little golden book of hymns (414c)
300-3    Mother Goose in the city (491a)
300-21   Little golden Mother Goose (423c)
300-22   Mother Goose, Eloise Wilkin's (488a)
300-41   Owl and the pussycat (567)
300-42   Old Mother Hubbard (554a)
301-2    Poky little puppy (600c)
301-4    Lassie and the big clean-up day (382a)
301-21   Poky little puppy follows his nose home (601a)
301-23   Lassie and her day in the sun (381b)
301-41   Sleepy book (682)
301-53   Hush, hush, it's sleepytime (342a)
302-3    Three little kittens (725d)
302-21   Four little kittens (251b)
302-22   Shy little kitten (678c)
302-24   Pussy Willow (611a)
302-32   Shy little kitten (678c)
302-41   Pussy Willow (611a)
302-44   Charlie (130a)
302-51   Little pussycat (434)
302-55   Polly's pet (603)
303-21   Old MacDonald had a farm (553b)
303-22   Jolly barnyard (369a)
303-23   Animals of Farmer Jones (030c)
303-44   Rags (624a)
304-2    My little dinosaur (514a)
304-4    Saggy baggy elephant (662b)
304-21   Large and growly bear (380a)
304-23   Tawny scrawny lion (711b)
```

```
304-25   Animal friends (021c)
304-25   Very best home for me (774)
304-41   Big brown bear (072b)
304-42   Large and growly bear (380a)
304-58   Cow and the elephant (167)
305-21   Scuffy the tugboat (671c)
305-41   We help Daddy (781a)
305-44   My home (512a)
305-55   Grandma and Grandpa Smith (296)
306-21   Tootle (747a)
306-22   Little red caboose (435b)
306-44   Where did the baby go? (794a)
306-51   When you were a baby (793b)
307-1    Three bears (722a)
307-22   Three bears (722c)
307-23   Jack and the beanstalk (356a)
307-41   Noah's ark (543a)
307-42   Tale of Peter Rabbit (707b)
307-47   Musicians of Bremen (500a)
307-56   Elves and the shoemaker (225)
308-1    Heidi (310c)
308-21   Heidi (310c)
308-22   Hansel and Gretel (302c)
308-41   Whales (786a)
308-44   Animal quiz book (025)
308-54   Animal quiz book (025)
308-55   How does your garden grow? (326)
308-56   My first book of the planets (509)
309-21   Little Red Riding Hood (437b)
309-22   Three little pigs (726a)
309-44   Cats (128a)
310-21   Gingerbread man (276c)
310-22   Wizard of Oz  (814a)
310-44   Scuffy the tugboat (671c)
311-1    Counting rhymes (165c)
311-5    Boy with a drum (092a)
311-7    Ginghams! The backwards picnic (278a)
311-22   Bedtime stories (058d)
311-23   Three bedtime stories (723a)
311-26   Just for fun (371a)
311-43   Bunny book (115a)
400-1    Noah's ark (543a)
401-1    David and Goliath (180b)
402-1    Stories of Jesus (696a)
403-1    Little golden book of hymns (414b)
404-1    Bible stories of boys and girls (068a)
405-1    Prayers for children (607b)
406-1    Heroes of the Bible (313a)
408-1    Where Jesus lived (797a)
409-1    Bible stories from the Old Testament (067a)
410-1    I think about God (346a)
411-1    Book of God's gifts (089a)
451-1    Frosty the snowman   (258a)
452-1    Rudolph the red-nosed reindeer (655a)
452-42   Rudolph the red-nosed reindeer shines again (656)
454-1    ABC is for Christmas (002a)
```

454-42   Twelve days of Christmas (763a)
455-1   My Christmas treasury (503a)
456-1   Animals' Christmas eve (028a)
457-1   Raggedy Ann and Andy help Santa Claus (620a)
459-1   Santa's surprise book (665a)
459-8   Biggest most beautiful Christmas tree (076)
459-9   Mickey's Christmas carol (480)
460-41   Christmas donkey (142)
471-21   Rabbit's adventure (617a)
472-21   Rabbit and his friends (615a)
473-21   Bunny book (115a)
474-1   Rabbit is next (616a)
477-21   Home for a bunny (319a)
478-21   Golden egg book (283a)
479-21   Tale of Peter Rabbit (707b)
482-21   Fuzzy duckling (263c)

---   Bialosk 's Christmas (065)
---   Jenny's surprise summer (361)
---   Poky little puppy's naughty day (602)
---   There's no such thing as a dragon (718)

LITTLE GOLDEN BOOK AND CASSETTE

Produced by Walt Disney Productions in 1976, this set
contained a cassette and a book.

Poky Little puppy (600cSR)
Thumbelina (729SR)

LITTLE GOLDEN BOOK AND RECORD

A series produced by Walt Disney Productions in 1976,
consisted of a 7 inch record accompanied by a LITTLE
GOLDEN BOOK.

Circus time (153SR)
Color kittens (156SR)
Happy man and his dump truck (308aSR)
Large and growly bear (380SR)
Little boy with a big horn (401SR)
Little fat policeman (406SR)
Lively little rabbit (441SR)
Poky little puppy (600cSR)
Pussycat tiger (612SR)
Rudolph the red-nosed reindeer (655SR)
Saggy baggy elephant (662SR)
Scuffy the tugboat (671SR)
Tawny scrawny lion (711SR)
Taxi that hurried (713SR)

LITTLE GOLDEN BOOK LIBRARY

These titles, published in 1969, were compilations of favorite
LITTLE GOLDEN BOOK titles. The compilation was necessarily in
a much larger format than the familiar LITTLE GOLDEN BOOK
series.

Bedtime stories (Ø57)
Fairy tales and rhymes (23Ø)
Golden favorites (284)

LITTLE GOLDEN BOOKS FILMSTRIPS AND BOOKS

This filmstrip series was produced by Miller-Brody, a
division of Random House. The set contained a color filmstrip
and cassette.

Neatos and the litterbugs (532FS)
Poky little puppy (6ØØFS)
Saggy baggy elephant (662FS)
Shy little kitten (678FS)
Tawny scrawny lion (711FS)
Tootle (747FS)

LITTLE GOLDEN READ ALONG

Produced by Western Publishing Co. in 1977, this series
consisted of a cassette, a LITTLE GOLDEN BOOK and a teacher's
guide written by Joanne Wylie. The series was designed to
allow the child to follow along in his book while the same
story was read on the cassette. This series had a unique
numbering system, but the books had the familiar binding.

3500   Bouncy baby bunny finds his bed (Ø9ØSR)
3501   Corky's hiccups (162SR)
3502   Forest hotel (25ØSR)
3503   Large and growly bear (38ØSR)
3504   Magic friend-maker (455SR)
3505   Neatos and the litterbugs (532SR)
3506   New friends for the saggy baggy elephant (536SR)
3507   Pano the train (569SR)
3508   Poky little puppy (6ØØSR)
3509   Pussycat tiger (612SR)
3510   Rags (624SR)
3511   Tawny scrawny lion and the clever monkey (712SR)

LITTLE GOLDEN RECORD

Simon & Schuster issued the first LITTLE GOLDEN RECORDS in
the Summer of 1948. The 78 rpm, yellow plastic records were
an instant success with the public. This new line had a
numbering system which appears to the left of the title in
the listing below.

```
 1  Scuffy the tugboat (671SR)
 2  Lively little rabbit (441SR)
 3  Shy little kitten (678SR)
 4  Tootle (747SR)
 5  Poky little puppy (600SR)
 6  Circus time (153SR)
 9  Little Peewee (432SR)
10  Golden egg (283SR)
11  Big brown bear (072SR)
13  Animals of Farmer Jones (030SR)
```

MICKEY MOUSE CLUB BOOK

Issued by Walt Disney Productions, the MICKEY MOUSE CLUB
BOOK series contained titles from the WALT DISNEY BOOK series.
This series utilized the same numbering system as the WALT
DISNEY BOOK series and was in the same format as the LITTLE
GOLDEN BOOK series. Rather than the traditional gold foil
spine, the MICKEY MOUSE CLUB BOOK series had a red foil
spine imprinted with pictures of Mickey Mouse. The use of
the "X" following D55 signifies that two titles were issued
with the same series number.

```
D3    Dumbo (223)
D4    Snow White and the seven dwarfs (689)
D6    Uncle Remus (771)
D7    Bambi (049)
D8    Pinocchio (592)
D9    Bongo (087)
D10   Three little pigs (727)
D13   Cinderella (146)
D14   Donald Duck's adventure (214)
D18   Donald Duck's toy train (219)
D33   Mickey Mouse goes Christmas shopping (477)
D35   Seven dwarfs find a house (672)
D41   Donald Duck's safety book (217)
D42   Lady (378)
D43   Disneyland on the air (195)
D44   Donald Duck in Disneyland (208)
D45   Davy Crockett, king of the wild frontier (181)
D46   Little man of Disneyland (430)
D47   Davy Crockett's keelboat race (182)
D48   Robin Hood (641)
D49   Donald Duck, prize driver (212)
D50   Jiminy Cricket (364)
D51   Mother Goose (491a)
D52   Goofy, movie star (295)
D53   Mickey Mouse flies the Christmas mail (476)
D54   Perri and her friends (578)
D55   Donald Duck and the Mouseketeers (203)
D55X  Day with Donald Duck (188)
D56   Peter and the wolf (580)
D57   Mickey Mouse and the missing Mouseketeers (473)
D58   Cinderella's friends (148)
```

READ AND HEAR

This series, issued with a Golden Record imprint, paired a
Golden Record with a LITTLE GOLDEN BOOK.

GR00151   Hansel and Gretel (302aSR)
GR00152   Heidi (310SR)
GR00154   Poky little puppy (600SR)
GR00155   Three bears (722SR)
GR00156   Little Red Riding Hood (437SR)
GR00158   Pat-a-cake (574SR)
GR00159   Litttle red caboose (435SR)
GR00162   Chicken little (133SR)
GR00163   Jack and the beanstalk (357aSR)
GR00164   Gingerbread man (276aSR)
GR00166   Little red hen (436aSR)
GR00167   Numbers (546SR)
GR00169   Bozo finds a friend (094SR)
GR00170   Smokey the Bear (687SR)
GR00175   Puss in boots (610aSR)
GR00176   Snow White and Rose Red (688SR)
GR00177   Musicians of Bremen (500SR)
GR00179   Frosty the snowman (258SR)
GR00181   Scuffy the tugboat (671aSR)
GR00182   Old MacDonald had a farm (553aSR)
GR00183   Little boy with a big horn (401SR)
GR00208   Tootle (747SR)
GR00209   Three little pigs (726SR)
GR00211   Ugly Duckling (768SR)
GR00212   Bozo the clown (095SR)
GR00213   Three little kittens (725SR)
GR00214   Seven little postmen (673SR)
GR00217   White bunny and his magic nose (800SR)
GR00218   Animals of Farmer Jones (030aSR)
GR00219   Happy man and his dump truck (308SR)
GR00220   Big brown bear (072SR)
GR00232   Visit to the children's zoo (775SR)
GR00233   ABC rhymes (003SR)
GR00234   Riddles, riddles from A to Z (632SR)
GR00235   Day on the farm (187SR)
GR00236   Child's garden of verses (134aSR)
GR00238   Chitty chitty bang bang (139SR)
GR00239   Circus time (153SR)
GR00241   Five little firemen (244SR)
GR00242   Shy little kitten (678SR)
GR00243   Lively little rabbit (441SR)
GR00244   When I grow up (792aSR)
GR00246   Little fat policeman (406SR)
GR00249   Ukelele and her new doll (769SR)
GR00250   Mister Dog (482SR)
GR00251   Naughty bunny (531SR)
GR00252   Happy days (304SR)
GR00253   Tiger's adventure (731SR)
GR00254   Boy with a drum (092SR)
GR00256   Fuzzy duckling (263SR)
GR00260   Bravest of all (099SR)

```
GR00261   Wacky Witch and the mystery of the king's gold (776SR)
GR00262   Corky's hiccups (162SR)
-------   Ali Baba and the forty thieves (009SR)
-------   Twelve days of Christmas (763SR)
-------   Who comes to your house? (801SR)
```

SESAME STREET BOOK

The SESAME STREET BOOK series is published by Western
Publishing Co. in conjunction with the Children's
Television Workshop. This is a subseries within the
LITTLE GOLDEN BOOK series and does not have a unique
numbering system. The format is the same as the LITTLE
GOLDEN BOOK series.

```
Amazing Mumford forgets the magic words (015)
Bert's hall of great inventions (061)
Big Bird brings Spring to Sesame Street (069)
Big Bird's day on the farm (070)
Big Bird's red book (071)
Cookie Monster and the cookie tree (160)
Count all the way to Sesame Street (163)
Ernie's work of art (227)
Four seasons (253)
Grover's own alphabet (298)
I think that it is wonderful (347)
Many faces of Ernie (462)
Monster at the end of this book (484)
Oscar's book (561)
Puppy love (609)
Together book (736)
```

TWIN VISION BOOK   [BRAILLE BOOKS]

This series was published by the American Brotherhood for
the Blind in Tarzana, California. The familiar LITTLE GOLDEN
BOOK stories have been represented in braille, with opposite
pages in traditional text.

```
ABC rhymes (003B)
Bambi (049B)
Bugs Bunny (104B)
Chitty Chitty Bang Bang (139B)
Cinderella's friends (148B)
Cindy Bear (149B)
Dumbo (223B)
How to tell time (328B)
Jenny's new brother (360B)
Little golden ABC (408B)
Little golden book of words (419B)
Little golden picture dictionary (425B)
Little Red Riding Hood (437B)
Mr. Puffer-Bill (496B)
Pepper plays nurse (577B)
```

Peter Pan and Wendy (583B)
Prayers for children (607B)
Taxi that hurried (713B)
Tom and Jerry meet Little Quack (738B)
Tootle (747B)

WALT DISNEY BOOK

This series was produced by Simon & Schuster in cooperation
with Walt Disney Productions. The numbering system was unique
to this series and the books retain the familiar LITTLE GOLDEN
BOOK binding.

D1	Through the picture frame (728)
D2	Cold-blooded penguin (155)
D3	Dumbo (223)
D4	Snow White and the seven dwarfs (689)
D5	Peter and the wolf (580)
D6	Uncle Remus (771)
D7	Bambi (049)
D8	Pinocchio (592)
D9	Bongo (087)
D10	Three little pigs (727)
D11	Johnny Appleseed (367)
D12	Once upon a wintertime (556)
D13	Cinderella (146)
D14	Donald Duck's adventure (214)
D15	Mickey Mouse's picnic (479)
D16	Santa's toy shop (666)
D17	Cinderella's friends (148)
D18	Donald Duck's toy train (219)
D19	Alice in Wonderland meets the white rabbit (011)
D20	Alice in Wonderland finds the garden of live flowers (010)
D21	Grandpa Bunny (297)
D22	Ugly Duckling (768)
D23	Mad Hatter's tea party (452)
D24	Peter Pan and Wendy (583)
D25	Peter Pan and the pirates (582)
D26	Peter Pan and the Indians (581)
D27	Donald Duck and Santa Claus (202)
D28	Noah's ark (544)
D29	Mickey Mouse and his space ship (469)
D30	Pluto Pup goes to sea (599)
D31	Hiawatha (316)
D32	Mickey Mouse and Pluto Pup (470)
D33	Mickey Mouse goes Christmas shopping (477)
D34	Donald Duck and the witch (205)
D35	Seven dwarfs find a house (672)
D36	Mother Goose (491)
D37	Ben and me (059)
D38	Chip 'n' Dale at the zoo (135)
D39	Donald Duck's Christmas tree (216)
D40	Donald Duck's toy sailboat (218)
D41	Donald Duck's safety book (217)

D42   Lady (378)
D43   Disneyland on the air (195)
D44   Donald Duck in Disneyland (208)
D45   Davy Crockett, king of the wild frontier (181)
D46   Little man of Disneyland (430)
D47   Davy Crockett's keelboat race (182)
D48   Robin Hood (641)
D49   Donald Duck, prize driver (212)
D50   Jiminy Cricket (364)
D51   Mother Goose (491a)
D52   Goofy, movie star (295)
D53   Mickey Mouse flies the Christmas mail (476)
D54   Perri and her friends (578)
D55   Donald Duck and the Mouseketeers (203)
D55X   Day with Donald Duck (188)
D56   Peter and the wolf (580a)
D57   Mickey Mouse and the missing Mouseketeers (473)
D58   Cinderella's friends (148a)
D59   Cinderella (146a)
D60   [not used]
D61   Sleeping Beauty (679)
D62   Bongo (087a)
D63   Scamp (668)
D64   Paul Revere (575)
D65   Old Yeller (555)
D66   Snow White and the seven dwarfs (689a)
D67   Seven dwarfs find a house (672a)
D68   Zorro (830)
D69   [not used]
D70   Scamp's adventure (669)
D71   Sleeping Beauty and the good fairies (680)
D72   Peter Pan and Wendy (583a)
D73   Peter Pan and the pirates (582a)
D74   Peter Pan and the Indians (581a)
D75   Manni the donkey (461)
D76   Mickey Mouse and Pluto Pup (470a)
D77   Zorro and the secret plan (831)
D78   Three little pigs (727a)
D79   Mother Goose (491b)
D80   Tonka (746)
D81   Darby O'Gill (179)
D82   Shaggy Dog (675)
D83   Goliath II (287)
D84   Donald Duck's Christmas carol (215)
D85   Uncle Remus (771a)
D86   Donald Duck, lost and found (210)
D87   Toby Tyler (735)
D88   Scamp's adventure (669a)
D89   Lucky puppy (448)
D90   Bambi (049a)
D91   Pollyanna (604)
D92   Donald Duck in Disneyland (208a)
D93   Bedknobs and broomsticks (056)
D94   Donald Duck, private eye (211)
D95   Swiss Family Robinson (705)
D96   Flying car (249)

D97   Babes in toyland (Ø36)
D98   Ludwig Von Drake (45Ø)
D99   Toy soldiers (751)
D1ØØ   Pinocchio (592a)
D1Ø1   Pinocchio and the whale (593)
D1Ø2   Big Red (Ø75)
D1Ø3   Lady (378a)
D1Ø4   Savage Sam (667)
D1Ø5   Surprise for Mickey Mouse (7Ø1)
D1Ø6   Sword in the stone (7Ø6)
D1Ø7   Wizards duel (815)
D1Ø8   Mickey Mouse and his space ship (469a)
D1Ø9   Donald Duck in Disneyland (2Ø8b)
D11Ø   Peter Pan and Wendy (583b)
D111   Bunny book (116)
D112   Mary Poppins: a jolly holiday (465)
D113   Mary Poppins (464)
D114   Cinderella (146b)
D115   Cinderella's friends (148b)
D116   Winnie-the-Pooh: the honey tree (813)
D117   Winnie-the-Pooh meets Gopher (812)
D118   Ugly dachshund (767)
D119   Thumper (73Ø)
D12Ø   Jungle book (37Ø)
D121   Winnie-the-Pooh and Tigger (811)
D122   Aristocats (Ø35)
D123   Disneyland parade with Donald Duck (196)
D124   Pluto and the adventure of the golden scepter (598)
D125   Favorite nursery tales (233)
D126   Robin Hood (641a)
D127   Donald Duck and the witch next door (2Ø6)
D128   Robin Hood and the daring mouse (642)
D129   Mickey Mouse and the great lot plot (472)
D13Ø   Love bug (446)
D131   Donald Duck in America on parade (2Ø7)
D132   Bambi, friends of the forest (Ø5Ø)
D133   Mickey Mouse: the kitten sitters (478)
D134   Mickey Mouse and the best-neighbor contest (471)
D135   Mickey Mouse and the Mouseketeers: Ghost town
         adventure (474)
D136   Rescuers (629)
D137   Pete's dragon (585)
D138   Mickey Mouse and Goofy: the big bear scare (468)
D139   Donald Duck and the one bear: a turn-about tale (2Ø4)
D14Ø   Donald Duck, instant millionaire (2Ø9)

Name Index

The number in parenthesis following the title refers to the entry number in the main TITLE LIST. Pseudonyms appear in brackets beneath the person's real name.

ABRANZ, FRED (illus)
Bugs Bunny at the county fair (106)

ALBANO, JOHN
Ronald McDonald and the tale of the talking plant (647)

ALDRICH, ANDY (illus)
Little Crow (403)

ALEXANDER, BEATRICE (pseud)
see RAYMOND, LOUISE 1907-

ALLEN, JOAN (illus)
Happy golden ABC (306,306a)

ALOISE, FRANK E. (illus)
Just watch me! (372)

ALSON, LAWRENCE
Leave it to Beaver (386)

ALVARADO, PETER (illus)
Bugs Bunny - too many carrots (111,111a)
New friends for the saggy baggy elephant (536, 536SR)
Tweety plays catch the puddy tat (761,761a)
Wacky Witch and the mystery of the king's gold (776, 776SR)

AMES, LEE J. 1921- (illus)
Lassie shows the way (005, 385,385a)

ANASTASIO, DINA 1941-
Count all the way to Sesame Street (163)

ANDERSEN, AL (illus)
Bravest of all (099, 099SR, 099a)
Smokey Bear finds a helper (686)
Tom and Jerry's photo finish (741)

ANDERSEN, HANS CHRISTIAN 1805-1875
Fairy tales (229)
Lisa and the eleven swans (395)
Princess and the pea (658)
Through the picture frame (728)
Thumbelina (729,729SR,729a)

ANDERSON, LEONE CASTELL 1923-
Good-by day (288)

ANGLUND, JOAN WALSH 1926- (illus)
Circus boy (151)
Stop and go (694)

ARCHER, PEGGY
    One of the family (557)

ARCHER, PETER
    (joint pseud. of Byron and
    Kathryn Jackson)
        Emerald City of Oz (226)
        Road to Oz (639)
        Tin Woodman of Oz (732)
        Tom and Jerry's merry
        Christmas (739)

ARENS, MICHAEL (illus)
    Scooby Doo and the pirate
    treasure (670)

ARIANE (pseud)
    see DUPLAIX, GEORGES

ARLANDSON, LEONE 1917-
    Mr. Puffer-Bill (496,496B)

ARMITAGE, FRANK (illus)
    Sleeping Beauty (679)
    Sleeping Beauty paper dolls
    (681)

ARMSTRONG, SAMUEL (illus)
    Day with Donald Duck (188)
    Disneyland on the air (195)
    Donald Duck and the
        Mousketeers (203)
    Donald Duck's toy sailboat
        (218)
    Goofy, movie star (295)
    Jiminy Cricket (364)
    Lady (378,378a,378b)
    Tom and Jerry's merry
        Christmas (739)
    Tom and Jerry's party (740)

ASBJORNSEN, PETER CHRISTEN
1812-1885
    Three billy goats gruff
        (724)
    Wolf and the kids (724)

ATENCIO, XAVIER (illus)
    Mickey Mouse goes Christmas
    shopping (477)

AUGUSTINY, SALLY (illus)
    ABC is for Christmas (002,
    002a)
    Fritzie goes home (256)

BACON, JOAN CHASE (pseud)
    see BOWDEN, JOAN CHASE

BAIRD, BIL 1904-
    Whistling Wizard (799)

BAKER, DARRELL (illus)
    Bugs Bunny, pioneer (110,
    110a)
    Pink Panther in the haunted
    house (591,591a)
    Rudolph the red-nosed
    reindeer shines again
    (656)

BANNERMAN, HELEN (BRODIE COWAN
WATSON) 1862(?)-1946
    Little black Sambo (398)

BANTA, MILTON (illus)
    Mickey Mouse and his space
    ship (469,469a)
    Three little pigs, Disney's
    (234,727,727a)

BARAN, DORIS (narrator)
    ABC rhymes (003SR)

BARRETT, OLIVER O'CONNOR
    Little Benny wanted a pony
    (396)

BARRIE, J(AMES) M(ATTHEW)
1860-1937
    Peter Pan and the Indians
    (581,581a)
    Peter Pan and the pirates
    (582,582a)
    Peter Pan and Wendy (583,
    583B,583a,583b,583c)

BARRITT, BOB (illus)
    Yogi Bear (828)

BARTKOWSKI, RENEE
    My home (512,512a)

BATTAGLIA, AURELIUS 1910-
(illus)
    Baby's Mother Goose (048,
    048a)
    Hiram's red shirt (317)
    Little boy with a big horn
    (401,401SR)
    Mr. Bell's fixit shop (493)

BATTAGLIA, AURELIUS (cont'd)
Old Mother Hubbard (554, 554a)
Pat-a-cake (574,574SR)
Pets for Peter (587)

BAUM, L(YMAN) FRANK 1856-1919
Emerald City of Oz (226)
Road to Oz (639)
Tin Woodman of Oz (732)
Wizard of Oz (814, 814a)

BECHDOLT, JACK
see BECHDOLT, JOHN ERNEST

BECHDOLT, JOHN ERNEST 1884-
1954 [Jack Bechdolt]
Little boy with a big horn
(401,401SR)

BECKETT, SHEILAH 1913- (illus)
My little golden Christmas
book (521)
Twelve dancing princesses
(762)

BEDFORD, ANNIE NORTH (pseud)
see WATSON, JANE WERNER 1915-

BEECHER, ELIZABETH
Bugs Bunny at the county
fair (106)
Bugs Bunny's birthday (112)
Hopalong Cassidy and the
Bar 20 cowboy (321)
Mickey Mouse and Pluto Pup
(470,470a)
Pollyanna (604)
Roy Rogers and Cowboy Toby
(651)
Tonka (746)

BEGLEY, EVELYN M.
Little red hen (436d)

BELLAH, MELANIE
Bow wow! Meow! (091,091a)

BEMELMANS, LUDWIG 1898-1962
(author/illus)
Madeline (453)

BENDEL, RUTH (illus)
Lucky rabbit (449)

BENSTEAD, VIVIENNE
Chicken Little (133,133SR)

BENVENUTI (illus)
Forest hotel (250,250SR, 250a)

BERIS, SANDRA
Inspector Gadget in Africa
(353)
Pink Panther and sons: fun
at the picnic (590)

BESTOR, DON (illus)
Lucky puppy (448)

BIALOSKY, ALAN
Bialosky's Christmas (065)
Bialosky's special picnic
(066)

BIALOSKY, PEGGY
Bialosky's Christmas (065)
Bialosky's special picnic
(066)

BIESTERVELD, BETTY (PARSONS)
1923-
Barbie (052)

BLACK, IRMA S(IMONTON)
1906-1972
Taxi that hurried (713, 713B,713SR)

BLAIR, MARY (ROBINSON) 1911-
(illus)
Baby's house (047,047a)
I can fly (343)

BLAKE, VIVIENNE (illus)
Alphabet from A to Z (013)

BLOOM, LLOYD (illus)
Elves and the shoemaker
(225)

BOLLE, FRANK (illus)
Gene Autry and Champion
(267)
Lassie and the lost
explorer (384)
Lone Ranger and the talking
pony (443)
Wagon train (777)

BOND, GLADYS BAKER 1912–
   Magic friend-maker (455,
   455SR)

BOONSHAFT, ROCHELLE (illus)
   Raggedy Ann and Fido (622,
   622FS,622SR)

BORDIGONI, IDELLETTE (illus)
   I sing a song of praise
   (089,089a)

BOSCHE, BILL (illus)
   Chip 'n' Dale at the zoo
   (135)

BOWDEN, JOAN CHASE 1925–
   [Joan Chase Bacon]
   Bear's surprise party (055)
   Boo and the flying Flews
   (088)
   Bouncy baby bunny finds his
   bed (090,090SR)
   Ginghams: The backward
   picnic (278,278a)
   Hat for the queen (309)
   New home for Snow Ball
   (537)
   Pussycat tiger (612,612SR)
   Waltons and the birthday
   present (780)
   Who took the top hat
   trick? (803)

BOYLE, NEIL (illus)
   Donald Duck, prize driver
   (212)
   Mickey Mouse flies the
   Christmas mail (476)
   Scamp's adventure (669,
   669a)

BRACKE, CHARLES (illus)
   Neatos and the litterbugs
   (532,532FS,532MP,532SR)

BRADFIELD, ROGER 1924– (illus)
   Bert's hall of great
   inventions (061,061a)
   Together book (736,736a)

BRAGG, MABEL CAROLINE 1870–
1945 [Watty Piper]
   Little engine that could
   (404,404SR)

BREITMEYER, LOIS
   Rabbit is next (616,616a)

BRIAN, BRUCE
   Cub scouts (172)

BROOKS, ANDREA (illus)
   Christmas donkey (142)

BROUN, EMILY (pseud)
   see STERNE, EMMA GELDERS
   1894–1971

BROWN, FERN G. 1918–
   Bugs Bunny, pioneer (110,
   110a)

BROWN, MARGARET WISE 1910–1952
   Color kittens (156,156FS,
   156SR,156a,156b,156c)
   Doctor Squash, the doll
   doctor (199)
   Five little firemen (244,
   244SR, 244a)
   Friendly book (255,255a,
   255b)
   Golden egg book (283,283FS,
   283SR,283a)
   Golden sleepy book (286,
   286a)
   Home for a bunny (319,319a)
   Little fat policeman (406,
   406SR)
   Little Indian (427)
   Little pussycat (434)
   Mister dog (482,482SR,482a)
   Pussy Willow (611,611a)
   Sailor dog (663,663VC)
   Seven little postmen (673,
   673SR,673a)
   Sleepy book (682)
   Train to Timbuctoo (754)
   Two little gardeners (765)
   Two little miners (766)
   Wonderful house (816)

BROWN, RICHARD (illus)
   Count all the way to Sesame
   Street (163)

BUELL, ELLEN LEWIS 1905–
   Treasury of little golden
   books (757,757a,758)

BUELL, MARJORIE HENDERSON
1904- [Marge]
Little Lulu (428)
Little Lulu and her magic
tricks (429)

BUETTNER, CARL
Bozo the clown (095,095SR)
Donald Duck, lost and found
(210)
Donald Duck, private eye
(211)
Pixie and Dixie and Mr.
Jinks (author/illus)
(594)
Woody Woodpecker drawing
fun for beginners (821)

BUNKY (illus)
Runaway squash (659)

BURROUGHS, EDGAR RICE 1875-
1950
Tarzan (710)

CABRAL, OLGA 1909-
Seven sneezes (674,674FS)

CALMENSON, STEPHANIE 1952-
Ten items or less (714)

CAMP, JOE
Benji, fastest dog in the
West (060,060a)

CANIFF, MILTON
Steve Canyon (692)

CARBE, NINO 1909- (illus)
Chip Chip (136)

CAREY, MARY (VIRGINIA) 1925-
Tawny, scrawny lion and the
clever monkey (712,712SR)
Wizard of Oz (814,814a)

CARLIN, STEVE
Rootie Kazootie, baseball
star (648)
Rootie Kazootie, detective
(649)
Rootie Kazootie joins the
circus (650)

CARLISLE, CLARK (pseud)
see HOLDING, JAMES 1907-

CARRICK, BRUCE R.
Cave kids (129)
Magilla Gorilla (458)

CARROLL, LEWIS (pseud)
see DODGSON, CHARLES
LUTWIDGE 1832-1898

CARY, LOUIS (Favreau) 1915-
(illus)
Words (824)

CASSEN, CHRISTIANE (illus)
I think about God (346,
346a)

CASSIDY, CLARA
We like kindergarten (783,
783a)
Who needs a cat? (802)

CAULEY, LORINDA BRYAN 1951-
(illus)
Best of all! (063,063a)
What Lily Goose found (789)

CELLINI, JOSEPH 1924- (illus)
Shaggy dog (675)

CERF, JONATHAN
Big Bird's red book (071,
071a)

CERF, PHYLLIS FRASER 1915-
[Phyllis Fraser]
Mother Goose (487,487a)
This little piggy (720)

CERF, ROSANNE
Big Bird's red book (071,
071a)

CHAIKO, TED
Giant little golden book
about plants and animals
(269)

CHAMBERS, SELMA LOLA 1908-
Little golden book of words
(419,419B,419a,419b,419c)
Words (824)

CHANDLER, JEAN
Poky little puppy's naughty
day (602)

CHARTIER, NORMAND (illus)
    Amazing Mumford forgets the
        magic words! (015)
    Many faces of Ernie (462)

CHERR, PAT
    Huckleberry Hound and his
        friends (338)
    Huckleberry Hound and the
        Christmas sleigh (339)
    Yakky Doodle and Chopper
        (825)

CLAMPETT, BOB
    Beany goes to sea (053)

CLARKE, BRENDA (illus)
    How does your garden grow?
        (326)

CLARKE, GRACE (illus)
    ABC rhymes (003,003B,003SR,
        003a)

CLASTER, NANCY
    Romper Room do bees (645)
    Romper Room exercise book
        (646)

COLE, ALAN (narrator)
    Little boy with a big horn
        (401SR)
    Old MacDonald had a farm
        (553aSR)
    Scuffy the tugboat (671aSR)

COLLODI, CARLO (pseud)
    see LORENZINI, CARLO
    1826-1890

COLLYER, BARBARA
    Christmas in the country
        (143)

COMBES, HERBERT (illus)
    Airplanes (006)
    Boats (084,084a,084b)

COMBES, LENORA FEES 1919-
    (illus)
    Airplanes (006)
    Boats (084,084a,084b)
    Let's go shopping with
        Peter and Penny (387)

CONGER, MARION 1915-
    All aboard! (012)
    Circus time (153,153FS,
        153SR,153a)
    Day at the zoo (185,185a)
    Little golden holiday book
        (422)
    Rainy day play book (626,
        626a)

CONN, MARTHA ORR
    Petey and I (586)

CONNER, EULALA (illus)
    What will I be? (790)

COOK, STEPHEN (illus)
    Our flag (563)

COOKE, TOM (illus)
    Four seasons (253)

CORWIN, DAVID
    Chipmunks' Merry Christmas
        (138)

CORWYN, DAVID
    Bullwinkle (114)

COSTANZA, JOHN (illus)
    Biskitts in double trouble
        (080)
    Robotman & friends at
        school (643)
    Road runner: mid-mesa
        marathon (638)
    Ronald McDonald and the
        tale of the talking plant
        (647)

COSTELLO, ANNE (narrator)
    Day on the farm (187SR)

COWLES, KATHLEEN KRULL (pseud)
    see KRULL, KATHLEEN 1952-

CRAGER, JOEL (narrator)
    Chitty Chitty Bang Bang
        (139SR)

CRAMPTON, GERTRUDE 1909-
    Large and growly bear (380,
        380FS,380SR,380a)
    Little golden funny book
        (421)

CRAMPTON, GERTRUDE (cont'd)
  Noises and Mr. Flibberty-
    Jib (545)
  Scuffy the tugboat (671,
    671SR,671a,671aSR,671b,
    671bVC,671c)
  Tootle (747,747B,747FS,
    747SR,747a)

CRAWFORD, MEL 1925- (illus)
  Animal quiz (024,024a)
  Annie Oakley and the
    rustlers (032)
  Big Red (075)
  Broken Arrow (100)
  Cats (128,128a)
  Cave kids (129)
  Cub scouts (172)
  Dale Evans and the lost
    gold mine (176)
  Davy Crockett, king of the
    wild frontier (181)
  Davy Crockett's keelboat
    race (182)
  Flintstones (author/illus)
    (247)
  Fury (261)
  Fury takes the jump (262)
  Gene Autry (266)
  Jungle book (370)
  Lassie and her day in the
    sun (381,381a,381b)
  Leave it to Beaver (386)
  Life and legend of Wyatt
    Earp (391)
  Little golden book of
    helicopters (412)
  Little golden book of
    Uncle Wiggly (418)
  Mister Ed (483)
  National Velvet (530)
  Pebbles Flintstone (576)
  Rin Tin Tin and Rusty (634)
  Rin Tin Tin and the outlaw
    (636)
  Rootie Kazootie, baseball
    star (648)
  Rootie Kazootie, detective
    (649)
  Rootie Kazootie joins the
    circus (650)
  Roy Rogers and Cowboy Toby
    (651)
  Roy Rogers and the Indian
    sign (652)

CRAWFORD, MEL (cont'd)
  Roy Rogers and the mountain
    lion (653)
  Roy Rogers and the new
    cowboy (654)
  Smokey and his animal
    friends (684)
  Smokey Bear and the campers
    (685)
  Supercar (699)
  Tarzan (710)
  Tommy's camping adventure
    (744)
  Ugly dachshund (767)
  Visit to the children's zoo
    (775)
  Where is the bear? (795,
    795a)
  Whistling wizard (799)

CREATIVE STUDIOS I (illus)
  Ginghams: The backward
    picnic (278,278a)
  Wild kingdom (808)

CROWNINSHIELD, ETHEL
  Day at the zoo (songwriter)
    (185,185a)
  Surprise for Sally (702)

CRUISE, BEN
  Musicians of Bremen (500a)

CUMMINS, JIM (illus)
  Who took the top hat trick?
    (803)

CURREN, POLLY 1917-
  Fire fighters' counting
    book (237)
  Raggedy Ann and Andy help
    Santa Claus (620,620a)
  Raggedy Ann and Andy: The
    little gray kitten (621,
    621a)

CUSHMAN, JEAN
  We help Mommy (782,782a)

DALY, EILEEN
  Just watch me! (372)
  Raggedy Ann and Andy. Five
    birthday parties in a row
    (618)
  Smokey Bear finds a helper
    (686)

DALY, EILEEN (cont'd)
    Tweety plays catch the
        puddy tat (761,761a)

DALY, KATHLEEN N(ORAH)
    Aladdin and his magic lamp
        (007)
    Animal stamps (026)
    Big Red (075)
    Bird stamps (077)
    Captain Kangaroo (119,120)
    Captain Kangaroo and the
        panda (119,122)
    Car and truck stamps (124)
    Cinderella paper dolls
        (147)
    Deep blue sea (189)
    Four little kittens (251,
        251a,251b)
    Giant little golden book
        of dogs (272)
    Good Humor man (290)
    Howdy Doody's animal
        friends (335)
    Jingle bells (366)
    Little golden book about
        colors (409)
    Little golden book about
        the seashore (410)
    Mickey Mouse Club stamp
        book (475)
    My little golden book about
        travel (518)
    New puppy (541,541a)
    Tammy (709)
    Trains - a little golden
        stamp book (755)
    Wild animal babies (805)

D'AMATO, ALEX 1919-
    Bunny's magic tricks (117)

D'AMATO, JANET 1925-
    Bunny's magic tricks (117)

DART, ELEANOR (illus)
    Happy days (304,304SR)
    How to tell time (328,328B,
        328a)
    Romper Room do bees (645)

DAUBER, ELIZABETH (illus)
[Liz Dauber]
    Howdy Doody's circus (336)

DAUBER, LIZ
    see DAUBER, ELIZABETH

d'AVIGNON, SUE (illus)
    Fun for Hunky Dory (259)

DAVIS, BARBARA STEINCROHN
    Forest hotel (250,250SR,
        250a)

DAWSON, DIANE (illus)
    Good night, Aunt Lilly
        (293)

DeJOHN, MARIE (illus)
    Little golden picture
        dictionary (425b)

DELANEY, A.
    see DELANEY, TONI

DELANEY, TONI (illus)
[A. Delaney]
    I think that it is
        wonderful (347)

DeLARA, PHIL (illus)
    Road Runner (637,637a)

deLUNA, TONY (illus)
    Twelve days of Christmas
        (763,763SR)

DEMPSTER, AL (illus)
    Alice in Wonderland meets
        the White Rabbit (011)
    Bugs Bunny (104,104B,104a,
        104b)
    Bugs Bunny's birthday (112)
    Cinderella's friends (148,
        148B,148a,148b)
    Donald Duck and Santa Claus
        (202)
    Mother Goose (490,490a,
        490b)
    Santa's toy shop (666)
    Snow White and the seven
        dwarfs (689,689a)
    Three little pigs, Disney's
        (727,727a)

De NUNEZ, BEN (illus)
    Huckleberry Hound and his
        friends (338)
    Huckleberry Hound and the
        Christmas sleigh (339)
    Rocky and his friends (644)
    Woody Woodpecker takes a
        trip (823,823a)

DeSANTIS, GEORGE (illus)
    Winnie-the-Pooh meets
        Gopher (812,812a)

DeWITT, CORNELIUS (HUGH) 1905-
    (illus)
    Johnny's machines (368)
    Little golden ABC (408,
        408B,408a)
    Night before Christmas (542)
    What am I? (787,787a)

DIAS, RON (illus)
    Mickey's Christmas carol
        (480,480SR)

DiSALVO-RYAN, DYANNE (illus)
    Best friends (062)

DISNEY, WALT(ER ELIAS)
    1901-1966 (author/illus)
    Alice in Wonderland finds
        the garden of live
        flowers (010)
    Alice in Wonderland meets
        the White Rabbit (011,
        011a)
    Aristocats (035)
    Babes in toyland (036)
    Bambi (049,049B,049a,049b)
    Bambi, friends of the
        forest (050,050a)
    Bedknobs and broomsticks
        (056)
    Ben and me (059)
    Big Red (075)
    Black cauldron - Taran
        finds a friend (081)
    Black hole (082)
    Bongo (087,087a)
    Bunny book (116)
    Chip 'n' Dale at the zoo
        (135)
    Cinderella (146,146a,146b,
        146c)
    Cinderella's friends (148,
        148B,148a,148b)
    Cold-blooded penguin (155)
    Darby O'Gill (179)
    Davy Crockett, king of the
        wild frontier (181)
    Davy Crockett's keelboat
        race (182)
    Day with Donald Duck (188)
    Disneyland on the air (195)

DISNEY, WALT(ER) ELIAS (cont'd)
    Disneyland parade with
        Donald Duck (196)
    Donald Duck and Santa Claus
        (202)
    Donald Duck and the
        Mousketeers (203)
    Donald Duck and the
        one-bear (204)
    Donald Duck and the witch
        (205,213)
    Donald Duck and the witch
        next door (206)
    Donald Duck in America on
        parade (207)
    Donald Duck in Disneyland
        (208,208a,208b)
    Donald Duck instant
        millionaire (209,209a)
    Donald Duck lost and found
        (210)
    Donald Duck, private eye
        (211)
    Donald Duck, prize driver
        (212)
    Donald Duck's adventure
        (213,214)
    Donald Duck's Christmas
        carol (215)
    Donald Duck's Christmas
        tree (216)
    Donald Duck's safety book
        (217)
    Donald Duck's toy sailboat
        (218)
    Donald Duck's toy train
        (213,219)
    Dumbo (223,223B,223a,234)
    Favorite nursery tales
        (233,233a)
    Favorite stories (234)
    Flying car (249)
    Fox and the hound - hide
        and seek (254)
    Goliath II (287,287SR)
    Goofy, movie star (295)
    Grandpa Bunny (297)
    Hiawatha (316)
    Jiminy Cricket (364)
    Johnny Appleseed (367)
    Lady (378,378a,378b)
    Little man of Disneyland
        (430)
    Love bug (446)
    Lucky puppy (448)
    Ludwig von Drake (450)

DISNEY, WALT(ER) ELIAS (cont'd)
Mad Hatter's tea party
(452)
Manni the donkey (461)
Mary Poppins (464)
Mickey Mouse and Goofy -
The big bear scare (468,
468a)
Mickey Mouse and his space
ship (469,469a)
Mickey Mouse and Pluto Pup
470,470a)
Mickey Mouse and the best-
neighbor contest (471)
Mickey Mouse and the great
lot plot (472)
Mickey Mouse and the
missing Mouseketeers
(473)
Mickey Mouse and the
Mouseketeers - ghost town
adventure (474)
Mickey Mouse flies the
Christmas mail (476)
Mickey Mouse goes Christmas
shopping (477)
Mickey Mouse - the kitten
sitters (478)
Mickey Mouse's picnic (479,
479a)
Mickey's Christmas carol
(480,480SR)
Mother Goose (490,490a,
490b)
Noah's ark (544)
Old Yeller (555)
Once upon a wintertime
(556)
Paul Revere (575)
Perri and her friends (578)
Peter and the wolf (580,
580a)
Peter Pan and the Indians
(581,581a)
Peter Pan and the pirates
(582,582a)
Peter Pan and Wendy (583,
583B,583a,583b,583c)
Pete's dragon (585)
Pinocchio (592,592a)
Pinocchio and the whale
(593)
Pluto and the adventure of
the golden scepter (598)
Pluto Pup goes to sea (599)
Pollyanna (604)
Rescuers (629,629a)

DISNEY, WALT(ER) ELIAS (cont'd)
Return to Oz - Dorothy
saves the Emerald City
(630)
Return to Oz - Escape from
the witch's castle (631)
Robin Hood (641,641a)
Robin Hood and the daring
mouse (642)
Santa's toy shop (666)
Savage Sam (667)
Scamp (668)
Scamp's adventure (669,
669a)
Shaggy dog (675)
Sleeping Beauty (679)
Sleeping Beauty and the
good fairies (680)
Sleeping Beauty paper dolls
(681)
Snow White and the seven
dwarfs (689,689a)
Sport Goofy and the racing
robot (691)
Storytime book (698)
Surprise for Mickey Mouse
(701)
Swiss Family Robinson (705)
Sword in the stone (706)
Three little pigs (234,727,
727a)
Through the picture frame
(728)
Thumper (730)
Toad flies high (734)
Toby Tyler (735)
Tonka (746)
Toy soldiers (751)
Treasury of Disney little
golden books (756)
Ugly dachshund (767)
Ugly duckling (768,768SR)
Uncle Remus (234,771,771a)
Winnie-the-Pooh and Tigger
(811,811a)
Winnie-the-Pooh meets
Gopher (812,812a)
Winnie-the-Pooh: the honey
tree (813)
Wizard's duel (815)
Zorro (830)
Zorro and the secret plan
(831)

DIXON, RACHEL TAFT (illus)
    Bible stories of boys and
        girls (068,068a)
    Heroes of the Bible (313,
        313a)
    Prayers for children (607)

DODGSON, CHARLES LUTWIDGE
1832-1898 [Lewis Carroll]
    Alice in Wonderland finds
        the garden of live
        flowers (010)
    Alice in Wonderland meets
        the white rabbit (011,
        011a)
    Mad Hatter's tea party
        (452)

DOUGLAS, SUSAN (narrator)
    Heidi (310SR)

DOWNS, DIANE FOX 1924-
    Charlie (130,130a)

DREANY, E. JOSEPH (illus)
    Annie Oakley, sharpshooter
        (033)
    Car and truck stamps (124)
    Dale Evans and the coyote
        (175)
    Gunsmoke (301)
    Lassie and the daring
        rescue (005,383)
    Lone Ranger (442)
    Old Yeller (555)
    Trains - a little golden
        stamp book (755)

DUGAN, WILLIAM J. (illus)
    Animal stamps (026)
    Cars (125,125a)
    I'm an Indian today (348)
    Let's go, trucks! (388,
        388a)
    Machines (author/illus)
        (451)
    My magic slate book (523)
    Rumpelstiltskin (658,658SR,
        658a)
    Tom Thumb (742)

DUKAS, JIM (narrator)
    Bravest of all (099SR)
    Corky's hiccups (162SR)
    White bunny and his magic
        nose (800SR)

DUNLEAVY, JANET EGLESON 1928-
[Janet Frank]
    Daddies (173)
    Happy days (304,304SR)

DUPLAIX, GEORGES 1895-
[Ariane; Nicole]
    Big brown bear (072,072SR,
        072a,072b)
    Gaston and Josephine (264)
    Giant little golden book
        of animal stories (270)
    Happy family (305,305a)
    Lively little rabbit (441,
        441SR,441a,441b)
    Merry shipwreck (467)
    Topsy turvy circus (749)

DUPLAIX, LILY
    White Bunny and his magic
        nose (800,800SR)

DWIGHT, RAVENA
    Bert's hall of great
        inventions (061,061a)
    Buck Rogers and the
        children of Hopetown
        (102)
    Together book (736,736a)

DYCKE, SAHULA
    see SAHULA-DYCKE

EAGLE, MIKE 1942- (illus)
    Twelve days of Christmas
        (763a)

EARLE, EYVIND 1916- (illus)
    Peter Pan and Wendy (583,
        583B,583a,583b,583c)

EBSUN, E.D.
    Little golden book of hymns
        (414c)
    Little golden book of jokes
        & riddles (415)

ED (narrator)
    Gingerbread man (276aSR)

EDMUNDS, ROBERT
    Cold-blooded penguin (155)
    Through the picture frame
        (728)

EDWARDS, BEVERLEY (illus)
  Ookpik, the Arctic owl
  (559)

EISENBERG, HARVEY (illus)
  Cindy Bear (149,149B)
  Huckleberry Hound builds a
    house (340)
  Ruff and Reddy (657,657a)
  Tom and Jerry (737,737a)
  Tom and Jerry meet Little
    Quack (738,738B,738a)
  Tom and Jerry's Merry
    Christmas (739)
  Tom and Jerry's party (740)
  Woody Woodpecker drawing
    fun for beginners (821)

ELFRIEDA (illus)
  Gingerbread man (276b)

ELLIOTT, GERTRUDE (illus)
  Gingerbread shop (277)
  Golden book of fairy tales
    281)
  Happy family (305,305a)
  Little golden book of words
    (419,419B,419a,419b,419c)
  Magic compass (454)
  Mother Goose (487,487a)
  Mr. Wiggs' birthday party
    (498)
  Nursery rhymes (548)
  Two little gardeners (765)

ELMO, HORACE
  Quiz fun (614)

ELWART, JOAN POTTER 1927-
  Santa's surprise book (665,
    665a)

EMERSON, CAROLINE (DWIGHT)
1891-1973
  Make way for the highway
    (459)
  Make way for the thruway
    (460)

EMRICH, SYLVIA (illus)
  My Christmas treasury (503,
    503a)

ENG, RITA
  When you were a baby (793,
    793a)

ESLEY, JOAN (illus)
  Jenny's new brother (360,
    360B)
  New brother, new sister
    (535)
  Play Street (596)

ESTRADA, RICK (illus)
  Fireman and fire engine
    stamps (239)

EUGENIE (pseud)
  see FERNANDES, EUGENIE

EVANS, ELAINE
  Jenny's new brother (360,
    360B)

EVANS, KATHERINE FLOYD 1901-
1964 (illus)
  Jingle bell Jack (365)

FAWCETT, GENE (illus)
  Dennis the menace and Ruff
    (191a)

FERAND, EMMY (illus)
  My first book of Bible
    stories (508)

FERGUSON, WALTER (W.) 1930-
(author/illus)
  Birds of all kinds (079)

FERN, MARY JANE
  Underdog and the disappear-
    ing ice cream (772)

FERNANDES, EUGENIE (illus)
[Eugenie]
  Adventures of goat (004)
  Good-by day (288)
  Jenny's surprise summer
    (author/illus) (361)

FERNIE, JOHN (illus)
  Pepper plays nurse (577,
    577B)

FIEDLER, JEAN (FELDMAN) 1923-
  New brother, new sister
    (535)

FILLMORE, HERB (illus)
  Gay purr-ee (265)

FLETCHER, STEFFI
    Gene Autry (266)
    Lone Ranger (442)
    Tom and Jerry's party (740)

FLOETHE, RICHARD 1901- (illus)
    Year on the farm (827,
        827FS)

FOLEY, JOHN R.
    Christmas in the country
        (143)

FORAY, JUNE (narrator)
    Neatos and the litterbugs
        (532MP)
    Poky little puppy (600MP)
    Tawny scrawny lion (711MP)

FORBERG, ATI 1925- (illus)
    Stories of Jesus (696,696a)

FOSTER, ANNE
    Superstar Barbie (700,700a)

FRANK, JANET (pseud)
    see DUNLEAVY, JANET EGLESON
    1928-

FRASER, PHYLLIS
    see CERF, PHYLLIS FRASER
    1915-

FRENCH, LAURA 1949-
    Cats (128,128a)
    Donny and Marie (220,220a)

FREUDBERG, JUDY
    Big Bird's day on the farm
        (screenplay) (070)
    Count all the way to Sesame
        Street (screenplay) (163)
    Many faces of Ernie (462)

FREUND, RUDOLF 1915-1969
    (illus)   [Rudolf]
    Animals of Farmer Jones
        (030,030SR)
    Little red hen (436)

FRY, ROSALIND (illus)
    Monster! Monster! (485)

GALE, LEAH
    Alphabet from A to Z (013)
    Animals of Farmer Jones
        (030,030SR,030a,030aSR,
        030b,030c)
    Bedtime stories (058,058a,
        058b,058c,058d)
    Golden book of fairy tales
        (280)
    Nursery songs (549,549a,
        549b)
    Prayers for children (607,
        607a,607aB,607b)

GANTZ, DAVID (illus)
    Darby O'Gill (179)
    Inspector Gadget in Africa
        (353)
    Pink Panther and sons: fun
        at the picnic (590)

GARIS, HOWARD R(OGER) 1873-
1962
    Little golden book of Uncle
        Wiggly (418)

GARO, HARRY (illus)
    Bullwinkle (114)

GASPARD, HELEN
    Doctor Dan the bandage man
        (198,198a)

GEISEL, HELEN 1898-1967
    [Marion Palmer; Helen Marion
    Palmer]
    Bobby and his airplanes
        (085)
    Johnny's machines (368)
    Tommy's wonderful rides
        (745)
    Uncle Remus (771,771a)

GEISS, TONY
    Big Bird's day on the farm
        (screenplay) (070)
    Count all the way to Sesame
        Street (screenplay) (163)
    Four seasons (253)
    Many faces of Ernie
        (scriptwriter) (462)

GEORGE (pseud)
    see WOLFSON, GEORGE

GERGELY, TIBOR 1900-1978
  (illus)
    Animal gym (022)
    Animal orchestra (023)
    Bobby and his airplanes
      (085)
    Christopher and the
      Columbus (145)
    Circus time (153,153FS,
      153SR,153a)
    Daddies (173)
    Day at the zoo (185, 185a)
    Day in the jungle (186)
    Deep blue sea (189)
    Exploring space (228)
    Fire engines (236,236a)
    Five little firemen (244,
      244SR,244a)
    From then to now (257)
    Giant little golden book of
      animal stories (270)
    Giant little golden book of
      dogs (272)
    Good Humor man (290)
    Happy little whale (307)
    Happy man and his dump
      truck (308,308SR,308a,
      308aSR)
    Houses (324)
    Jolly barnyard (369,369a)
    Little golden book about
      the seashore (410)
    Little golden book of dogs
      (411,411a,411b,411c)
    Little golden picture
      dictionary (425,425B,
      425a)
    Little gray donkey (426)
    Little pond in the woods
      (433)
    Little red caboose (435,
      435SR,435a,435b)
    Little Yip Yip and his bark
      (439)
    Make way for the highway
      (459)
    Make way for the thruway
      (460)
    Merry shipwreck (467)
    Mr. Puffer-Bill (496,496B)
    My little golden book about
      the sky (517)
    My little golden book about
      travel (518)
    My little golden book of
      jokes (519)

GERGELY, TIBOR (cont'd)
    Noah's ark (543,543SR,543a)
    Quiz fun (614)
    Rupert the rhinoceros (660)
    Scuffy the tugboat (671,
      671SR,671a,671aSR,671b,
      671bVC,671c)
    Seven little postmen (673,
      673SR,673a)
    Seven sneezes (674,674FS)
    Taxi that hurried (713,
      713B,713SR)
    Tootle (747,747B,747FS,
      747SR,747a)
    Year in the city (826)

GIACOMINI, OLINDO (illus)
    Hat for the queen (309)

GIANNINI (illus)
    Pano the train (569,569SR,
      569a)

GIBEAULT, KATHI
    Susan in the driver's seat
      (703)

GILBERT, JOHN MARTIN (illus)
    Dragon in a wagon (221,
      221FS)

GILL, TOM (illus)
    Steve Canyon (692)

GIORDANO, JOSEPH (illus)
    I have a secret (344)

GIPSON, FREDERICK B(ENJAMIN)
  1908-1973
    Old Yeller (555)
    Savage Sam (667)

GODFREY, JANE (pseud)
    see BOWDEN, JOAN CHASE

GOLBERG, TOM
    Bozo finds a friend (094)
    Wally Gator (779)

GOLDSBOROUGH, JUNE 1923-
  (illus)
    Chicken Little (133a)
    Raggedy Ann and Andy and
      the rainy-day circus
      (619,619a)

GOLDSBOROUGH, JUNE (cont'd)
   Raggedy Ann and Andy help
      Santa Claus (620,620a)
   Raggedy Ann and Andy: the
      little gray kitten (621,
      621a)
   Raggedy Ann and the cookie
      snatcher (623,623a)
   Three bears (722b,722c)

GOLDSMITH, JANE
   Fireman and fire engine
      stamps (239)

GONZALES, MANUEL (illus)
   Donald Duck's safety book
      (217)

GOODMAN, JOAN ELIZABETH
   (author/illus)
   Amanda's first day of
      school (014)
   Right's animal farm (633)

GORMLEY, DAN (illus)
   Howdy Doody's circus (336)

GOTTLIEB, WILLIAM P(AUL)
   (author/illus)
   Farmyard friends (232,232a)
   Laddie and the little
      rabbit (376)
   Laddie the superdog (377)
   New kittens (539)
   Pal and Peter (568)
   Pony for Tony (605)
   Tiger's adventure (731,
      731SR,731a)

GRACEY, YALE (illus)
   Mickey Mouse and Pluto Pup
      (470a)
   Pluto Pup goes to sea (599)

GRAHAM, KENNON (pseud)
   see HARRISON, DAVID LEE
      1937-

GRAHAME, KENNETH 1859-1932
   Toad flies high (734)

GRANGER, PAUL
   Swiss family Robinson (705)

GRANT, BOB (illus)
   Bambi (049,049B,049a,049b)
   Donald Duck, lost and found
      (210)
   Storytime book (698)
   Uncle Remus (234,771,771a)

GRANT, CAMPBELL 1909- (illus)
   Alice in Wonderland finds
      the garden of live
      flowers (010)
   Ben and me (059)
   Bongo (087,087a)
   Cinderella (146,146a,146b,
      146c)
   Donald Duck in Disneyland
      (208,208a,208b)
   Donald Duck's adventure
      (213,214)
   Mickey Mouse and Pluto Pup
      (470)
   Noah's ark (544)
   Pinocchio (592,592a)
   Storytime book (698)
   Ukelele and her new doll
      (769,769SR)

GRANT, CLARA LOUISE
   Ukelele and her new doll
      (769,769SR)

GRANT, LEIGH 1947- (illus)
   Where will all the animals
      go? (798,798a)

GRAY, LES (illus)
   Little Red Riding Hood
      (437a,437b)

GRAYBILL, DURWARD B.
   (photographer)
   Cleo (154)

GREENE, HAMILTON 1904- (illus)
   Buffalo Bill, Jr. and the
      Indian chief (103)
   Horses (322,322a)
   Rin Tin Tin and the lost
      Indian (635)
   Savage Sam (667)
   Zorro and the secret plan
      (831)

GREENE, WARD 1892-1956
   Lady (378,378a,378b)

GRIDER, DOROTHY (illus)
    We love Grandpa (785)

GRIFFITH, DON (illus)
    Mad Hatter's tea party
        (452)

GRIMM, JACOB LUDWIG KARL
  1785-1863
    Brave little tailor (098)
    Giant with the three golden
        hairs (275)
    Golden goose (285,285a)
    Hansel and Gretel (302,
        302a,302aSR,302b,302c)
    Musicians of Bremen (500,
        500SR,500a)
    Rumpelstiltskin (658,658SR,
        658a)
    Snow White and Rose Red
        (688,688SR)
    Snow White and the seven
        dwarfs (689,689a)
    Twelve dancing princesses
        (762)

GRIMM, WILHELM KARL 1786-1859
    Brave little tailor (098)
    Giant with the three golden
        hairs (275)
    Golden goose (285,285a)
    Hansel and Gretel (302,
        302a,302aSR,302b,302c)
    Musicians of Bremen (500,
        500SR,500a)
    Rumpelstiltskin (658,658SR,
        658a)
    Snow White and Rose Red
        (688,688SR)
    Snow White and the seven
        dwarfs (689,689a)
    Twelve dancing princesses
        (762)

GROCE, LARRY (songwriter)
    Color kittens (156SR)
    David and Goliath (180SR)
    Happy man and his dump
        truck (308aSR)
    Little fat policeman
        (406SR)
    Lively little rabbit
        (441SR)
    Noah's ark (543SR)
    Poky little puppy (600cSR)

GROCE, LARRY (cont'd)
    Saggy baggy elephant
        (662SR)
    Scuffy the tugboat (671SR)
    Seven little postmen
        (673SR)
    Smokey the bear (687SR)
    Tawny, scrawny lion
        (711SR)
    Taxi that hurried (713SR)
    There's no such thing as a
        dragon (718SR)
    Thumbelina (729SR)
    Tootle (747SR)

GROSS, MICHAEL (illus)
    Oscar's book (561,561a)

GUY, ANNE WELSH
    Good-bye tonsils (289)

H., M. (pseud)
    see HARSHBERGER, MAC

HALL, NANCY
    Big enough helper (073,
        073a)

HALL, PATRICIA (narrator)
    Visit to the children's zoo
        (775SR)

HAMMOND, LUCILLE
    Adventures of goat (004)
    Polly's pet (603)

HANNA-BARBERA (author/illus)
    Cindy Bear (149,149B)
    Hey there - it's Yogi Bear
        (314)
    Hokey Wolf and Ding-a-Ling
        (318)
    Huckleberry Hound safety
        signs (341)
    Jetsons (363)
    Lippy Lion and Hardy Har
        Har (394)
    Pixie and Dixie and Mr.
        Jinks (594)
    Top Cat (748)
    Touche Turtle (750)
    Yakky Doodle and Chopper
        (825)

HANNON, RUTH
    Book of God's gifts (089,
        089a)

HARMON, LARRY (narrator)
  Bozo finds a friend (094SR)
  Bozo the clown (095SR)
  Tootle (747SR)

HARRIS, JOEL CHANDLER 1848-
1908
  Uncle Remus (234,771,771a)

HARRISON, DAVID L(EE) 1937-
[Kennon Graham]
  Boy with a drum (092,092SR,
    092a)
  Circus is in town (152,152a)
  Land of the lost (379)
  Lassie and the big clean-up
    day (382,382a)
  Let's go, trucks (388,388a)
  Little boy and the giant
    (400)
  Monster! Monster! (485)
  Pink Panther in the haunted
    house (591,591a)
  Woodsy owl and the trail
    bikers (819)

HARSHBERGER, MAC (illus)
[m.h.]
  Golden book of flowers
    (282)

HARTIG, HERBERT
  Many faces of Ernie
    (scriptwriter) (462)

HARTWELL, MARJORIE (illus)
  Bible stories of boys and
    girls (068,068a)
  Heroes of the Bible (313,
    313a)

HAUGE, CARL (illus)
  Little red hen (436d)

HAUGE, MARY (illus)
  Little red hen (436d)

HAUMAN, DORIS 1898- (illus)
  Little engine that could
    (404,404SR)

HAUMAN, GEORGE 1890-1961
(illus)
  Little engine that could
    (404,404SR)

HAYES, SHEILAH
  Where did the baby go?
    (794,794a)

HAYWARD, LINDA 1943-
  When you were a baby (793b)

HAZEN, BARBARA SHOOK 1930-
  Animal alphabet from A to Z
    (016)
  Animal daddies and my daddy
    (019,019a)
  Animals and their babies
    (027)
  Babes in toyland (036)
  Blue book of fairy tales
    (083)
  Charmin' Chatty (131)
  David and Goliath (180,
    180SR,180a,180b)
  Fireball XL5 (238)
  Mister Ed (483)
  Noah's ark (543,543SR,
    543a)
  Ookpik, the Arctic owl
    (559)
  Raggedy Ann and Andy and
    the rainy-day circus
    (619,619a)
  Raggedy Ann and Fido (622,
    622FS,622SR)
  Raggedy Ann and the cookie
    snatcher (623,623a)
  Rudolph the red-nosed
    reindeer (655,655SR,655a)
  Tiny tawny kitten (733)
  Toy soldiers (751)
  Visit to the children's zoo
    (775,775SR,775a)

HEATHERS, ANNE
  Four puppies (252,252a)

HEDSTROM, KAREN (illus)
  Pollyanna (604)

HEIMDAHL, RALPH 1909- (illus)
  Bugs Bunny's birthday (112)

HELWEG, HANS H. 1917- (illus)
  Roy Rogers and the new
    cowboy (654)

HENDERSON, DORIS (illus)
  Party in Shariland (572)
  Trim the Christmas tree
    (759,759a)

HENDERSON, MARION (illus)
    Party in Shariland (572)
    Trim the Christmas tree
        (759,759a)

HESS, LOWELL (illus)
    Aladdin and his magic lamp
        (007)
    Ali Baba and the forty
        thieves (009,009SR)
    Fairy tales (229)
    My Christmas treasury (504)

HIGGINS, LOYTA
    Let's save money (389)
    Stop and go (694)

HILL, MONICA (pseud)
    see WATSON, JANE WERNER
    1915-

HILLERT, MARGARET 1920-
    I like to live in the city
        (345)
    Who comes to your house?
        (801,801SR)

HITTE, KATHRYN 1919-
    Bugs Bunny at the Easter
        party (107)
    I'm an Indian today (348)
    Loopy de Loop goes west
        (445)
    National Velvet (530)

HOCKERMAN, DENNIS (illus)
    Giant who wanted company
        (274)

HOFFMAN, BETH GREINER
    Animal gym (022)
    Giant little golden book
        of animal stories (270)

HOFFMANN, HILDE 1927- (illus)
    Wonderful school (817)

HOFMANN, GINNIE (illus)
    Betsy McCall (064)

HOGAN, CECILY RUTH
    Best of all! (063,063a)
    Remarkably strong Pippi
        Longstocking (628)

HOLAVES, SHARON
    ABC around the house (001,
        001a,001b,001c)
    Pano the train (569,569SR,
        569a)
    Where will all the animals
        go? (798,798a)

HOLDING, JAMES 1907-
[Clark Carlisle]
    Bugs Bunny's carrot machine
        (113,113a)

HOLL, ADELAIDE (HINKLE) 1910?-
    Colors are nice (157,157a)
    Dragon in a wagon
        (teacher's guide) (221FS)
    Golden egg book (teacher's
        guide) (283FS)
    Jamie looks (359)
    Large and growly bear
        (teacher's guide) (380FS)
    New friends for the saggy
        baggy elephant (536,
        536SR)
    Poky little puppy follows
        his nose home (601,601a)
    Tawny scrawny lion
        (teacher's guide) (711FS)

HOLLEY, LEE (illus)
    Dennis the Menace. A quiet
        afternoon (190)
    Dennis the Menace and Ruff
        (191)

HOLLOWAY, STERLING 1905-
(narrator)
    Goliath II (287SR)

HORVATH, SHERL
    Little book (399,399a)

HORWICH, FRANCES R., DR.
    Here comes the band (311)
    Jingle bell Jack (365)
    Lucky rabbit (449)
    Magic wagon (457)
    Mr. Meyer's cow (494)
    My daddy is a policeman
        (505)
    Our baby (562)
    We love Grandpa (785)

HOSKINS, WINFIELD (SCOTT)
   (illus)
   Golden book of fairy
      tales (280)

HUBBARD, ALLEN (illus)
   Bozo and the hide 'n' seek
      elephant (093)
   Lucky puppy (448)

HUBERMAN, ED
   Indian stamps (351)

HUBKA, BETTY 1924-
   Where is the bear? (795,
      795a)

HULICK, NANCY FIELDING
   Animal quiz (024,024a)
   Day on the farm (187,187SR,
      187a)
   Little golden picture
      dictionary (425,425B,
      425a,425b)
   Quiz fun (614)

HUMBERT, CLAUDE (illus)
   Littlest raccoon (440)
   My word book (528)

HURD, EDITH THACHER 1910-
   Five little firemen (244,
      244SR,244a)
   Jack's adventure (358)
   Little fat policeman (406,
      406SR)
   Seven little postmen (673,
      673SR,673a)
   Two little gardeners (765)
   Two little miners (766)

HURFORD, ARCH (illus)
   Daniel Boone (177)

HURFORD, MIRIAM STORY 1894-
   (illus)
   Daniel Boone (177)

HYATT, S(TUART) QUENTIN
   Hokey Wolf and Ding-a-Ling
      (318)
   Smokey Bear and the campers
      (685)
   Yogi Bear (828)
   Yogi Bear: a Christmas
      visit (829)

HYMAN, TRINA SCHART 1939-
   (illus) [Trina Schart]
   Bow wow! Meow! (091,091a)
   I do my best (346,346a)
   Riddles, riddles, from
      A to Z (632,632SR)

IKE, JANE (illus)
   Susan in the driver's seat
      (703)

INGOGLIA, GINA
   see WEINER, GINA INGOGLIA

IRVIN, FRED (MADDOX) 1914-
   (illus)
   ABC around the house (001,
      001a,001b,001c)
   Barbie (052)
   Flying car (249)
   Land of the lost (379)
   Petey and I (586)
   Superstar Barbie (700,700a)

IRVING, JAMES GORDON
   Animal stamps (026)
   Bird stamps (077)

IRWIN, KATHLEEN
   Fury (261)

JACKSON, BYRON 1889-1949
see also ARCHER, PETER
   Animal babies (017)
   Brave cowboy Bill (096)
   Busy Timmy (118,118a)
   Christopher and the
      Columbus (145)
   Day at the beach (183)
   Duck and his friends (222,
      222a)
   Jerry at school (362)
   Katie the kitten (373,
      373FS)
   Little galoshes (407)
   Little trapper (438)
   Little Yip Yip and his bark
      (439)
   Party pig (573)
   Saggy baggy elephant (662,
      662FS,662SR,662a,662b)

JACKSON, KATHRYN 1907-
see also ARCHER, PETER
   Animal babies (017)
   Animals' merry Christmas
      (029,029a)

JACKSON, KATHRYN (cont'd)
    Brave cowboy Bill (096)
    Busy Timmy (118,118a)
    Cars (125)
    Christopher and the
        Columbus (145)
    Circus ABC (150)
    Day at the beach (183)
    Duck and his friends (222,
        222a)
    Farm stamps (231)
    Here comes the parade (312)
    Jerry at school (362)
    Katie the kitten (373,
        373FS)
    Little Eskimo (405)
    Little Galoshes (407)
    Little Trapper (438)
    Little Yip Yip and his
        bark (439)
    Nurse Nancy (547,547a,547b)
    Off to school (552)
    Pantaloon (570)
    Party pig (573)
    Puss in boots (610,610a,
        610SR)
    Saggy baggy elephant (662,
        662FS,662SR,662a,662b)
    Sly little bear and other
        bears (683)
    Tawny scrawny lion (711,
        711FS,711MP,711SR,711a,
        711b)
    Trucks (760)
    Wheels (791)

JACKSON, PAULINE 1918- (illus)
    [Polly Jackson]
    Out of my window (566)

JACKSON, POLLY
    see JACKSON, PAULINE 1918-

JANCAR, MILLI (illus)
    Bozo and the hide 'n' seek
        elephant (093)
    Cindy Bear (149,149B)
    Tawny scrawny lion and the
        clever monkey (712,712SR)

JASON ART STUDIOS (illus)
    Mary Poppins - a jolly
        holiday (465)
    Mr. Rogers' neighborhood -
        Henrietta meets someone
        new (497)

JASON ART STUDIOS (cont'd)
    Pink Panther in the
        haunted house (591,591a)
    Underdog and the disappear-
        ing ice cream (772)
    Wizard of Oz (814,814a)

JOHNSON, AUDEAN (illus)
    Who needs a cat? (802)

JOHNSON, FLORENCE
    Christmas ABC (140)

JOHNSTON, SCOTT (illus)
    Sly little bear and other
        bears (683)
    Sticks (693)

JOHNSTON, WILLIAM
    Bozo and the hide 'n'
        seek elephant (093)

JONAS, HOMER (illus)
    Donald Duck, private eye
        (211)

JONAS, NITA
    Little golden book of dogs
        (411,411a,411b,411c)

JONES, ELIZABETH ORTON 1910-
    (author/illus)
    Little Red Riding Hood
        (437,437B,437SR,437a,
        437b)

JOYNER, JERRY 1938- (illus)
    Bialosky's Christmas (065)
    Bialosky's special picnic
        (066)

JUSTICE, BILL (illus)
    Bunny book, Walt Disney's
        (116)
    Donald Duck's toy train
        (213,219)
    Grandpa Bunny (297)

JUSTUS, MAY 1898-
    Fun for Hunky Dory (259)
    Wonderful school (817)

KALER, JAMES OTIS 1848-1912
    Toby Tyler (735)

KANE, SHARON (illus)
    Counting rhymes (165b)
    Little Mommy
        (author/illus) (431)

KANE, WILMA
    Little golden paper dolls
        (424,424a,424b,424c)
    Paper doll wedding (571)

KARI (narrator)
    Chicken Little (133SR)
    Little red caboose (435SR)
    Pat-a-cake, a baby's Mother
        Goose (574SR)

KAUFMAN, CAROL
    Reading, writing and
        spelling stamps (627)

KAUFMAN, JOE 1911-
    (author/illus)
    Things in my house (719,
    719a)

KAWAGUCHI, M. (illus)
    Yogi Bear (828)

KAYE, DANNY 1913- (narrator)
    Musicians of Bremen (500SR)
    Snow White and Rose Red
        (688SR)
    Ugly duckling (768SR)

KEAN, EDWARD (GEORGE) 1924-
    Howdy Doody and Clarabell
        (329)
    Howdy Doody and his magic
        hat (330)
    Howdy Doody and Mr. Bluster
        (331)
    Howdy Doody and Santa Claus
        (332)
    Howdy Doody and the
        Princess (333)
    Howdy Doody in funland
        (334)
    Howdy Doody's circus (336)
    Howdy Doody's lucky trip
        (337)
    It's Howdy Doody time (354)

KELSEY, DICK
    see KELSEY, RICHMOND I.

KELSEY, RICHMOND I. (illus)
[Dick Kelsey]
    Bugs Bunny and the Indians
        (105,105a)
    Bunny book, Walt Disney's
        (116)
    Donald Duck and the witch
        (205)
    Donald Duck's toy train
        (219)
    Grandpa Bunny (297)
    Little man of Disneyland
        (430)
    Mad Hatter's tea party
        (452)
    Peter and the wolf
        (580,580a)

KENNEL, MORITZ (illus)
    Animal counting book (018)
    Big little book (074)
    My little golden animal
        book (515,515a)
    Old MacDonald had a farm
        (553a,553aSR,553b)

KENT, JACK
    see KENT, JOHN WELLINGTON
    1920-1985

KENT, JOHN WELLINGTON 1920-
    1985 (author/illus)
[Jack Kent]
    There's no such thing as a
        dragon (718,718SR)

KENWORTHY, CATHERINE
    Best friends (062)

KETCHAM, HANK
    see KETCHAM, HENRY KING
    1920-

KETCHAM, HENRY KING 1920-
[Hank Ketcham]
    Dennis the Menace. A quiet
        afternoon (190)
    Dennis the Menace and Ruff
        (191,191a)
    Dennis the Menace waits for
        Santa (192)

KIMBRELL, WOODY (illus)
    Little Lulu (428)

KINNEY, DICK (illus)
    Peter Pan and the Indians
        (581,581a)

KLINORDLINGER, JEAN
    Cindy Bear (149,149B)

KOENIG, JOANNE E. (illus)
    Ginghams: The backward
        picnic (278,278a)

KOESTER, SHARON (illus)
    My baby sister (502,502a)

KORMAN, JUSTINE
    Robotman & friends at
        school (643)

KORR, DAVID
    Cookie Monster and the
        cookie tree (160,160SR,
        160a)
    I think that it is
        wonderful (347)

KRAUSS, RUTH (IDA) 1911-
    I can fly (343)

KRINSLEY, JEANETTE
    Cow went over the mountain
        (168)

KRULL, KATHLEEN 1952-
[Kathleen Krull Cowles]
    What will I be? (790)

KRUSH, BETH 1918- (illus)
    Count to ten (164,164a)

KUDO, BEN (illus)
    Bugs Bunny at the Easter
        party (107)

KUNHARDT, DOROTHY M(ESERVE)
1901(?)-1979
    Little Peewee (432,432SR)
    Lucky Mrs. Ticklefeather
        (447)

KUNHARDT, EDITH T.
    Animal quiz book (025)
    Grandma and Grandpa Smith
        (296)

KURTZ, ELAINE (illus)
    Aren't you glad? (034)

LACHMAN, RUTH MABEE
    Airplanes (006,006a)
    Boats (084,084a,084b)

LAINE, MISS (narrator)
    Animals of Farmer Jones
        (030aSR)

LAITE, GORDON 1925- (illus)
    Blue book of fairy tales
        (083)
    Chitty Chitty Bang Bang
        (139,139B,139SR)
    Cinderella paper dolls
        (147)
    Lisa and the eleven swans
        (395)

LaMONT, VIOLET (illus)
    Let's save money (389)
    Mother Goose (489)
    Numbers (546,546SR,546a,
        546b)
    Off to school (552)

LAMSWEERDE, FRANS VAN (illus)
    Hokey Wolf and Ding-a-Ling
        (312)

LANDE, KAY (narrator)
    Little boy with a big horn
        (401SR)
    Lively little rabbit
        (441SR)
    Puss in boots (610aSR)
    Seven little postmen
        (673SR)
    Shy little kitten (678SR)
    Smokey the Bear (687SR)
    Three little kittens
        (725SR)
    Three little pigs (726SR)
    Twelve days of Christmas
        (763SR)

LANTZ, WALTER 1900- (illus)
    Woody Woodpecker at the
        circus (820,820a)
    Woody Woodpecker drawing
        fun for beginners (821)
    Woody Woodpecker joins the
        circus (822,822a)
    Woody Woodpecker takes a
        trip (823,823a)

LAWSON, ROBERT 1892-1957
    Ben and me (059)

LAZARE, JACK (narrator)
    Little Red Riding Hood
        (437SR)

LAZARUS, LEON
    Lassie and the lost
        explorer (384)
    Tales of Wells Fargo (708)

LEAKE, DONALD (illus)
    Boo and the flying Flews
        (088)

LEAR, EDWARD 1812-1888
    Owl and the pussycat (567)

LEDER, DORA (illus)
    Jack and the beanstalk
        (356,356a)
    Mother Goose in the city
        (491,491a)

LEE, ROBERT J. 1921- (illus)
    David and Goliath (180,
        180SR,180a,180b)

LEE, SING (pseud)
    see MULLAN, CAROL

LEITHAUSER, GLADYS 1925-
    Rabbit is next (616,616a)

LEON, RUTH HOPE 1888-
    What am I? (787,787a)

LEONE, JOHN (illus)
    Maverick (466)
    Tales of Wells Fargo (708)

LEONE, SERGIO 1921- (illus)
    Romper Room exercise book
        (646)

LERCH, STEFFIE E. 1908-
    (illus)
    Little golden Christmas
        manger (420)
    Story of Jesus (697)
    We like to do things (784,
        784FS)

LESLIE, SARAH
    Rainbow Brite and the brook
        meadow deer (625,625SR)

LETTEW, RONALD (illus)
    Where Jesus lived (797,
        797a)

LEVENTHAL, JOHN PHILIP
    From then to now (257)

LEVINE, MILTON I(SRA) 1902-
    Tommy visits the doctor
        (743)

LEWIS, JEAN 1924-
    Bamm-Bamm, with Pebbles
        Flintstone (051)
    Bugs Bunny - too many
        carrots (111,111a)
    Chitty Chitty Bang Bang
        (139,139B,139SR)
    Dogs (201)
    Little golden book of
        holidays (413)
    Pebbles Flintstone (576)
    Scooby Doo and the pirate
        treasure (670)
    Swiss family Robinson (705)
    Tom and Jerry's photo
        finish (741)
    Wacky Witch and the mystery
        of the king's gold (776,
        776SR)

LEWIS, SINCLAIR 1885-1951
    Bongo (087,087a)

LINDGREN, ASTRID 1907-
    Remarkably strong Pippi
        Longstocking (628)

LINDQUIST, WILLIS 1908-
    Cowboys and Indians (171)
    Old Yeller (555)

LINDSAY, BARBARA
    Captain Kangaroo's surprise
        party (119,123)

LLOYD, ANNE (narrator)
    Little Red Riding Hood
        (437SR)
    Three bears (722SR)
    Three little kittens
        (725SR)

LOCKWOOD, HAZEL
    Golden book of birds (279)

LORDIER, PAT (narrator)
  Wacky Witch and the mystery
    of the king's gold
    (776SR)

LORENCZ, BILL
  see LORENCZ, WILLIAM

LORENCZ, WILLIAM (illus)
  [Bill Lorencz]
    Beaney goes to sea (053)
    Scooby Doo and the pirate
      treasure (670)
    Touche Turtle (750)
    Tweety plays catch the
      puddy tat (761,761a)
    Wally Gator (779)

LORENZINI, CARLO 1826-1890
  [Carlo Collodi]
    Pinocchio (592,592a)
    Pinocchio and the whale
      (593)

LOW, ALICE 1926-
  Open up my suitcase (560)
  Out of my window (566)

LOWREY, JANETTE SEBRING 1892-
  Baby's book (044)
  Day in the jungle (186)
  Poky little puppy (600,
    600FS,600MP,600SR,600a,
    600b,600c,600cSR)
  Where is the poky little
    puppy? (796)

LUHRS, PAUL
  Paul Revere (575)

LUNT, ALICE
  Little gray donkey (426)

M.H. (pseud)
  see HARSHBERGER, MAC

MGM CARTOONS (author/illus)
  Tom and Jerry (737,737a)
  Tom and Jerry meet Little
    Quack (738,738B,738a)
  Tom and Jerry's merry
    Christmas (739)
  Tom and Jerry's party (740)

McCANN, GERALD (illus)
  Play ball (595)

McCLAIN, MARY S.   (illus)
  Raggedy Ann and Andy. Five
    birthday parties in a row
    (618)

MacCOMBIE, TURI (illus)
  Dogs (201)

McCULLEY, JOHNSTON 1883-1958
  Zorro (830)
  Zorro and the secret plan
    (831)

McDERMOTT, CAROLINE
  Little Crow (403)

McELROY, MARGARET JULIA 1889-
  [Hilda K. Williams]
    Up in the attic (773)

McGARY, NORM (illus)
  Bamm-Bamm, with Pebbles
    Flintstone (051)
  Donald Duck's Christmas
    carol (215)
  Lippy the Lion and Hardy
    Har Har (394)
  Scamp (668)
  Sword in the stone (706)
  Touche turtle (750)
  Woody Woodpecker drawing
    fun for beginners (821)

McGINLEY, PHYLLIS (LOUISE)
1905-1978
  Name for kitty (529)

McGOVERN, ANN
  Annie Oakley and the
    rustlers (032)
  Dog stamps (200)
  Huckleberry Hound builds
    a house (340)
  Huckleberry Hound safety
    signs (341)
  Party in Shariland (572)
  Rocky and his friends (644)
  Roy Rogers and the mountain
    lion (653)
  Ruff and Reddy (657,657a)
  Winky Dink (810)
  Woody Woodpecker takes a
    trip (823,823a)

McGUIRE, LESLIE (SARAH) 1945-
    Bialosky's Christmas (065)
    Bialosky's special picnic
        (066)

McHUGH, GELOLO 1907-
    Baby's house (047,047a)

McKIM, SAM (illus)
    Toby Tyler (735)

McKIMSON, TOM 1907- (illus)
    Bugs Bunny (104,104B,104a,
        104b)
    Bugs Bunny and the Indians
        (105,105a)
    Porky Pig and Bugs Bunny.
        Just like magic! (606,
        606a)

MACLANE, KERRY (narrator)
    Poky little puppy (600MP)
    Tawny scrawny lion (711MP)

MacLAUGHLIN, DON (illus)
    Bugs Bunny at the county
        fair (106)
    Bugs Bunny gets a job (108)
    Tom and Jerry (737,737a)
    Tom and Jerry meet Little
        Quack (738,738B,738a)
    Ugly duckling (768,768SR)

McLENIGHAN, VALJEAN 1947-
    Ernie's work of art (227)

McNAUGHT, HARRY (illus)
    Emerald City of Oz (226)
    Howdy Doody's lucky trip
        (337)
    Road to Oz (639)
    Tin Woodman of Oz (732)

MacPHERSON, ELIZABETH (H.)
    My little golden animal
        book (515,515a)

McQUEEN, LUCINDA (illus)
    Gull that lost the sea
        (300)
    Theodore Mouse goes to sea
        (717,717VC)

McSAVAGE, FRANK (illus)
    Woodsy owl and the trail
        bikers (819)

McSAVAGE, FRANK (cont'd)
    Woody Woodpecker at the
        circus (820,820a)

MACE, HARRY (F.) 1922-
    When I grow up (792,792a,
        792aSR)

MACE, KAY (KATHERINE KEELER)
    1921-
    When I grow up (792,792a,
        792aSR)

MACK, BRICE (illus)
    Peter Pan and the Indians
        (581,581a)

MACK, GILBERT (songwriter)
    Scuffy the tugboat (671aSR)

MADIGAN, MARGARET
    Good night, Aunt Lilly
        (293)

MAGON, JYMN (songwriter)
    There's no such thing as
        a dragon (718SR)

MAHONY, ELIZABETH WINTHROP
    1948- [Elizabeth Winthrop]
    My first book of the
        planets (509)
    Shoelace box (677)

MALVERN, CORINNE 1905-1956
    (illus)
    All aboard! (012)
    Christmas carols (141,141a)
    Counting rhymes (165,165a)
    Day at the beach (183)
    Doctor Dan the bandage man
        (198,198a)
    5 pennies to spend (245)
    Frosty the snowman (258,
        258SR,258a)
    Fun with decals (260)
    Happy family (305,305a)
    Heidi (310,310SR,310a,310b,
        310c)
    How big? (author/illus)
        (325)
    Jerry at school (362)
    Little golden book of hymns
        414,414a,414b)
    Little golden book of
        poetry (416)

MALVERN, CORINNE (cont'd)
  Little golden book of
    singing games (417)
  Night before Christmas
    (542a)
  Nurse Nancy (547,547a,547b)
  Nursery songs (549)
  Off to school (552)
  Open up my suitcase (560)
  Rainy day play book (626)
  Robert and his new friends
    (640)
  Surprise for Sally (702)
  Susie's new stove (704)
  Tex and his toys (716)
  Uncle Mistletoe (770)
  Up in the attic (773)
  When I grow up (792)
  When you were a baby (793,
    793a)

MARGE
  see BUELL, MARJORIE
  HENDERSON 1904-

MARGE, ELIAS (illus)
  Howdy Doody and Mr.
    Bluster (331)

MARKHAM, MARY BETH
  Willie found a wallet (809)

MARSHALL, CAROL (illus)
  Babes in toyland (036)

MARSHALL, EARL (illus)
  Babes in toyland (036)

MARTIN, BARRY (illus)
  Bunny's magic tricks (117)
  Hansel and Gretel (303)

MARTIN, JUDY (illus)
  Bunny's magic tricks (117)
  Hansel and Gretel (303)

MARTIN, RICHARD A.
  Insect stamps (352)

MARTIN, SARAH CATHERINE
  1768-1826
  Old Mother Hubbard (554,
    554a)

MARX, HILDA (songwriter)
  I can fly (343)

MASHA (pseud)
  see STERN, MARIE SIMCHOW
  1909-

MASON, WALTER M.
  We like to do things (784,
    784FS)

MATHIEU, JOE
  see MATHIEU, JOSEPH

MATHIEU, JOSEPH (illus)
  [Joe Mathieu]
  Cookie Monster and the
    cookie tree (160,160SR,
    160a)
  Ernie's work of art (227)

MATTINSON, BURNETT (illus)
  Pixie and Dixie and Mr.
    Jinks (594)
  Yogi Bear: a Christmas
    visit (829)

MATTINSON, SYLVIA (illus)
  Pixie and Dixie and Mr.
    Jinks (594)
  Yogi Bear: a Christmas
    visit (829)

MAY, ROBERT LEWIS 1905-1976
  Rudolph the red-nosed
    reindeer (655,655SR,
    655a)
  Rudolph the red-nosed
    reindeer shines again
    (656)

MAZZA, ADRIANA
  see SAVIOZZI, ADRIANA MAZZA
  1928-

MEGARGEE, EDWIN (illus)
  Dog stamps (200)

MEIER, ESTA
  Wild kingdom (808)

MEMLING, CARL 1918-1969
  ABC rhymes (003,003B,003SR,
    003a)
  Captain Kangaroo and the
    beaver (121)
  Dennis the Menace. A quiet
    afternoon (190)

MEMLING, CARL (cont'd)
  Dennis the Menace and Ruff
    (191,191a)
  Dennis the Menace waits for
    Santa (192)
  Dick Tracy (193)
  Gay purr-ee (265)
  Hey there - it's Yogi Bear
    (314)
  I have a secret (344)
  Jetsons (363)
  Little Cottontail (402)
  Little golden book of
    helicopters (412)
  Maverick (466)
  My magic slate book (523)
  Our flag (563)
  Peter Potamus (584)
  Quick Draw McGraw (613)
  Riddles, riddles, from
    A to Z (632,632SR)
  Rupert the rhinoceros
    (660)
  Savage Sam (667)
  Steve Canyon (692)
  Sword in the stone (706)
  10 little animals (715)
  Toby Tyler (735)
  Tom Thumb (742)
  Top Cat (748)
  Touche turtle (750)
  Ugly dachshund (767)
  Wizard's duel (815)

MEYER, LOIS
  Store-bought doll (695)

MICLAT, ALEX C. (illus)
  Poky little puppy follows
    his nose home (601,601a)

MILANO, FRANK
  (narrator)
  Poky little puppy (600SR)

MILLER, J(OHN) P(ARR)
  1913- (illus)
  Brave little tailor (098)
  Circus ABC (150)
  Day on the farm (187,187SR,
    187a)
  Doctor Squash, the doll
    doctor (199)
  House that Jack built (323)
  Jack's adventure (358)
  Jingle bells (366)

MILLER, J(OHN) P(ARR) (cont'd)
  Large and growly bear (380,
    380FS,380SR,380a)
  Little galoshes (407)
  Little golden funny book
    (421)
  Little Peewee (432,432SR)
  Little red hen (436a,
    436aSR,436b,436c)
  Lucky Mrs. Ticklefeather
    (447)
  Marvelous merry-go-round
    (463)
  Musicians of Bremen (500,
    500SR)
  Puss in boots (610,610a,
    610aSR)
  Rags (624,624SR,624a)
  Tommy's wonderful rides
    (745)
  What if? (788)
  Wonderful house (816)

MILLER, MITCH 1911-
  (music director)
  Little Red Riding Hood
    (437SR)
  Poky little puppy (600SR)
  Three bears (722SR)

MILLER, ROBERTA
  Chipmunk's ABC (137)
  My word book (528)

MILNE, A(LAN) A(LEXANDER)
  1882-1956
  Winnie-the-Pooh and Tigger
    (811,811a)
  Winnie-the-Pooh meets
    Gopher (812,812a)
  Winnie-the-Pooh: the
    honey tree (813)

MILOCHE, HILDA
  Little golden paper dolls
    (424,424a,424b,425c)
  Paper doll wedding (571)

MIRYAM (pseud)
  see YARDUMIAN, MIRYAM

MITCHELL, FRANCES SCORE
  (illus)
  Little golden book of hymns
    (414c)

MITCHELL, LUCY SPRAGUE 1878-
    Fix it, please! (246,246FS)
    New house in the forest
        (538)
    Taxi that hurried (713,
        713B,713SR)
    Year in the city (826)
    Year on the farm (827,
        827FS)

MOORE, BOB (illus)
    Donald Duck's Christmas
        tree (216)
    Dumbo (223,223B,223a,234)
    Mickey Mouse goes Christmas
        shopping (477)
    Peter Pan and the pirates
        (582,582a)

MOORE, CLEMENT CLARKE 1779-
1863
    Night before Christmas
        (542,542a,542b)

MOORE, LILIAN
    Count to ten (164,164a)
    My first counting book
        (510,510a,510b)

MOSS, JEFFREY
    Oscar's book (561,561a)

MOWERS, PATRICIA
    Baby's birthday (043,
        043a)

MULFORD, CLARENCE E(DWARD)
1883-1956
    Hopalong Cassidy and the
        Bar 20 cowboy (321)

MULLAN, CAROL
[Sing Lee]
    Bible stories from the Old
        Testament (067,067a)

MUNTEAN, MICHAELA
    Theodore Mouse goes to sea
        (717,717VC)

MURDOCCA, SAL(VATORE) (illus)
    Grover's own alphabet (298)

NAGEL, STINA 1918-1969 (illus)
    Magic friend-maker (455,
        455SR)

NAST, ELSA RUTH (pseud)
    see WATSON, JANE WERNER
    1915-

NATHAN, STELLA WILLIAMS
    Chicken Little (133a)
    Jack and the beanstalk
        (356, 356a)
    Porky Pig and Bugs Bunny.
        Just like magic! (606,
        606a)
    Woody Woodpecker at the
        circus (820,820a)

NEEBE, WILLIAM (illus)
    Mr. Meyer's cow (494)

NEELY, JAN (illus)
    Donny and Marie (220,220a)
    New friends for the saggy
        baggy elephant (536,
        536SR)

NEZ, JOHN (illus)
    My first book of the
        planets (509)

NICKLAUS, CAROL (illus)
    Mrs. Brisby and the magic
        stone (499)
    Puppy love (609)

NICOLE (pseud)
    see DUPLAIX, GEORGES 1895-

NINA
    Kitten's surprise (375)

NOLTE, NANCY
    Gingerbread man (233,233a,
        276,276a,276aSR,276aVC,
        276b,276c)

NONNAST, MARIE 1924- (illus)
    Captain Kangaroo and the
        beaver (121)

NORRIS, KENNETH (STAFFORD)
1924-
    Happy little whale (307)

NORTON, MIRIAM
    Kitten who thought he was
        a mouse (374)

NUNEZ, BEN DE
  see DE NUNEZ, BEN

OBLIGADO, LILIAN (ISABEL)
1931- (illus)
  Animals and their babies
    (027)
  Charlie (130,130a)
  Four puppies (252,252a)
  Golden egg book (283,283FS,
    283SR,283a)
  I like to live in the
    city (345)
  If I had a dog
    (author/illus) (349)
  Little black puppy (397)
  Little Cottontail (402)
  New puppy (541,541a)
  Pussycat tiger (612,612SR)
  Reading, writing and
    spelling stamps (627)
  Wait-for-me kitten (778)
  Willie found a wallet (809)

O'BRIEN, JOHN (illus)
  Little golden book of jokes
    & riddles (415)

O'BRIEN, KEN (illus)
  Snow White and the seven
    dwarfs (689,689a)

OECHSLI, KELLY 1918- (illus)
  Animal quiz book (025)

OHLSSON, IB 1935- (illus)
  Rainy day play book (626a)

OREB, TOM (illus)
  Once upon a wintertime
    (556)

ORLEANS, ILO (LOUIS) 1897-1962
  Animal orchestra (023)

OSSWALD, EDITH
  Come play house (158)
  Come play with me (159)
  My little golden
    dictionary (522,522a)
  Numbers (546,546SR,546a,
    546b)
  Toys (752)

O'SULLIVAN, TOM (illus)
  Big enough helper (073,
    073a)
  Cat who stamped his feet
    (127)
  Corky's hiccups (162,162SR)
  Who comes to your house?
    (801,801SR)

OTTUM, BOB
  Cars (125a,125b)
  Shazam! (676)

PAFLIN, ROBERTA (pseud)
  see PETTY, ROBERTA HARRIS
  PFAFFLIN 1903-

PALMER, HELEN MARION
  see GEISEL, HELEN 1898-1967

PALMER, MARION
  see GEISEL, HELEN 1898-1967

PARISH, PEGGY 1927-
  Hush, hush, it's sleepytime
    (342,342a)
  Littlest raccoon (440)
  My little golden book of
    manners (520)

PARKER, BERTHA MORRIS 1890-
  Deep blue sea (189)

PARMALEE, TED (illus)
  Johnny Appleseed (367)

PARSONS, VIRGINIA
(author/illus)
  Fly high (248)
  Sam the firehouse cat (664)

PATTERSON, PAT
  How does your garden grow?
    (326)

PEET, BILL
  see PEET, WILLIAM BARTLETT
  1915-

PEET, WILLIAM BARTLETT 1915-
(author/illus) [Bill Peet]
  Goliath II (287,287SR)

PELTZMAN, RONNE
  Mr. Bell's fixit shop (493)

PEREGOY, WALT (illus)
    Sleeping Beauty (679)
    Sleeping Beauty paper dolls
        (681)

PERNA, DEBI (illus)
    How does your garden grow?
        (326)

PERRAULT, CHARLES 1628-1703
    Puss in boots (610,610a,
        610aSR)

PERRIN, BLANCHE CHENERY
1894-1973
    Horses (322,322a)
    New pony (540)

PETTY, ROBERTA HARRIS PFAFFLIN
1903- [Roberta Paflin]
    This little piggy (720)

PFLOOG, JAN (illus)
    Animals on the farm
        (author/illus) (031,031a)
    Tiny tawny kitten (733)

PFLOOG, PIET (illus)
    Pick up sticks (588)

PINCHEVSKY, LEONID (illus)
    Hush, hush, it's sleepytime
        (342,342a)

PIPER, WATTY (pseud)
    see BRAGG, MABEL CAROLINE
    1870-1945

POGUE, KATE EMERY
    Bravest of all (099,099SR,
        099a)
    Fritzie goes home (256)

POINTER, PRISCILLA (illus)
    Our baby (562)

PORTER, ELEANOR H. 1868-1920
    Pollyanna (604)

POTTER, BEATRIX
1866-1943
    Tale of Peter Rabbit (707,
        707a,707b)

POTTER, MARIAN 1915-
    Little red caboose (435,
        435SR,435a,435b)

POWELL, ED (narrator)
    Puss in boots (610aSR)

POWELL, LINDA (illus)
    Rabbit is next (616,616a)

PRATT, HAWLEY (illus)
    Bamm-Bamm, with Pebbles
        Flintstone (051)
    Beaney goes to sea (053)
    Bozo finds a friend (094,
        094SR)
    Bullwinkle (114)
    Dennis the Menace and Ruff
        191,191a)
    Dick Tracy (193)
    Fireball XL5 (238)
    Gay purr-ee (265)
    Hey there - it's Yogi Bear
        (314)
    Jetsons (363)
    Lippy the Lion and Hardy
        Har Har (394)
    Ludwig Von Drake (450)
    Magilla Gorilla (458)
    Peter Potamus (584)
    Quick Draw McGraw (613)
    Top Cat (748)
    Wally Gator (779)
    Wizard's duel (815)
    Yakky Doodle and Chopper
        (825)

PRAY, RUPERT
    Whistling Wizard (799)

PRICKETT, HELEN (illus)
    My daddy is a policeman
        (505)

PRIESTLY, LEE (SHORE) 1904-
    Giant who wanted company
        (274)

PROBST, PIERRE 1913-
(author/illus)
    Bobby the dog (086)
    Puff the blue kitten (608)
    Rusty goes to school (661)

PROKOFIEFF, SERGE 1891-1953
    Peter and the wolf (580,
        580a)

PROVENSEN, ALICE 1918- (illus)
    Color kittens (156,156FS,
        156SR,156a,156b,156c)
    Fuzzy duckling (263,263FS,
        263SR,263a,263b,263c)
    Katie the kitten (373,
        373FS)
    Little fat policeman (406,
        406SR)
    Mr. Noah and his family
        (495)

PROVENSEN, MARTIN 1916-
    (illus)
    Color kittens (156,156FS,
        156SR,156a,156b,156c)
    Fuzzy duckling (263,263FS,
        263SR,263a,263b,263c)
    Katie the kitten (373,
        373FS)
    Little fat policeman (406,
        406SR)
    Mr. Noah and his family
        (495)

PYK, JAN (illus)
    New home for Snow Ball
        (537)

QUIGLEY, RAY (illus)
    Trucks (760)

RAINWATER, JANETTE
    Dragon in a wagon (221,
        221FS)

RAYMOND, LOUISE 1907-
    [Beatrice Alexander]
    Story of Jesus (697)

REED, MARY MAUD 1880-1960
    My little golden
        dictionary (522,522a)
    Numbers (546,546SR,546a,
        546b)

REIT, SEYMOUR
    Fury takes the jump (262)
    Gunsmoke (301)

RICHARDS, JEAN H.
    Stories of Jesus (696,696a)

RINALDI, JOE (illus)
    Scamp (668)
    Scamp's adventure (669,
        669a)

RITA (narrator)
    Gingerbread man (276aSR)
    Little red hen (436aSR)
    Numbers (546SR)

ROBERTS, JERRY (narrator)
    Big brown bear (072SR)
    Happy man and his dump
        truck (308SR)

ROBERTS, LAINE (narrator)
    Who comes to your house
        (801SR)

ROBINSON, SELMA 1899?-1977
    Betsy McCall (064)

ROBISON, JIM (illus)
    Animals' Christmas eve
        (028,028a)
    Bible stories from the Old
        Testament (067,067a)
    Superstar Barbie (700,700a)

RODEGAST, ROLAND (illus)
    ABC rhymes (003,003B,003SR,
        003a)

ROFry (illus)
    Little boy and the giant
        (400)
    My home (512,512a)
    Three little pigs (726,
        726SR,726a)

ROGERS, FRED (McFEELY) 1928-
    Mr. Rogers' neighborhood -
        Henrietta meets someone
        new (497)

ROJANKOVSKY, FEODOR
    (STEPANOVICH) 1891-1970
    (illus)
    Animal dictionary (020,
        020a,020b)
    Cow went over the mountain
        (168)
    Gaston and Josephine (264)
    Golden book of birds (279)
    Hop, little kangaroo (320)
    Kitten's surprise (375)
    Little golden Mother Goose
        (423,423a,423b,423c)
    More Mother Goose rhymes
        (486)
    Mother Goose rhymes (492)

ROJANKOVSKY, FEODOR (cont'd)
Name for kitty (529)
Our puppy (564,564a)
10 little animals (715)
Three bears (722,722SR,
722a)
Treasury of little golden
books (757,757a)
White Bunny and his magic
nose (800,800SR)
Wild animal babies (805)
Wild animals (806)

ROSENBERG, AMYE (illus)
Biggest most beautiful
Christmas tree
(author/illus) (076)
Polly's pet (603)

ROSENBERG-TUROW, CATHI
Big Bird's day on the farm
(070)

ROSS, ELIZABETH
Three little pigs (726,
726SR,726a)

ROSS, LARRY 1943- (illus)
Circus is in town (152,
152a)

RUDOLF (pseud)
see FREUND, RUDOLF
1915-1969

RUMELY, LOUISE (illus)
Brownie scouts (101)

RUTH, ROD 1912- (illus)
Feelings from A to Z
(235)
Whales (786,786a)

RUTHERFOORD, WILLIAM de
J(ANETTE) (illus)
Dinosaurs (194,194a)

RYERSON, JOHN (narrator)
Five little firemen (244SR)

SAHULA-DYCKE (illus)
Hopalong Cassidy and the
Bar 20 cowboy (321)

SALTEN, FELIX
see SALZMANN, SIEGMUND
1869-1945

SALVA, ADA (illus)
Tammy (709)

SALZMANN, SIEGMUND 1869-1945
[Felix Salten]
Bambi (049,049B,049a,049b)
Bambi, friends of the
forest (050,050a)
Manni the donkey (461)
Perri and her friends (578)

SAMPSON, KATHERINE (illus)
Doctor Dan at the circus
(197)

SANDERSON, RUTH (L.) 1951-
(illus)
One of the family (557)
Owl and the pussycat (567)
Store-bought doll (695)
When you were a baby (793b)

SANDPIPERS (singers)
Little boy with a big horn
(401SR)
Scuffy the tugboat (671aSR)
Twelve days of Christmas
(763SR)

SANTOS, GEORGE (illus)
Loopy de Loop goes west
(445)

SATTERFIELD, C.W. (illus)
Sleeping Beauty and the
good fairies (680)
Sleeping Beauty paper dolls
(681)

SATTERFIELD, CHARLES (illus)
Bozo the clown (095,095SR)
Huckleberry Hound and the
Christmas sleigh (339)

SATZMAN, BEN
Cub Scouts (foreword)
(172)

SAVAGE, STEELE 1900- (illus)
Airplanes (006a)

SAVIOZZI, ADRIANA MAZZA 1928-
(illus) [Adriana Mazza]
Farm stamps (231)
Four little kittens (251,
251a,251b)

SAVIOZZI, ADRIANA MAZZA
 (cont'd)
    Nursery songs (549a,549b)
    Tale of Peter Rabbit (707,
      707a,707b)

SAXON, GLADYS R(ELYEA)
    Cowboy ABC (169)
    Tommy's camping adventure
      (744)

SAYLES, WILLIAM (illus)
    First golden geography
      (241)
    Our world (565)

SCARRY, PATRICIA (MURPHY)
  1924- [Patsy Scarry]
    Bunny book (115,115a)
    Corky (161)
    Country mouse and the city
      mouse (166)
    Danny Beaver's secret (178)
    Giant little golden book of
      kittens (273)
    Good night, Little Bear
      (294)
    Hop, little kangaroo (320)
    Just for fun (371,371a)
    Let's visit the dentist
      (390)
    My baby brother (501)
    My baby sister (502,502a)
    My dolly and me (506)
    My kitten (513,513a,513b)
    My pets (524)
    My puppy (525,525a)
    My snuggly bunny (526)
    My teddy bear (527,527a)
    Pierre Bear (589)
    Rags (624,624SR,624a)
    Wait-for-me kitten (778)

SCARRY, PATSY
    see SCARRY, PATRICIA MURPHY
    1924-

SCARRY, RICHARD (McCLURE)
  1919- (illus)
    Albert's zoo (008)
    Animals' Merry Christmas
      (029,029a)
    Animals of Farmer Jones
      (030a,030aSR,030b,030c)
    Brave cowboy Bill (096)
    Bunny book (115,115a)

SCARRY, RICHARD (cont'd)
    Cars and trucks
      (author/illus) (126,126a)
    Chicken little (133,133SR)
    Chipmunk's ABC (137)
    Chipmunks' merry Christmas
      (138)
    Country mouse and the city
      mouse (166)
    Cowboy stamps (170)
    Cowboys and Indians (171)
    Danny Beaver's secret (178)
    Duck and his friends (222,
      222a)
    Gingerbread man (233,233a,
      276,276a,276aSR,276aVC,
      276c)
    Good night, Little Bear
      (294)
    Here comes the parade (312)
    Just for fun (371,371a)
    Little Benny wanted a pony
      (396)
    Little golden book about
      colors (409)
    Little Indian (427)
    My little golden book of
      manners (520)
    My little golden Christmas
      book (cover illus) (521)
    My little golden dictionary
      (522,522a)
    Naughty bunny (author/
      illus) (531,531SR)
    Nursery tales (551)
    Party pig (573)
    Pierre Bear (589)
    Rabbit and his friends
      (author/illus) (615,615a)
    Rudolph the red-nosed
      reindeer (655,655SR,655a)
    Smokey the Bear (687,
      687SR,687a,687b)
    Three billy goats gruff
      (724)
    Tommy visits the doctor
      (743)
    Two little miners (766)
    Winky Dink (810)

SCHAAR, BOB (illus)
    Lassie and the big clean-up
      day (382,382a)

SCHAFFENBERGER, KURT 1920-
   (illus)
   Buck Rogers and the
      children of Hopetown
      (102)
   Shazam! (676)

SCHART, TRINA
   see HYMAN, TRINA SCHART
   1939-

SCHLEIN, MIRIAM 1926-
   Day at the playground (184)

SCHMIDT, AL (illus)
   Cheyenne (132)

SCHMIDT, EDWIN (illus)
   Captain Kangaroo and the
      panda (119,122)
   Captain Kangaroo's surprise
      party (119,123)
   Indian stamps (351)
   J. Fred Muggs (355)
   Lone Ranger and Tonto (444)
   Old Yeller (555)

SCHNEIDER, NINA (ZIMET) 1913-
   Robert and his new friends
      (640)

SCHRETER, RICK (illus)
   Book of God's gifts (089,
      089a)

SCHROEDER, RUSSELL K.
   Mickey Mouse and the great
      lot plot (472)
   Road Runner (637,637a)

SCHROEDER, TED (illus)
   Elephant on wheels (224)

SCHURR, CATHLEEN 1916-
   Giant little golden book
      of kittens (273)
   Shy little kitten (273,678,
      678FS,678a,678b,678c)

SCHWENINGER, ANN 1951- (illus)
   Musicians of Bremen (500a)

SCOTT, CECELIA (narrator)
   Circus time (153SR)
   Fuzzy duckling (263SR)
   Happy days (304SR)

SCOTT, CECELIA (cont'd)
   Naughty bunny (531SR)
   Tiger's adventure (731SR)
   Ukelele and her new doll
      (769SR)
   When I grow up (792aSR)

SCOTT, JERRY (illus)
   Bear's surprise party (055)
   Elephant on wheels (224)

SEIDEN, ART (illus)
   Captain Kangaroo (119,120)
   Howdy Doody and Clarabell
      (329)
   Howdy Doody and his magic
      hat (330)
   Howdy Doody and Santa Claus
      (332)
   Howdy Doody and the
      Princess (333)
   Howdy Doody in funland
      (334)
   Howdy Doody's animal
      friends (335)
   It's Howdy Doody time (354)
   Never pat a bear (533)
   Train to Timbuctoo (754)

SELIGMANN, JEAN H(ORTENSE)
   Tommy visits the doctor
      (743)

SEWARD, JAMES (illus)
   Wild kingdom (808)

SHANE, HAROLD (GRAY) 1914-
   New baby (534,534a,534b,
      534c)
   Twins (764)

SHANE, RUTH
   New baby (534,534a,534b,
      534c)
   Twins (764)

SHAPIRO, IRWIN 1911-1981
   Circus boy (151)
   Cleo (154)
   Daniel Boone (177)
   Davy Crockett, king of the
      wild frontier (181)
   Davy Crockett's keelboat
      race (182)
   J. Fred Muggs (355)
   Paul Revere (575)

SHARP, MARGERY 1905–
Rescuers (629,629a)

SHERMAN, GEORGE
Ludwig Von Drake (450)
Supercar (699)

SHIMEK, JOHN LYLE
Cowboy stamps (170)

SHORTALL, LEONARD W. (illus)
Colors are nice (157,157a)

SLATER, TEDDY
Road runner: mid-mesa marathon (638)

SMARIDGE, NORAH 1903–
I do my best (346,346a)
Neatos and the litterbugs
(532,532FS,532MP,532SR)

SMATH, JERRY (illus)
Cowboy ABC (169)

SMITH, BOB
see SMITH, ROBERT EVERETT
1910–

SMITH, CLAUDE CLAYTON
Cow and the elephant (167)
Gull that lost the sea
(300)

SMITH, DOROTHY HALL
Big little book (074)

SMITH, ROBERT EVERETT 1910–
(illus) [Bob Smith]
Baby's book (044)
My first book (507)

SMOLLIN, MICHAEL J. (illus)
Big Bird's red book (071,
071a)
Monster at the end of this
book (484,484a)

SOLONEVICH, GEORGE 1915–
(illus) [George Solonewitsch]
Exploring space (cover
illus) (228)

SOLONEWITSCH, GEORGE
see SOLONEVICH, GEORGE
1915–

SOSKIN, LILLIAN GARDNER
Brownie scouts (101)

SPECTER, A.J. (illus)
Wacky Witch and the mystery
of the king's gold (776,
776SR)

SPYRI, JOHANNA (HEUSSER)
1827–1901
Heidi (310,310SR,310a,
310b,310c)

STACK, NICOLETE MEREDITH
(McGUIRE) 1896–
Corky's hiccups (162,162SR)

STANG, JUDIT 1921–1977
(illus) [Judy Stang]
Magic next door (456)
Pet in the jar
(author/illus) (579)

STANG, JUDY
see STANG, JUDIT 1921–1977

STANTON, JESSIE
Taxi that hurried (713,
713B,713SR)

STEEL, JOHN (illus)
Zorro (830)

STEIN, MINI
We help Daddy (781,781a)

STEIN, RALPH (music director)
Animals of Farmer Jones
(030aSR)
Big brown bear (072SR)
Happy man and his dump
truck (308SR)
White bunny and his magic
nose (800SR)
Who comes to your house
(801SR)

STERN, ALAN
Whistling wizard (799)

STERN, JEFF (songwriter)
Circus time (153SR)

STERN, MARIE SIMCHOW 1909–
(illus) [Masha]
Giant little golden book
of kittens (273)

STERN, MARIE SIMCHOW (cont'd)
   Nursery tales (550)
   Three little kittens
     (273,725)
   Toys (752)

STERNE, EMMA GELDERS 1894-1971
  [Emily Broun]
   Lone Ranger and the talking
     pony (443)
   Manni the donkey (461)
   Wagon train (777)

STEVENSON, ROBERT LOUIS
  1850-1894
   Child's garden of verses
     (134,134a,134aSR)

STEWART, PAT (illus)
   Fire fighters' counting
     book (237)

STONE, JON 1931-
   Monster at the end of this
     book (484,484a)

STOTT, HERBERT (illus)
   Ludwig Von Drake (450)

STREBE, DOROTHY
   Sleeping Beauty and the
     good fairies (680)

STROBL, ANTHONY (illus)
  [Tony Strobl]
   Bugs Bunny at the Easter
     party (107)
   Bugs Bunny gets a job (108)
   Bugs Bunny's carrot machine
     (113,113a)

STROBL, TONY
   see STROBL, ANTHONY

SUBEN, ERIC
   Elves and the shoemaker
     (225)

SUMERA, ANNABELLE
   What Lily Goose found (789)

SUNSHINE, MADELINE
   Puppy love (609)

SUPER, TERRI (illus)
   Ten items or less (714)
   Grandma and Grandpa Smith
     (296)

SUSCHITZKY, WOLFGANG 1912-
  (author/illus)
   Wild animals (806)

SVENDSEN, JULIUS 1919- (illus)
   Mickey Mouse and the
     missing Mouseketeers
     (473)
   Mickey Mouse Club stamp
     book (475)
   Mickey Mouse flies the
     Christmas mail (476)
   Seven Dwarfs find a house
     (672,672a)
   Sleeping Beauty (679)
   Sleeping Beauty and the
     good fairies (680)
   Sleeping Beauty paper dolls
     (681)

SWANSON, MAGGIE (illus)
   Big Bird's day on the farm
     (070)
   Rabbit's adventure (617,
     617a)

SWETNAM, EVELYN
   Magic next door (456)

SWINDLER, LAUREN COLLIER
   Big Bird brings Spring to
     Sesame Street (069,069VC)

TANOUS, HELEN (NICOL) 1917-
   What if? (788)

TANOUS, HENRY
   What if? (788)

TAYLOR, T. WILLIAM
   Christmas donkey (142)

TEIG, DAVID (narrator)
   Boy with a drum (092SR)
   Little fat policeman
     (406SR)
   Mister dog (482SR)

TENGGREN, GUSTAF (ADOLF)
  1896-1970 (illus)
   Bedtime stories (058,058a,
     058b,058c,058d)

TENGGREN, GUSTAF (cont'd)
    Big brown bear (072,072SR,
        072a,072b)
    Five bedtime stories (243)
    Giant little golden book
        of kittens (273)
    Giant with the three golden
        hairs (275)
    Golden goose (285,285a)
    Jack and the beanstalk (357,
        357a,357aSR,357b,357c)
    Lion's paw (393)
    Little black Sambo (398)
    Little trapper (438)
    Lively little rabbit (441,
        441SR,441a,441b)
    Old MacDonald had a farm
        (553,553a,553aSR,553b)
    Poky little puppy (600,
        600FS,600MP,600SR,600a,
        600b,600c,600cSR)
    Saggy baggy elephant
        (662,662FS,662SR,662a,
        662b)
    Shy little kitten (273,678,
        678FS,678SR,678a,678b,
        678c)
    Snow White and Rose Red
        (688,688SR)
    Tawny scrawny lion (711,
        711FS,711MP,711SR,711a,
        711b)
    Thumbelina (729,729SR,729a)
    Topsy turvy circus (749)
    Where is the poky little
        puppy? (796)

THACHER, ALIDA McKAY
    Elephant on wheels (224)

THACKRAY, PATRICIA
    Amazing Mumford forgets the
        magic words! (015)

THOMPSON, ROBERT
    Toy soldiers (751)

THOMSON, RILEY (illus)
    Woody Woodpecker joins the
        circus (822,822a)

TIMMINS, WILLIAM (illus)
    Here comes the band (311)

TOTTEN, BOB (illus)
    Bugs Bunny - too many
        carrots (111,111a)
    Bugs Bunny's carrot machine
        (113,113a)
    Donald Duck, lost and found
        (210)
    Huckleberry Hound and his
        friends (338)
    Mickey Mouse and the
        missing Mouseketeers
        (473)
    Porky Pig and Bugs Bunny.
        Just like magic! (606,
        606a)
    Road Runner (637,637a)
    Wacky Witch and the mystery
        of the king's gold (776,
        776SR)
    Winnie-the-Pooh: the honey
        tree (813)

TRAVERS, P(AMELA) L(YNDON)
1906-
    Gingerbread shop (277)
    Magic compass (454)
    Mr. Wiggs' birthday party
        (498)

TREMAYNE, LES 1913- (narrator)
    Neatos and the litterbugs
        (532MP)
    Poky little puppy (600MP)
    Tawny scrawny lion (711MP)

TURNER, DON (illus)
    Remarkably strong Pippi
        Longstocking (628)
    Wizard of Oz (814,814a)

UPA CARTOONS
    Howdy Doody and his magic
        hat (330)

UPA PICTURES
    Gay purr-ee (265)

USHLER, JOHN (illus)
    Mickey Mouse and his space
        ship (469,469a)

VAL, SUE
    I think about God (346,
        346a)

VANDERLAAN, SI (illus)
  Brave Eagle (097)

VAUGHN, FRANK (illus)
  Good-bye tonsils (289)

VERRAL, CHARLES SPAIN 1904-
  Annie Oakley, sharpshooter
    (033)
  Brave Eagle (097)
  Broken arrow (100)
  Cheyenne (132)
  Flying car (249)
  Lassie and her day in the
    sun (005,381,381a,381b)
  Lassie and the daring
    rescue (005,383)
  Lone Ranger and Tonto (444)
  Play ball (595)
  Rin Tin Tin and the outlaw
    (636)
  Shaggy dog (675)
  Smokey and his animal
    friends (684)
  Zorro (830)
  Zorro and the secret plan
    (831)

VISSER, PAT
  Feelings from A to Z (235)

VOGEL, ILSE-MARGRET 1914-
  (author/illus)
  Animal daddies and my daddy
    (illus. only) (019,019a)
  Bear in the boat (054)
  Daisy Dog's wake-up book
    (174)
  My little dinosaur (514)
  1,2,3, juggle with me (558,
    558a)
  When I grow up (792a,
    792aSR)

WALT DISNEY STUDIO
  see DISNEY, WALT(ER ELIAS)
  1901-1966

WALTON, MARY ANN
  My first book of Bible
    stories (508)

WARD, MURIEL
  Little pond in the woods
    (433)

WARNER BROTHERS
  Cheyenne (132)

WARNER BROTHERS CARTOONS
  (author/illus)
  Bugs Bunny (104,104B,104a,
    104b)
  Bugs Bunny and the Indians
    (105,105a)
  Bugs Bunny at the county
    fair (106)
  Bugs Bunny at the Easter
    party (107)
  Bugs Bunny gets a job (108)
  Bugs Bunny's birthday (112)

WATSON, JANE WERNER 1915-
  [Annie North Bedford, Monica
  Hill, Elsa Ruth Nast, Jane
  Werner, Elsa Jane Werner]
  ABC is for Christmas (002,
    002a)
  Albert's zoo (008)
  Alice in Wonderland finds
    the garden of live
    flowers (010)
  Alice in Wonderland meets
    the White Rabbit (011,
    011a)
  Animal dictionary (020,
    020a,020b)
  Animal friends (021,021a,
    021b,021c)
  Baby Jesus stamps (040)
  Beaney goes to sea (053)
  Bible stories of boys and
    girls (068,068a)
  Birds (078, 078a)
  Bugs Bunny and the Indians
    (105,105a)
  Bugs Bunny gets a job (108)
  Bunny book, Walt Disney's
    (116)
  Chip 'n' Dale at the zoo
    (135)
  Christmas story (144)
  Cinderella's friends (148,
    148B,148a,148b)
  Dale Evans and the lost
    gold mine (176)
  Darby O'Gill (179)
  Day with Donald Duck (188)
  Dinosaurs (194,194a)
  Disneyland on the air (195)
  Donald Duck and Santa Claus
    (202)

WATSON, JANE WERNER (cont'd)
Donald Duck and the
Mousketeers (203)
Donald Duck and the witch
(205,213)
Donald Duck in Disneyland
(208,208a,208b)
Donald Duck, prize driver
(212)
Donald Duck's adventure
(214)
Donald Duck's Christmas
carol (215)
Donald Duck's Christmas
tree (216)
Donald Duck's safety book
(217)
Donald Duck's toy sailboat
(218)
Donald Duck's toy train
(213,219)
First Bible stories (240)
First golden geography
(241)
Frosty the snowman (258,
258SR,258a)
Fun with decals (260)
Fuzzy duckling (263,263FS,
263SR,263a,263b,263c)
Gene Autry and Champion
(267)
Giant little golden book
about plants and animals
(269)
Giant little golden book
of birds (271)
Good morning and good night
(292)
Goofy, movie star (295)
Grandpa Bunny (297)
Happy little whale (307)
Heroes of the Bible (313,
313a)
Houses (324)
How to have a happy
birthday (327,327a)
How to tell time (328,328B,
328a)
Jiminy Cricket (364)
Jolly barnyard (369,369a)
Jungle book (370)
Lassie shows the way (005,
385,385a)
Life and legend of Wyatt
Earp (391)
Lion's paw (393)

WATSON, JANE WERNER (cont'd)
Little golden book of hymns
(414,414a,414b,414c)
Little golden Christmas
manger (420)
Little man of Disneyland
(430)
Lucky puppy (448)
Mad Hatter's tea party
(452)
Marvelous merry-go-round
(463)
Mary Poppins (464)
Mary Poppins - a jolly
holiday (465)
Mickey Mouse and his space
ship (469,469a)
Mickey Mouse and Pluto Pup
(470a)
Mickey Mouse and the
missing Mouseketeers
(473)
Mickey Mouse flies the
Christmas mail (476)
Mickey Mouse goes Christmas
shopping (477)
Mickey Mouse's picnic (479,
479a)
Mike and Melissa and their
magic mumbo jumbo (481)
Mr. Noah and his family
(495)
My little golden book about
God (516)
Noah's ark (543,543SR,543a)
Old MacDonald had a farm
(553,553a,553aSR,553b)
Our puppy (564,564a)
Our world (565)
Perri and her friends (578)
Peter Pan and the Indians
(581,581a)
Peter Pan and Wendy (583,
583B,583a,583b,583c)
Pets for Peter (587)
Pluto Pup goes to sea (599)
Rin Tin Tin and Rusty (634)
Rin Tin Tin and the lost
Indian (635)
Robin Hood (641,641a)
Roy Rogers and the new
cowboy (654)
Scamp (668)
Scamp's adventure (669,
669a)
Seven dwarfs find a house
(672,672a)

WATSON, JANE WERNER (cont'd)
  Sleeping Beauty (679)
  Sleeping Beauty and the
    good fairies (680)
  Smokey the bear (687,687SR,
    687a,687b)
  Susie's new stove (704)
  Tex and his toys (716)
  This world of ours (721)
  Trim the Christmas tree
    (759,759a)
  Twelve dancing princesses
    (762)
  Ugly duckling (768,768SR)
  Uncle Mistletoe (770)
  Very best home for me (774)
  Whales (786,786a)
  Where Jesus lived (797,
    797a)
  Wonders of nature (818)
  Woody Woodpecker joins the
    circus (822,822a)

WATTS, MABEL (PIZZEY) 1906-
  Hiram's red shirt (317)
  Little Red Riding Hood
    (437a)
  Never pat a bear (533)
  Three bears (722b)

WEBBE, ELIZABETH (illus)
  Magic wagon (457)

WEIHS, ERIKA 1917- (illus)
  Hansel and Gretel (302)

WEINER, GINA INGOGLIA
[Gina Ingoglia]
  Benji, fastest dog in the
    West (060,060a)
  Biskitts in double trouble
    (080)
  Lippy the Lion and Hardy
    Har Har (394)
  Little Lulu (428)
  Ludwig Von Drake (450)
  Mrs. Brisby and the magic
    stone (499)
  Pepper plays nurse (577,
    577B)
  Pinocchio and the whale
    (593)
  Tarzan (710)

WEISGARD, LEONARD (JOSEPH)
1916- (illus)
  Indian, Indian (350)
  Little Eskimo (405)
  Little Pussycat (434)
  Pantaloon (570)
  Pussy Willow (611,611a)
  Wheels (791)

WEISMAN, AL (illus)
  Dennis the Menace waits for
    Santa (192)

WERBER, ADELE (illus)
  Animal alphabet from A to Z
    (016)
  Animal babies (017)

WERNER, ELSA JANE (pseud)
  see WATSON, JANE WERNER
  1915-

WERNER, JANE
  see WATSON, JANE WERNER
  1915-

WESSELLS, KATHARINE TYLER
  Little golden book of
    singing games (417)

WESTERBERG, CHRISTINE 1950-
(illus)
  Bouncy baby bunny finds
    his bed (090,090SR)

WHEELER, GEORGE (illus)
  Donald Duck's safety book
    (217)

WHITE, AL (illus)
  Bozo finds a friend (094,
    094SR)
  Bozo the clown (095,095SR)
  Dick Tracy (193)
  Donald Duck, private eye
    (211)
  Fireball XL5 (238)
  Hey there - it's Yogi Bear
    (314)
  Huckleberry Hound builds a
    house (340)
  Huckleberry Hound safety
    signs (341)
  Jetsons (363)
  Little Lulu (428)
  Magilla Gorilla (458)

WHITE, AL (cont'd)
Mary Poppins (464)
Pinocchio and the whale
(593)
Quick Draw McGraw (613)
Rocky and his friends
(644)
Ruff and Reddy (657,657a)
Touche turtle (750)
Wizard's duel (815)
Woody Woodpecker takes a
trip (823,823a)
Yakky Doodle and Chopper
(825)

WHITE, ANNE TERRY 1896-
Fairy tales (229)

WHITE, MARY MICHAELS
I sing a song of praise
(089,089a)

WHITLOCK, R. Z.
Cow and the elephant (167)

WIERSUM, GALE
Animals' Christmas eve
(028,028a)
My Christmas treasury (503,
503a)
Runaway squash (659)

WILBURN, KATHY (illus)
Little golden book of
holidays (413)
Shoelace box (677)

WILDE, IRMA (illus)
Corky (161)

WILDER, ALEC 1907-
(songwriter)
I can fly (343)

WILE, JOAN (narrator)
Riddles, riddles, from
A to Z (632SR)

WILKIN, ELOISE (BURNS)
1904- (illus)
Baby Dear (038,038a)
Baby Jesus stamps (040)
Baby listens (041)
Baby looks (042)
Baby's birthday (043,043a)

WILKIN, ELOISE (cont'd)
Baby's first Christmas
(046)
Birds (078, 078a)
Boy with a drum (092,092SR,
092a)
Busy Timmy (118,118a)
Child's garden of verses
(134,134a,134aSR)
Christmas ABC (140)
Christmas story (144)
Come play house (158)
Come play with me (159)
Day at the playground (184)
First Bible stories (240)
Fix it, please (246,246FS)
Georgie finds a Grandpa
(268)
Giant little golden book
of birds (271)
Giant little golden book
of kittens (273)
Good little, bad little
girl (291)
Good morning and good
night (292)
Guess who lives here (299)
Hansel and Gretel (302a,
302aSR,302b,302c)
Hi ho! Three in a row (315)
Jamie looks (359)
Linda and her little sister
(392)
Little book (399,399a)
Little golden holiday book
(422)
Mother Goose (488,488a)
My baby brother (501)
My dolly and me (506)
My kitten (513,513a,513b)
My little golden book about
God (516)
My pets (524)
My puppy (524,525,525a)
My snuggly bunny (524,526)
My teddy bear (527,527a)
New baby (534,534a,534b,
534c)
New house in the forest
(538)
Night before Christmas
(542b)
Noises and Mr. Flibberty-
Jib (545)
Play with me (597)

WILKIN, ELOISE (cont'd)
    Prayers for children (607a,
        607aB,607b)
    So big (690,690a)
    This world of ours (721)
    Twins (764)
    We help Daddy (781,781a)
    We help Mommy (782,782a)
    We like kindergarten (783,
        783a)
    Where did the baby go?
        (794,794a)
        Wiggles (804)
    Wonders of nature (818)

WILKIN, ESTHER
    Baby Dear (038,038a)
    Baby listens (041)
    Baby looks (042)
    Baby's first Christmas
        (046)
    Good little, bad little
        girl (291)
    Linda and her little sister
        (392)
    Play Street (596)
    Play with me (597)
    So big (690,690a)

WILKINS, PAULINE
    Doctor Dan at the circus
        (197)
    Pick up sticks (588)
    Sticks (693)

WILLIAMS, GARTH (MONTGOMERY)
1912- (illus)
    Animal friends (021,021a,
        021b,021c)
    Baby animals (author/illus)
        (037,037a,037b)
    Baby farm animals
        (author/illus) (039,039a,
        039b)
     Baby's first book
        (author/illus) (045,045a)
    Friendly book (255,255a,
        255b)
    Golden sleepy book (286,
        286a)
    Home for a bunny (319,319a)
    Kitten who thought he was
        a mouse (374)
    Mister Dog (482,482SR,482a)
    My first counting book
        (510,510a,510b)

WILLIAMS, GARTH (cont'd)
    Sailor dog (663,663VC)
    Sleepy book (682)
    Three bedtime stories (723,
        723a)
    Very best home for me (774)

WILLIAMS, HILDA K. (pseud)
    see McELROY, MARGARET JULIA

WILLIS, WERNER (illus)
    Benji, fastest dog in the
        West (060,060a)

WILSON, DAGMAR 1916- (illus)
    Charmin' Chatty (131)
    Let's visit the dentist
        (390)
    New pony (540)

WILSON, ROY (illus)
    Rainbow Brite and the brook
        meadow deer (625,625SR)

WINBORN, MARSHA (illus)
    Big Bird brings Spring to
        Sesame Street (069,069VC)

WINSHIP, FLORENCE SARAH
    Santa's surprise book
        (665,665a)

WINTHROP, ELIZABETH
    see MAHONY, ELIZABETH
    WINTHROP 1948-

WITMAN, MABEL FOOTE
    Golden book of flowers
        (282)

WITMAR, THELMA
    Sleeping Beauty paper dolls
        (681)

WOLFSON, GEORGE
[George]
    My little golden book of
        jokes (519)

WOODCOCK, LOUISE (PHINNEY)
1892-
    Guess who lives here (299)
    Hi ho! Three in a row (315)
    Wiggles (804)

WORCESTER, RETTA (illus)
  Christmas in the country
    (143)
  How to have a happy
    birthday (327,327a)

WRIGHT, BETTY REN 1927-
  Cat who stamped his feet
    (127)
  Rabbit's adventure (617,
    617a)

WRIGHT, NORMAN
  Chip Chip (136)

WYATT, GLADYS
  Buffalo Bill, Jr. and the
    Indian chief (103)
  Dale Evans and the coyote
    (175)
  Roy Rogers and the Indian
    sign (652)

WYCKOFF, MARJORIE (ELAINE
MORRISON) 1915-
  Christmas carols (141,141a)

WYLER, ROSE 1909-
  Exploring space (228)
  My little golden book about
    the sky (517)

WYLIE, JOANNE
  Bouncy baby bunny finds his
    bed (teacher's guide)
    (090SR)
  Corky's hiccups (teacher's
    guide) (162SR)
  Forest hotel (teacher's
    guide) (250SR)
  Large and growly bear
    (teacher's guide) (380SR)
  Magic friend-maker
    (teacher's guide) (455SR)
  Neatos and the litterbugs
    (teacher's guide) (532SR)
  New friends for the saggy
    baggy elephant (teacher's
    guide) (536SR)
  Pano the train (teacher's
    guide) (569SR)
  Poky little puppy
    (teacher's guide) (600SR)
  Pussycat tiger (teacher's
    guide) (612SR)

WYLIE, JOANNE (cont'd)
  Rags (teacher's guide)
    (624SR)
  Tawny scrawny lion and the
    clever monkey (teacher's
    guide) (712SR)

WYSS, JOHANN DAVID VON
1743-1818
  Swiss family Robinson (705)

YARDUMIAN, MIRYAM
[Miryam]
  Giant little golden book of
    animal stories (270)
  Happy man and his dump truck
    (308,308SR,308a,308aSR)

YOUNG, HARLAND (illus)
  Gay purr-ee (265)

YOUNG, MIRIAM (BURT) 1913-1974
  5 pennies to spend (245)
  Georgie finds a Grandpa
    (268)

YOUNG, NATALIE
  Rainy day play book (626,
    626a)

YOUNG, SUSAN
  Rainy day play book (626a)

ZALLINGER, JEAN (DAY)
1918- (illus)
  Fish (242)
  Insect stamps (352)

ZIM, HERBERT S(PENCER) 1909-
  Fish (242)

ZOLOTOW, CHARLOTTE (SHAPIRO)
1915-
  Aren't you glad? (034)
  Indian, Indian (350)
  Little black puppy (397)

Format Index

Items listed in this index are grouped according to the format in which they were published. A cross reference to the main TITLE LIST is provided by the entry number following each title.

BRAILLE

ABC rhymes (003B)
Bambi (049B)
Bugs Bunny (104B)
Chitty Chitty Bang Bang (139B)
Cinderella's friends (148B)
Cindy bear (149B)
Dumbo (223B)
How to tell time (328B)
Jenny's new brother (360B)
Little golden ABC (408B)
Little golden book of words (419B)
Little golden picture dictionary (425B)
Little Red Riding Hood (437B)
Mr. Puffer Bill (496B)
Pepper plays nurse (577B)
Peter Pan and Wendy (583B)
Prayers for children (607aB)
Taxi that hurried (713B)
Tom and Jerry meet Little Quack (738B)
Tootle (747B)

CASSETTE

Bouncy baby bunny finds his bed (090SR)
Cookie Monster and the cookie tree (160SR)

Corky's hiccups (162SR)
Forest hotel (250SR)
Happy man and his dump truck (308aSR)
Large and growly bear (380SR)
Little engine that could (404SR)
Little fat policeman (406SR)
Magic friend-maker (455SR)
Neatos and the litterbugs (532FS,532SR)
New friends for the saggy baggy elephant (536SR)
Pano the train (569SR)
Poky little puppy (600FS, 600SR,600cSR)
Pussycat tiger (612SR)
Raggedy Ann and Fido (622FS, 622SR)
Rags (624SR)
Rainbow Brite and the brook meadow deer (625SR)
Rumpelstiltskin (658SR)
Saggy baggy elephant (662FS, 662SR)
Scuffy the tugboat (671SR)
Seven little postmen (673SR)
Shy little kitten (678FS)
Tawny scrawny lion (711SR)
Tawny scrawny lion and the clever monkey (712SR)
Taxi that hurried (713SR)
There's no such thing as a dragon (718SR)

Thumbelina (729SR)
Tootle (747FS,747SR)

FILMSTRIP

Circus time (153FS)
Color kittens (156FS)
Dragon in a wagon (221FS)
Fix it, please (246FS)
Fuzzy duckling (263FS)
Golden egg book (283FS)
Katie the kitten (373FS)
Large and growly bear (380FS)
Neatos and the litterbugs
  (532FS)
Poky little puppy (600FS)
Raggedy Ann and Fido (622FS)
Saggy baggy elephant (662FS)
Seven sneezes (674FS)
Shy little kitten (678FS)
Tawny scrawny lion (711FS)
Tootle (747FS)
We like to do things (784FS)
Year on the farm (827FS)

MOTION PICTURE

Neatos and the litterbugs
  (532MP)
Poky little puppy (600MP)
Tawny scrawny lion (711MP)

RECORDING

ABC rhymes (003SR)
Ali Baba and the forty
  thieves (009SR)
Animals of Farmer Jones
  (030SR,030aSR)
Big brown bear (072SR)
Boy with a drum (092SR)
Bozo finds a friend (094SR)
Bozo the clown (095SR)
Bravest of all (099SR)
Chicken Little (133SR)
Child's garden of verses
  (134aSR)
Chitty Chitty Bang Bang
  (139SR)
Circus time (153SR)
Color kittens (156SR)
Cookie Monster and the cookie
  tree (160SR)
Corky's hiccups (162SR)

David and Goliath (180SR)
Day on the farm (187SR)
Dragon in a wagon (221FS)
Five little firemen (244SR)
Fuzzy duckling (263FS)
Gingerbread man (276aSR)
Golden egg book (283FS,283SR)
Goliath II (287SR)
Hansel and Gretel (302aSR)
Happy days (304SR)
Happy man and his dump truck
  (308SR,308aSR)
Heidi (310SR)
Jack and the beanstalk
  (356aSR)
Large and growly bear
  (380FS,380SR)
Little boy with a big horn
  (401SR)
Little fat policeman (406SR)
Little Peewee (432SR)
Little red caboose (435SR)
Little red hen (436aSR)
Little Red Riding Hood (437SR)
Lively little rabbit (441SR)
Mickey's Christmas carol
  (480SR)
Mister Dog (482SR)
Musicians of Bremen (500SR)
Naughty bunny (531SR)
Neatos and the litterbugs
  (532FS)
Noah's ark (543SR)
Numbers (546SR)
Old MacDonald had a farm
  (553aSR)
Pat-a-cake (574SR)
Poky little puppy (600SR,
  600cSR)
Puss in boots (610aSR)
Pussycat tiger (612SR)
Rainbow Brite and the brook
  meadow deer (625SR)
Riddles, riddles from A to Z
  (632SR)
Rudolph, the red-nosed
  reindeer (656SR)
Saggy baggy elephant (662SR)
Scuffy the tugboat (671SR,
  671aSR)
Seven little postmen (673SR)
Shy little kitten (678SR)
Smokey the bear (687SR)
Snow White and Rose Red
  (688SR)

Tawny scrawny lion (711FS,
711SR)
Taxi that hurried (713SR)
There's no such thing as a
dragon (718SR)
Three bears (722SR)
Three little kittens (725SR)
Three little pigs (726SR)
Tiger's adventure (731SR)
Tootle (747SR)
Twelve days of Christmas
(763SR)
Ugly duckling (768SR)
Ukelele and her new doll
(769SR)
Visit to the children's zoo
(775SR)
Wacky Witch and the mystery
of the king's gold (776SR)
When I grow up (792aSR)
White Bunny and his magic
nose (800SR)
Who comes to your house?
(801SR)

VIDEOCASSETTE

Big Bird brings Spring to
Sesame Street (069VC)
Gingerbread man (276aVC)
Sailor dog (663VC)
Scuffy the tugboat (671bVC)
Theodore Mouse goes to sea
(717VC)

ABOUT THE COMPILER

DOLORES BLYTHE JONES is Curator of the de Grummond Collection at
the University of Southern Mississippi. Her earlier works include *Children's
Literature Awards and Winners* and *An "Oliver Optic" Checklist: An Annotated Catalog-Index to the Series, Nonseries Stories, and Magazine Publications of William Taylor Adams* (Greenwood Press, 1985).